Packaging
YOUR HOME
FOR PROFIT

Packaging
YOUR HOME

FOR PROFIT

*How to Sell Your House or Condo
for More Money in Less Time*

Bruce A. Percelay
Peter Arnold

LITTLE, BROWN AND COMPANY
BOSTON   TORONTO

FIRST EDITION

Library of Congress Cataloging-in-Publication Data

Percelay, Bruce A.
  Packaging your home for profit.

  Includes index.
  1. Home selling.   I. Arnold, Peter, 1943 Jan. 25–
II. Title.
HD1379.P375   1986   333.33′8′0688   85-19761
ISBN 0-316-69895-4

BP

DESIGNED BY JEANNE F. ABBOUD

*Published simultaneously in Canada
by Little, Brown & Company (Canada) Limited*

PRINTED IN THE UNITED STATES OF AMERICA

Dedication

To my family, friends, and brother James,
Alicia Lee,
and the City of Boston.
B. A. P.

Contents

Foreword

For most Americans, the home is our largest personal investment. In fact, recent government statistics show that 60 percent of American families would have no net worth at all were it not for their homes.

With so much at stake in home ownership, the selling process becomes all the more critical. It is this step where people have the choice between maximizing the return on their investment or letting thousands of dollars slip between their fingers.

Packaging Your Home for Profit provides a revolutionary approach to getting the absolute top dollar for your home. By applying proven consumer marketing techniques to the home selling process, this book shows people not only how to sell their home for more money but in less time.

In *Packaging Your Home for Profit,* Messrs. Percelay and Arnold introduce ideas never before addressed in conventional "How to Sell Your Home" books. These include how to use certain colors, sounds, and even smells to enhance the selling environment. The book also details which inexpensive cosmetic improvements are most effective at making your house or condominium seem most valuable and which major expenditures you should consider.

Beyond showing readers what improvements to make to a home, the book also provides valuable advice on whether or not to use a broker and how best to handle a sale under either circumstance. There is, for example, a detailed section on advertising strategies that can help you generate not only more inquiries about your home but more qualified leads. There is also a section on how to make sure the broker is working for and not against you.

The information in *Packaging Your Home for Profit* is impressively documented by leading experts not only in the real estate field but in the areas of psychology, consumer behavior, interior design, and more.

Packaging Your Home for Profit is like no other book on the subject. It shatters much of the conventional wisdom on how to make a home more salable and will place those who use it at a distinct advantage over those who are content to settle for an average return on their home.

Given the results Mr. Percelay has achieved using the methods described in the book, it should be required reading for anyone contemplating selling a home or those who have any interest in maximizing the value of real estate.

Robert Allen

1

Introduction

Your perception of how to sell a home is about to change. And what you will learn in place of conventional methods will put you at a distinct advantage over most home sellers.

There is nothing conventional about this book or the results you will achieve by applying the information in it. By going beyond the obvious ways to sell your house, condominium, or cooperative apartment and focusing on underlying purchase motivators shared by almost all buyers, I will show you how to sell your home in less time for more money.

With so much already written and discussed about selling real estate, you may question how there could possibly be a new method more effective than those already in use.

As surprising as it may sound, there exists a wealth of information and proven techniques that has never been directly applied to home sales but that can dramatically change the way property is sold. This body of knowledge is loosely referred to as consumer marketing. It has been used for years by advertising executives on Madison Avenue and marketing experts at major consumer-products companies all across the country and has been refined to a virtual science.

We experience the results of effective consumer-marketing techniques everyday. This is why we select one brand of soap over another, why we must own a particular appliance that yesterday we didn't need, or why we will borrow more than we planned to buy that special new car.

If these techniques are so effective in marketing consumer products, why not apply them to the most important consumer product of all — your home? The point is: you can, and that is the theme of this book.

By thinking like a marketing professional and selling your home as if it were a consumer product, you will find yourself at a distinct advantage over the competition.

To make marketing your home both easy and profitable, I have developed a five-point system, which will be introduced in Chapter 2. This system is easy to understand and can require as little or as much time and money as you choose to spend. You should use it the moment you decide to sell your home. And it should also be used when you purchase a new home, so you will know what improvements will and won't pay off when you decide to resell.

This home marketing system covers a broad range of ideas and applies to houses, condominiums, cooperatives, and even investment property. It is designed for use whether you are selling the home yourself or with the help of a broker. For, no matter who is selling your property, the product should speak for itself.

Recognizing the Subtle Persuaders

Marketing experts have long recognized the impact of subtle visual, audible, and olfactory suggestions in selling products. From the use of color to make a package more appealing to the use of certain smells to increase sales of automobiles, seemingly small details can have dramatic influence on a product's success. These same elements can have dramatic impact on the sale of your home.

Chapters 3 through 5 show how you can apply sensory selling tools to the marketing of your home. By understanding how to harness the power of light, color, sound, and smell, you will benefit from what marketing professionals have known for years. Best of all, these marketing tools are often inexpensive but can have as much impact on selling a home as many more costly improvements.

Avoiding Critical Marketing Mistakes

One of the easiest traps sellers fall into is to prepare their homes as though they were selling to themselves. Focusing on aspects most important to you — like repainting the bedroom your favorite color, adding the final touches to a do-it-yourself construction project, or putting up your favorite wallpaper — may make you feel satisfied, but it usually does little for the person who really counts, the buyer.

Overpersonalizing a home can actually make it more difficult for the buyer to visualize it as his or her own home. Research done in this area has shown that sellers can create psychological barriers that make buyers feel uncomfortable in the home. We will show you how to avoid doing this and increase buyer comfort instead.

A sophisticated consumer marketing company would never risk second-guessing what the consumer wants. Rather than imposing their preferences on the consumer, marketing professionals go through a deliberate process to try to understand in advance what the buyer is looking for; then they package their product accordingly.

Let's hypothesize for a moment that the president of Procter and Gamble absolutely loved the color red. Would it seem logical if every box of detergent, tube of toothpaste, or bottle of shampoo featured his favorite color? While red may appeal to him, it may not appeal to the vast majority of consumers who buy Procter and Gamble products. That's the reason why, for example, the company spent over one year on research and interviewed nearly 3,000 customers just to determine what color to make Dawn dishwashing liquid.

Nothing about a well-marketed consumer product is accidental. From the color of the box to the logo to the name itself, everything is carefully planned. The same should hold true for the marketing of your home. But you don't have to go to such great lengths to market your house or condominium. All you have to do is gain an understanding of the basics by following the five-step system developed in this book.

Another way sellers often hurt their sale is by failing to recognize the weaknesses of their homes. It is difficult to be objective about a place you have lived in for some time. Because it often takes an impartial eye to suggest improvements that you simply cannot see, you may need a third party to help you identify them.

Consumer-products companies use this approach whenever they introduce a new product or upgrade an existing one. Before Miller Brewing introduced Lite Beer, for example, the company interviewed consumers and adapted the product on the basis of their criticisms and suggestions. A product manager, much like a home owner, can be so taken with his or her product that he or she needs an outsider to step back and critique it objectively.

Another common mistake sellers make is to allow a home to get lost in the crowd. Whether you realize it or not, your home is a commodity, which is competing against scores of relatively similar properties and is fighting for recognition. By failing to set it apart from the pack, you may cause it to sell later and for less money. The better able you are to make your home stand out, the more valuable it will seem and the more quickly it will sell.

This is the same strategy a consumer package-goods company goes through when it introduces a new product. If a company decides to launch a new bar of soap, there has to be something special about it in order for it to be successful. If if doesn't differ in price, quality, or promotion, or doesn't offer some unusual benefit, it will just sit on the supermarket shelf. Marketing experts put great emphasis on making their product stand out in the mind of the buyer, and so should you.

Effective packaging is one way to assure that a product stands out. Good packaging can cost little more than ordinary packaging but can change the viewer's perception of a product. Leggs (TM) panty hose, for example, might be just another stocking were it not for that clever egg-shaped container. Players cigarettes could be just another smoke were it not for the elegant black and gold box.

The packaging of your home can have the same effect yet cost far less than conventional approaches. We will show you how to apply these and other principles to each room of the home in chapters 7 through 15.

Last, we will discuss the final steps in selling your home, including advice on using brokers, ways to deal directly with prospects, and proven advertising techniques to assure the best exposure for your property.

The difference between simply selling your home and marketing it can mean thousands of dollars. There is an abundance of proof that consumer marketing methods work, and it is time that you took advantage of these methods to get the highest return on your largest personal investment.

The following chapter will introduce you to the basics of our proven home marketing system and start you toward a more profitable home sale.

2

The Home Marketing System

Using consumer marketing principles to sell your home requires no special skills or background. To make the process as easy and efficient as possible, I have developed a five-step system that can be applied to any or all parts of your home.

Take your time to become comfortable with each of the five basic marketing points in the system, since they will be the tools that enable you to get the highest return from your home sale.

Remember that what you will be learning represents a new approach to selling homes. For this reason, the terms and concepts discussed may seem foreign to you and even to your real estate broker, if you decide to use one. But, by the time you have read several chapters, this system should have become part of your thinking process.

On the basis of the prices received for homes sold through this system, you should plan to ask between 5 and 15 percent or more for your property than what the market suggests it is worth today. Exactly how much of a premium you ask for depends upon how many of the improvement ideas discussed in the book you decide to apply to your home. I will advise you throughout which improvements can yield the highest returns under given circumstances.

THE FIVE-STEP SYSTEM
Step 1. Consider the Competition

If you were a product manager at a major packaged-goods company and were in charge of marketing a new laundry detergent, wouldn't you first want to know something about the competition? For example, wouldn't it help to know how many competitors you had, what was special about their products, and what price they charged?

Without these facts, you could find yourself marketing a product that was less attractive than those already on the market.

The same holds true for marketing your home. By not knowing the competition, you won't have much of an idea what improvements are necessary to make your house or condo sell first and for the most money.

To eliminate this risk, you need to learn a little about the marketplace. Specifically, how many homes like yours are on the market, at what prices are they being offered, and in what ways is your property different?

Take a Firsthand Look

To get a clear picture of what buyers will be comparing your home with, go into the market, talk to those who know it well, and then tour comparable properties for yourself. There are a number of information sources that will make your survey a snap.

A good first source is a local real estate broker, whose job it is to stay on top of the market. (See "Selecting a Broker," p. 253.) He or she will have information about similar homes for sale in your area and how much they are selling for.

When evaluating other properties, look for two basic kinds of information.

Features or Aspects That Your Home Lacks

These will help you determine where your property needs improvement. For example, if the homes you are competing with are similar to yours with the exception of having much newer kitchens, you will find yourself at a major disadvantage. Your goal should be to make your house not simply as good as the competition but better.

Features Your Home Has That Others Don't

These will help you in sales presentations to prospects and brokers and will give you the necessary ammunition to set the highest reasonable asking price. If, for example, you were able to convert an underused area of your home into a third bedrooom while your competition has only two bedrooms, you can translate this information into revenue.

Go through competing homes paying particular attention to the age, condition, and appeal or lack of appeal of the following:

Exterior: location, landscape, painting, yard.
Interior: bedrooms, bathrooms, kitchen, living room, major mechanical systems.

Pricing It Right

Only after you have applied the methods in this book are you ready to price your home. Pricing beforehand would be unwise, since your product will be much more desirable after you have applied the five points of the home marketing system.

As discussed, after you have made the improvements appropriate for your home, you should be asking between 5 and 15 percent or more than the market suggests your home is currently worth.

So now is the time to find out the base price to which you will add your profit premium. If you determine today that your house or condo is worth $100,000, then, after applying the system, it should sell for between $105,000 and $115,000 or more.

The most accurate method to determine your current market value is to use recent sales prices on comparable properties in your area. This can be done by asking brokers what individual properties actually sold for, not simply what the asking price was.

If you can't get this information through a broker, ask your neighbors if they have any idea what a particular home sold for, because this information tends to spread quickly. If they don't know or you are unsure about the accuracy of their responses, go to your local registry of deeds and look up this public information.

Step 2: Consider the Buyer

Every buyer has underlying reasons for his or her home purchase decision. Some of these are specific to certain types of buyers while others are shared by all.

Experts in marketing and advertising have known for years that by appealing to certain buyer instincts, products sell better. It's no accident, for example, that life insurance advertisements play up to people's fears of being unprotected or that automobile ads show how envious the neighbors are when you pull up in your new car. You can use this approach to sell your home.

To do so, it's important to know who your buyer is, what his or her needs are, and how you can satisfy them.

Identifying Your Buyer

It would take a crystal ball to predict exactly who will buy your home. A suburban split-level ranch house, for example, could be purchased by a young first-time buyer, a couple transferring from out of town, or an elderly couple. But by looking around at your neighborhood and identifying recent arrivals, as well as recognizing those who already live there, you can get a pretty good sense of who is most likely to be your buyer.

If you need additional information on new arrivals in your neighborhood, ask a local broker. With the knowledge of where your house or condo is located, what style and size it is, and roughly how much you are asking for it, a good broker should be able to describe the type or types of buyer to expect.

The mailman can also be a good source. He or she is a walking census report, who will not only have an accurate idea of the current composition of the neighborhood but also up-to-the-minute information on the age, number of people in the family, location of previous home, and other characteristics of people moving into the area.

And don't forget to look at yourself. What type of buyer were you when you moved in? The new buyer may be very similar.

In real estate, there are commonly used classifications that cover the bulk of home buyers. While not all-inclusive, these categories can be very helpful in establishing a framework for the type of buyer you are likely to encounter.

Studies conducted by *Professional Builder* magazine and *Real Estate Quarterly,* as well as the Joint Center for Urban Studies at Harvard University and the Massachusetts Institute of Technology (M.I.T.) combine to provide a good composite of these groups.

First-Time Buyers

More than one third of all home buyers fit into this "first-time buyer" category. The average age of this group is about thirty. One quarter are single, 35 percent are couples without children, and the remaining 40 percent are married with young children. The homes they look for are modestly priced, often 30 percent less than the average price of a "trade-up" home.

You will want to consider the specific needs of this group when marketing your house or condominium to them.

They are much more nervous than seasoned buyers about all aspects of the real estate purchase process. A special effort has to be made to assure first-time buyers that they are considering a sound investment which they will have no trouble selling in later years. We will cover some of the hand-holding techniques that will give confidence to this type of buyer.

Peer influence plays an important role in their decision, and advice from friends who already own a home is also an important factor.

Nearly two thirds of this group want three bedrooms in their home, even though they expect to pay a relatively low purchase price.

Sheer prestige of ownership and not having to pay rent anymore head the list of reasons why these people buy a house or condominium. Privacy is another requirement for the home they select.

Trade-up Buyers

This group is the largest and fastest growing segment of the market, accounting for over 50 percent of all purchases.

The growth in this group is projected to come from the "baby-boom" generation. Their sheer numbers, combined with their relative prosperity, will make the trade-up market the hottest part of the real estate market from now into the 1990s.

The average age of trade-up buyers is about thirty-four, and most of them have one child. Their principal goal is to find a larger home. Price is not as important to this segment as the size of monthly payments, a motive that provides the opportunity for creative financing ideas.

Specific features this group considers important include a formal living room with a separate family room and a formal dining room, extra closet and pantry space, and an impressive entry.

Empty Nesters/Trade-down Buyers

There is a growing category of buyers who, for various reasons, are moving from larger homes to smaller ones. This group includes "empty nesters," whose children have grown up and left a home that has become too large for two people. The other component is the people who — because of divorce or financial difficulty — have decided to move into a more manageable space.

Empty Nesters

Fifteen percent of buyers are classified as empty nesters. The Housing Futures Study, conducted by the Joint Center for Urban Studies at Harvard and M.I.T., reports that nearly 80 percent of people fifty-five or older who plan to move, do so to smaller homes. They are seeking the advantage of lower cost and maintenance, better security, and more convenience.

Empty nesters also prefer more casual living space. They would, for example, opt for a "great room" rather than a formal living room, and they prefer a combined kitchen and eating area as compared with a separate, formal dining room. Empty nesters also want a smaller yard or none at all because yards require maintenance.

By making specific improvements or adding certain features to your home, you can appeal to the special needs of this important market segment.

Trade-down Buyers

With over one third of all marriages ending in divorce, there has been enormous increase in single-parent households. Trade-down buyers, who constitute 7 percent of the market, often have the emotionally difficult task of facing a cut in their standard of living. These buyers want to have the shock minimized by being offered similar life-style statements provided to the trade-up buyers.

Universal Buyer Needs

There are certain needs shared by almost all purchasers. While some of these may appear obvious, sellers often fail to realize how crucial certain points can be in influencing the outcome of a sale.

Physical Safety and Security

It is no surprise that people want to feel that the homes they purchase are safe from burglary and fire. But what may be surprising is the intensity of this need and how much it can determine whether or not a home is purchased. Studies conducted by numerous organizations, including the Joint Center of Urban Studies, as well as the National

Association of Home Builders, show that home security ranks among the most important concerns of both young and old, male and female buyers.

Especially in urban areas, a house or condo that looks vulnerable or has telltale signs of attempted break-ins can be very difficult to sell. We will discuss ideas on proven ways to deal with this throughout the book, but you should always keep physical safety and security near the top of your priority list.

Economic Safety and Security

Safety and security extend to all buyers' economic needs. A home is likely to be a person's largest single investment, and he or she wants to feel that it is a wise one. *Professional Builder* magazine reports this to be among the most important attractions in buying a particular home.

Buyers want to feel comfortable about affording the home, achieving high appreciation on it, and being able to get their money out quickly in case of an unforeseen problem. Financial jitters are particularly common among the less seasoned first-time buyers.

Privacy

A home isn't your castle if the neighbors can peer into your living room or if you can hear footsteps through your condominium ceiling. People want to feel in control of their space and want to know they can turn off the outside world when they're at home.

Research on the motivations of home buyers reveals that the need for privacy ranks among the highest considerations. By virtue of their design, some homes — particularly condominiums and cooperatives — can appear to lack privacy. As we will show, there are steps you can take to counteract this effect.

Peer Recognition and Life-Style Needs

A home is more than just a place to live. It can provide a sense of accomplishment and satisfy the desire for peer recognition.

Home ownership can be satisfying in itself, especially with the first-time buyer, but beyond that, people want to feel that they have bettered themselves and have tangible evidence of that accomplishment.

We will show you how to add to your home relatively inexpensive features that suggest a much higher life-style and can appeal to all market segments.

Step 3. Evaluate Your Product

You'll want to recognize the strengths and weaknesses of your home so you will know which improvements are needed to maximize its selling power. Objective evaluation of your home is also important to help you prevent seemingly small problems from becoming big deterrents to your home sale.

Like criticizing your own cooking or evaluating the way you look, making impartial judgments about your home can be very difficult. You are simply too close to the situation to see it clearly. Furthermore, the longer people remain in their environment, the harder it becomes to notice its deficiencies.

Has anyone ever visited your home for the first time and reacted to something that you take for granted, such as a handsomely framed picture, a striking fireplace, or unusually high ceilings? It's not that you don't like these features; it's simply that you've grown accustomed to them.

The same holds true when you don't stay on top of routine home maintenance. When the windows start getting dirty, the paint gradually begins to fade, or the smell of cigarettes starts permeating your home, it's easy for you not to notice.

Although these or other aspects of your environment may not bother you, don't assume they won't concern the buyer. Objective opinions should be sought to spot problems that you no longer notice.

Getting a Fresh Perspective

Consumer marketing professionals have long recognized the need for objective product evaluation. With this in mind, they have developed an effective technique called "focus group" testing, which requires assembling a group of prospective purchasers and getting their first impressions on a particular product. Often, this process can yield comments and concerns that the people who conceived the product totally missed. Consumer products are rarely introduced to the market without going through this step, and the same should apply to your home.

To do your own focus-group test, enlist the help of two or three neighbors, and offer them breakfast or cocktails. Tell them beforehand what you are doing, and when they arrive, ask them to pretend they are looking at your house as if they were thinking of buying it.

Start at the sidewalk in front of your house or condo, just as your prospect would, and walk with them to the front. At that point, ask each of them to describe their first impressions.

Encourage them to be as frank as possible and whatever you do, don't act offended by anything they say, since that would inhibit honest feedback.

The following is a series of open-ended questions you should consider asking just before you are ready to walk into your home.

What was your first impression from the street?

What impressed you most?

What impressed you least?

If you had $1,000 to improve the exterior, what would you spend it on?

Carry a pad of paper and jot down notes, even comments that you don't agree with. Then proceed inside and tour the home as you would with a buyer.

After you have shown them through your house or condo, bring them back to the entryway and ask the following series of questions.

What was your first impression when you walked in?

What did you like the most and least about what you first saw?

What rooms of the house did you like the best and which the least?

Was there any single feature of the home that stood out in your mind, either positive or negative?

If you had $1,000 to spend on improvements to the interior, where would you spend it?

You can conduct this focus-group test with brokers as well. Take all feedback very seriously. If both neighbors and brokers suggest the same improvements, chances are you should act on them.

Step 4. Eliminate Territorial Anxiety

Humans are basically territorial creatures. We feel most comfortable when we are on our own turf. When we are in a space that is clearly marked by someone else, our feelings can range from slight uneasiness to downright discomfort, and discomfort can turn a hot prospect into a lost opportunity.

In order for prospects to appreciate fully the benefits of your home, they must feel comfortable in it and be able to visualize it as theirs. They must be able to imagine their family eating in the dining room, their friends socializing in the living room, and they themselves sleeping in the bedroom.

Pierre L. van den Berghe, professor of sociology and anthropology at the University of Washington in Seattle, has done considerable research in this area. "Walking into a home which contains strong territorial statements, produces a feeling of discomfort in those entering the environment," he says. "This feeling of discomfort can negatively affect a person's attitude toward a particular environment. Visual, audible and olfactory messages can contribute to this."

Because few sellers recognize this need, they inadvertently commit one of the most critical home marketing mistakes by creating what we term "territorial anxiety." However, if you learn what it is and how to prevent your prospect from experiencing it, you can gain a distinct advantage when selling your home.

Since the natural tendency among people selling their homes is to accentuate those features that are most important to them, people often create an environment that is highly personal. Assuming that what you like is what the buyer likes can be a costly mistake.

The Model Unit Effect

Walk into a house or condominium that's for sale and see how you feel when you enter the owner's bedroom or master bedroom. You probably feel a little uneasy, and if the bed is unmade and the bathroom has an unpleasant odor, you will feel even more like an intruder.

Now do the same thing in the model unit of a new condominium project or suburban housing development. Would you think twice about examining the master bedroom or bathroom? Probably not, because there is no sense that this territory belongs to any one individual. It does not look "lived in" because everything is new and immaculate.

It does not have any personal odors, but rather has that distinctive "new" smell. It probably doesn't even *sound* inhabited: the only noise may be a broker in the background and some pleasant music. Notice that the colors of the walls, carpeting, and accessories are quite neutral, so you don't feel at odds with a strong personal design statement.

The fact that "model units" are almost always the first to sell, and at prices that more than pay for their furnishings, should say something very important to you about the packaging strategy of your home.

By keeping certain aspects — sights, sounds, and smells — of your home neutral, you not only reduce territorial anxiety but help the buyer visualize his or her own preferences. A person who loves pink has a much easier time visualizing it against a neutral backdrop than does a person who loves white or beige trying to imagine it against a pink backdrop.

Step 5. Maximize Packaging Appeal

To get the highest possible price for your home, you will want it to seem as valuable as possible. This can be done easily and inexpensively by making certain tested "cosmetic" packaging improvements. These are the low-cost, high-return upgrades that significantly improve the perceived value of your house or condo.

The hallmark of good packaging is its ability to draw attention to a product and increase the perceived value of what lies within. Products that are packaged in gold foil, for example, take on a much more expensive look than those wrapped in paper. While the foil may cost only pennies more, the price that the manufacturer can charge may be many times that amount.

By applying methods learned by packaging experts to your home, you can increase its selling price. These methods include many small and inexpensive improvements — like the creative use of molding, paint, and lighting — to improve dramatically the perception of both the interior and exterior of your home. We will show you, for example, how to add certain fixtures and hardware to doors and cabinets to create the impression of entirely new ones. The ideas are simple and easy to apply and, most important of all, they will add to the profit of your home sale.

Establish a Focal Point

Every room in your home should have one star attraction that makes it memorable. By establishing a focal point, you'll help set the tone for the room and leave a lasting impression in the buyer's mind. Whether you opt for a spotlight aimed at an exposed brick wall, a set of brass accessories in front of a handsome fireplace, or an especially attractive front doorway, you can make your home a winner by making each area exciting.

Dual Use of Rooms

How many gadgets have you seen in hardware stores that boast "3 in 1"? These are products that offer multiple uses, like a screwdriver that can also be used as a canopener and corkscrew. The marketing concept behind products like this is that they seem more valuable yet may cost only slightly more than single-use products. The same idea can be applied when marketing individual rooms of your home.

By suggesting dual uses for a room, you can increase the impression of value. A den that doubles as a bedroom or a living room that has a section that serves as a study can add to the usefulness of the home. Whenever possible, creating dual uses from certain rooms can prove an effective marketing strategy.

Differentiate Your Product

When Minnetonka, Inc. introduced Softsoap, the liquid soap in pump dispensers, the industry was taken by storm. The soap itself may have been nothing special, but by differentiating the packaging, Softsoap was able to set itself apart from the scores of competing soap products on the shelves. This same concept can be applied to marketing your home.

Offer some unique benefit, and your home will stand out from the competition. There are many small features you can add to your home that will differentiate it from others on the market.

If your home happens to be a condominium or co-op, there may be special ways to make it outstanding. The last element of the home marketing system deals with ways to maximize the value of your condo or co-op.

INTRODUCING C.U.M.E.: THE COMMON-AREA UPGRADE MULTIPLIER EFFECT

Condominiums and cooperatives present unique problems and opportunities relative to the improvement of lobbies, lawns, parking garages, and other common areas.

The very nature of condo or co-op bylaws usually prevents an individual from acting alone in authorizing improvement expenditures. Limiting individual decisions can be useful if someone voices a wild idea like installing a rooftop swimming pool or carpeting an underground garage. But management by committee can be frustrating when you try to get agreement on essential improvements.

What condo and co-op governments or associations seldom realize is how beneficial improvements to common areas can be in enhancing the value of individual units and how attractive the payoff can be when reselling. This is what I call the Common-Area Upgrade Multiplier Effect, or C.U.M.E.

If, for example, a condominium contains 20 units valued at $75,000 each, and the exterior of the building is in serious need of repainting, the return on investment for this painting can be dramatic. According to an independent study conducted by Dutch Boy Paints and based on a poll of real estate brokers in seven areas of the country, repainting the exterior can increase the resale value by a minimum of 5 percent.

Using this information, the following numbers demonstrate the C.U.M.E. effect:

Total Number of Units		20
Repainting Cost per Unit		$500
Total Cost of Repainting	=	$10,000
Value Increase per Unit (based on 5% appreciation)		$3,750
Return on Investment per Unit		+750%

Even more dramatic is the fact that the investment of $10,000 for the entire building will yield a total increase in value of $3,750 times 20 units, or $75,000.

The C.U.M.E. approach to looking at the economics of condo or co-op improvements is so compelling that it is difficult to understand why developers and governing associations so often cut corners on common-area maintenance and improvements. Keith Romney, pioneer of condominium development in the U.S., comments, "Of all the mistakes that can be made in the development, conversion or ownership of condominiums or co-ops, shortchanging work to the common areas can be among the most costly yet the easiest to avoid."

The C.U.M.E. effect will be addressed where appropriate throughout the book, as will all of the concepts discussed in this chapter. But first, there are basic tools you need to understand that will help you package your home effectively. These concern the use of color, lighting, smell, and sound. The next three chapters will show you how to use these elements to your best advantage.

3

Coloring
Perceptions

Color can be one of the most influential elements of your home's packaging. It can also be one of the most cost-effective.

Colors can influence how large your home looks, how well cared for it seems, and how easy it may be for a buyer to visualize him- or herself owning it. In addition, color can be used to minimize the effects of cosmetic problems and maximize the curb appeal of your property. From the smallest application of color to brightening a bathroom to a major project like exterior painting, improvements involving color will yield an exceptional return.

Consumer marketing experts have long recognized how powerful color can be in enhancing the appeal of consumer packaged goods. Every time a new product is designed and packaged, the color is carefully selected to make sure it gives the right message to the consumer.

You can use this same approach to help make your home sell for more money, without spending a fortune in the process.

In the study by Dutch Boy Paints mentioned in Chapter 2, the value of a particular home before interior and exterior painting, according to independent appraisal, was $75,400. After painting, the appraisal was $86,100, and this does not include any other changes or improvements. That's an increase of $10,700 on an investment of approximately $3,000.

When we talk about color in this chapter, think about the various forms it can take. It can mean the color of kitchen appliances, fresh flowers, or a newly stained hardwood floor. The way in which colors are introduced in a room can be as important as the colors themselves.

To learn how to harness the power of color, first go through the five steps of the system so you can recognize what improvements your home may need.

THE FIVE-STEP SYSTEM
Step 1. Consider the Competition

There are two important points to bear in mind when you compare your home with the competition.

The first is the general theme of the area you live in. Most neighborhoods tend to be consistent in the style and general appearance of their homes. And color has a great deal to do with establishing this consistency.

I recommend against trying to be the odd house out on the block. People are buying the feeling of the area as well as your home, and if your home is totally out of keeping with the neighborhood, you may have trouble selling it. The easiest way to avoid this is to keep the color of your home within the color scheme of the neighborhood.

The second point concerns the condition of the painted surfaces. Homes with blistering or peeling exterior paint or faded and soiled interior paint are likely to make a negative impression on the buyer. Moreover, if the competition has a fresh look as a result of new painting or papering, take a hard look at your home.

Step 2. Consider the Buyer

Different types of buyers have different types of color preference. While they are not dramatic, research indicates that subleties do exist.

First-Time Buyers

Younger buyers tend to respond favorably to bright colors. The purchase of a first home is an exciting and happy event, and bright colors can symbolize this.

Although virtually all buyers respond to bright homes, "fun" colors are much more appropriate for this group than for other segments of the market.

Trade-up Buyers

This group is generally more sophisticated and responds to more understated and sophisticated tones, such as the new pastels and high-tech colors. The urban buyer is closer to the leading-edge colors than the suburban buyer. But historical colors, where appropriate, can also be very appealing to this group.

Empty Nesters/Trade-down Buyers

Older people tend to like more traditional colors rather than stylish shades. Empty nesters are very comfortable with historic colors or conservative beiges, antique whites, or plain white. They are less comfortable with the bright colors that a first-time buyer might appreciate.

Since most empty nesters and trade-down buyers purchase smaller homes, it is important to stick with light colors so as to maximize the appearance of size.

Step 3. Evaluate Your Product

When your focus group of friends, neighbors, or brokers tours your property, listen for comments about the color of particular areas of your home.

Also pay attention to comments about the condition of the wallpaper or paint on your walls and ceiling, since it is so easy to become desensitized to their appearance. For example, soot from an oil heating system can gradually dull the color of a room; you may never notice it, and it may take an outsider to point this out to you.

It is far better for this sort of cosmetic problem to be picked up by your focus group than by a potential prospect.

Focus groups can also alert you to potentially offensive colors or wallpaper patterns. If comments about color don't surface and you are unsure about a certain part of your home, ask your group, "If you had the chance to change the color of any room in this house, which one would it be?"

Make sure you pay particular attention to feedback about the exterior color of your home, since this has a tremendous impact on the first impression of your property.

Step 4. Eliminate Territorial Anxiety

Color can either help you sell your home faster and for more money or make the sale more difficult. To avoid making critical mistakes with color, you must be able to recognize how it can work for or against you.

We all have favorite colors or patterns and feel comfortable when surrounded by them. But like the example of the president of Procter and Gamble who loved the color red, what's good for you is not necessarily good for the buyer.

Strong personal color or design statements can mark territory and subconsciously reinforce the buyer's feeling that he or she is an outsider. Your goal is to use color as a way of making the buyer more comfortable in your home.

Step 5. Maximize Packaging Appeal

Color may be the ultimate packaging tool. It has no effect on the substance of the product, yet for relatively little money, it can dramatically alter its perceived value.

A red sports car, for example, can look faster than a blue one, cigarettes in a gold foil box may seem more expensive than those in a plain generic carton, and a sleek black stereo system can appear more "state-of-the-art" than one that's brushed chrome. Materially, they may all be the same, but the difference in packaging can decide which will sell faster and for more money. The same holds true with your home.

UNDERSTANDING THE EFFECTS OF COLOR

Color can influence us in a number of ways. It can affect our emotions and the way we perceive the size of objects. By understanding the effects of color, you can use it to package your house or condo more effectively.

The Emotional Response

Despite the fact that individuals may have different color preferences, extensive research conducted by Dr. Max Lusher, one of the world's foremost experts on color, has shown that each color generates the same physiological response in all of us.

Red, for example, has a proven stimulating effect, while dark blue is relaxing. Yellow generates a cheerful feeling because of its association with sunlight, and certain shades of green evoke feelings of stability and peacefulness. Whether or not a person likes one or more of these colors has no bearing on how his or her body responds to it.

The Reflective Value of Colors

Colors can either absorb or reflect light. In cases where you want a room to seem brighter and larger, highly reflective colors can make all the difference. At the high end of the spectrum, white reflects 70 to 90 percent of the light directed toward it, ivory reflects 55 to 78 percent, and yellow reflects 65 to 75 percent. (There are shades of yellow that can reflect more light than white, but they would not be recommended for use in a home.)

At the opposite end is black, which may reflect less than 5 percent. It is followed by deep purple, olive, and browns.

Additionally, glossy surfaces reflect significantly more light than do flat finishes, which is why darkrooms often have matte black surfaces and laboratories have shiny white ones.

Unfortunately, many home sellers inadvertently decrease the value of their property by using colors that are too dark. The impact of light is simply too valuable to lose, and color is one of the easiest ways to enhance this.

THE CARDINAL RULES OF COLOR

There are two cardinal rules about the use of color: first, keep it neutral, and second, err on the side of caution.

As previously mentioned, it is far easier for a prospect who likes hot pink to visualize it against a white wall, for example, than it is for someone looking for white walls to visualize them against a hot pink surface.

And as boring as plain white may sound, Ken Charbonneau, color and merchandising manager of Benjamin Moore & Company, reports, "Plain white outsells any other single paint color by a factor of five." In addition, he states that white tones — including "Bone," "Antique," "Cameo," and "Off White" — are among the company's top sellers, as are different shades of beige.

These are the "safe" colors, which should be the basis of your interior wall color scheme. You can introduce accent colors to rooms or use more adventurous colors in transitional areas like hallways. But you can always rely on safe colors as a visual "retreat" that the prospect can fall back on if he or she objects to the accent color you've selected. Otherwise, you risk the prospective buyer's turning off to an entire room just because of the color.

The Color of Mistakes

Certain colors are risky. Black, violet, and pink top the list, according to Beverly Trupp, president of Color Design Art, a major California interior design firm. "While they may be fine for clothing, they generally do little for most home buyers," she comments. Even colors generally considered popular, like blue, red, and green, can be risky because they are either strongly liked or disliked.

But playing it safe is the only way to go when marketing your home. You can use colors as accents, but by using them as the primary focal point of a room or the exterior of your home, you are gambling for high stakes.

I once bought a two-family house that was painted Kelly green. Not only did it look like a float in a St. Patrick's Day parade, it was totally inconsistent with the rest of the neighborhood. It had sat on the market for several months, though it was fairly priced and in good condition.

I immediately repainted it light gray with white trim, and was offered 15 percent more for the property three months after I purchased it. It's hard to say if all of that appreciation came about from just the new color, but the light gray with white trim appealed to a much larger segment of the market.

A Warning on Wallpaper

If you have ever shopped for wallpaper, you know there are thousands of styles for just about every conceivable taste. Beware of expressing individuality through wallpaper.

Wallpaper can be useful if, for example, it covers up a cosmetic problem or adds to the historic charm of a home. But use it with caution.

Always avoid loud patterns, including those with strong colors or designs and unusual textures. Buyers will invariably tear these down when they buy your home. If your wallpaper could cause territorial anxiety, by all means strip it and paint the wall.

COLOR IT LARGE OR SMALL

Color can make small spaces seem to expand or large areas appear to contract, depending upon how you apply it. Interior decorators and designers have long used these principles in home design, and you can do the same.

Faber Birren, an internationally known color expert, says, "The perception of size is a function of brightness." Accordingly, he points out that the size of an object is magnified the most when it is painted yellow, and then in decreasing degrees when the same object is painted white, red, green, blue, and black. He adds that "pastels seem larger than most other color shades."

According to Birren, the scientific explanation for this is quite simple. "Brightness, when it strikes the nerves on the retina of the eye, tends to spread out like a drop of water on blotting paper. Thus it forms a larger image than anything dark." This effect is most profound in the interior of the home because you are completely surrounded by the color, as opposed to the exterior, where you are looking at it against a background of many other colors.

Changing Room Dimensions

As a general rule, lighter cool colors contribute to an expensive airy feeling, while warmer dark colors cause a room to close in.

Without moving a single piece of plaster, you can change the perceived shape of a room with color, too. If a room is uncomfortably long and narrow, paint the walls at either end a dark, warm color like deep brown, to draw them toward the center of the room. This will help make the room seem more square.

If you have a small room with one or more dark walls, painting them a light cool color — like a light gray or plain white — will make them recede from the center of the room.

Hallways

A small patterned wallpaper helps make wall surfaces recede, while large patterns draw wall surfaces toward the center of a room. Vertical stripes make a room seem taller and long hallways seem shorter. Horizontal stripes help make rooms seem wider and hallways longer.

As always, use caution with wallpaper to avoid making strong personal statements.

Ceilings

A ceiling that is too high can be "brought down" by making it darker. Coffee tones, grays, and dark greens can be used, but make sure there is enough light in the room to compensate for these dark shades.

If the ceiling is too low, painting the walls a darker color than the ceiling will make it seem higher. The more dramatic the contrast, the stronger this effect will be. But don't forsake the airiness of the room itself just to raise the ceiling.

Floors

Dark floors can absorb an enormous amount of light, thereby making a room look smaller than is necessary. If you have dark stained hardwood floors that need refinishing, for example, redo them with clear polyurethane to brighten up the room. Glossy urethane will reflect more light than a low-gloss finish will.

Enlarging the Exterior

It is much easier to use color to increase the perception of the size of the interior than of the exterior of your home. In both cases, lighter colors make surfaces seem larger. Since white is by far the most popular exterior color, most people are already maximizing the impression of the size of their homes.

But there is another equally important rule for the exterior that many homeowners ignore. The greater the unbroken expanse of one particular color, the larger the area will seem.

If the exterior of a tan house, for example, is broken up with dark brown trim around doors, windows, and the frame, the home will seem smaller. People often use this approach to highlight architectural detail, but there is another way to do this and still make the home seem larger. Use white as an accent against a darker background. The overall effect is more harmonious and creates a more expansive appearance.

CORRECTING PROBLEMS WITH COLOR

Color is one of the most cost-effective tools in solving problems in your home. From small cosmetic weaknesses to design flaws, color can detract from their impact. Here is a variety of common household problems you can correct.

Busy Walls

Rooms often have walls that are broken up by radiators, doors, windows, or vents. These can make a small room look smaller and a large room appear poorly designed.

By selecting a color in a flat tone and applying it to all elements of the wall, you can make the different elements seem to blend together, and the distractions will disappear. This will not only make the wall more pleasing to the eye, but will also make the wall seem larger. Once again, the larger a continuous expanse of any single color, the larger an area will appear to be.

Uneven Ceilings

In homes where normal settling has occurred, uneven ceilings are common. Since these may create an unwarranted concern in the mind of the buyer, you may want to draw attention away from the ceiling.

Darker paint will help do this by reflecting less light up toward the ceiling and indirectly shifting the focus of attention to brighter areas of the room. Another method, which is probably most appropriate in the kitchen or foyer, is to wallpaper the ceiling. There are patterns that are designed to go on both walls and ceilings that can cover up any cosmetic flaw.

Uneven Walls

Settling can play havoc with your walls. As long as this is not caused by a structural problem, you can take measures to draw attention away from this cosmetic flaw. Wallpaper can be ideal for this since it provides a uniform surface yet may have a pattern that makes slight irregularities indiscernible.

If the problem is severe, have it corrected by a plasterer. A bulging wall that has been recently covered with wallpaper will look very suspicious and cast doubts about the rest of your home.

Water Stains

You may have found that a stain caused by a ceiling leak keeps reappearing, even though you have corrected the problem. A buyer will notice this and may immediately fear that you have a major roof or plumbing problem.

To prevent this, apply a coat of polyurethane over the affected area, let it dry, and then paint as usual.

Soot Marks

It is not uncommon to have soot stains around heat vents. This may be the result of a poorly adjusted heating system or simply a condition that has developed over time.

Once you have corrected the problem, if any, be sure to repaint carefully so you don't create unwarranted concerns about the conditions of the systems in your home.

COLOR IT NEW

The perception of newness can be a real asset to your home. Newness can eliminate territorial anxiety, increase the feeling of value, and suggest a well-maintained property. Color can be used to suggest all three, and do so without your spending a great deal of money.

A freshly painted interior can create the same feeling of newness projected by model units. Painting can create a crisp, clean feeling that can also eliminate many of the personal clues that can create discomfort to potential buyers.

Fresh paint can also bring back to life the surface to which it is applied. For example, worn and weathered shingle siding can look brand new after a fresh coat of paint; even in the basement tired walls and ceilings can be improved dramatically by simply applying a coat of color.

A good test to determine the condition of painted walls is to remove any pictures or paintings you may have on them. If the area behind a picture, for example, is brighter and cleaner than the remainder of the wall, seriously consider repainting the area.

Not only does a fresh coat of paint suggest newness but so, too, can the color itself. Like fashions, automobile design, and music, colors change with the times. Although some colors, like white and beige, are timeless, others, like chocolate brown or harvest gold, are often associated with certain eras.

By applying up-to-date colors to older items in your home, you can avoid the question of age. Obviously there are some aspects of your home whose charm and character you will want to emphasize. But certain rooms in a house or condo, like kitchens or bathrooms, are looked upon more favorably by buyers when they are new.

In or Out?

There are some significant color trends that are reflected in anything from clothing to automobiles. According to Mr. Everett Call, president of the nonprofit Color Marketing Group, an international organization of leading color experts, "There seems to be a definite correlation between the mood and economy of the country and the popularity of certain colors." In the seventies, a period marked by economic slump and political upheaval, dark heavy earthtone colors like chocolate brown, for example, were very widely used.

The eighties appear to be a time of optimism and economic growth, and the color trends reflect this. Soft pastels and elegant traditional colors are replacing the heavy hues. There is a real renaissance in the historic color themes, as proven by the success of the Benjamin Moore and Pittsburgh historic paint lines.

The following list describes the color trends as applied to individual rooms. You will note that certain colors, most notably dark brown, are considered passé for the interior but are still big sellers for exterior use.

By no means rush out and apply every "in" color to your home. Nor need you tear out a bath fixture that features a dated color.

Our recommendation is to accent the staples listed with "in" colors. We will next suggest how you can add today's colors to your home inexpensively.

INEXPENSIVE WAYS TO INTRODUCE ACCENT COLOR

For the budget-conscious, there are many ways to introduce new accent colors into the home without replacing expensive fixtures and, in many cases, without repainting.

Best of all, most of these items are designed to be taken with you when you sell the house. A good strategy for purchasing one or more of these is to decide what you would like to have in your new home, so that these items will then fit right in. Don't forget to buy them in colors that will help brighten up or update the look of the room.

Kitchens

Countertop canisters, tablecloths, dishtowels, framed prints, drapes, window blinds, wallpaper trim, green plants, and flowers all add color.

Bathrooms

Matching towel sets, throw rugs, shower curtains and rod covers, toilet seats, decorative hand soaps, silk flowers, curtains or window blinds, and framed prints can brighten up this room.

Bedrooms

Comforters, sheets, curtains, window blinds, area rugs, flowers, plants, and wallpaper trim can enliven any bedroom.

COLORS

ROOM	Fashionable	Staple	Outdated
KITCHEN			
Appliances	sand, toast, platinum, silver	almond, white	harvest gold, avocado, brown
Cabinets	white/oak, almond/oak, platinum, gray	oak, maple	dark brown, pine, gold
Countertops	almond, ceramic red, platinum	white, butcher-block	gold speckled, gold, avocado, brown
Sinks	crimson, rose, almond, sand	stainless, white	brown, gold
Floors	vanilla, peach, rose, seafoam, buff, oak, slate gray	white, beige, terra-cotta, almond, umber	gold, dark brick

COLORS

ROOM	Fashionable	Staple	Outdated
BATHROOMS			
Tubs, Toilets, Sinks	peach, gray, taupe, jade, rose, French vanilla, sea mist, cerulean blue	white, almond, blue, beige, marblized China	gold, brown, green, marble
Floors	sepia, sand, wheat, sea mist, peach, rose, taupe	white, beige, tan	yellow, powder blue
LIVING ROOM			
Carpets	mauve, ivory, gray	beige, tan	gold, brown, green
Drapery	aquamarine, celadon, turquoise, lavender, pale yellow	ivory, tan, natural	
Walls	cream, ivory, peach, putty, gray, bisque	white, beige, tan	brown, deep red, reflective foil

ROOM	COLORS		
	Fashionable	*Staple*	*Outdated*
BEDROOMS			
Walls	Wedgewood blue, peach, taupe, rose, ivory	white, cream, beige	deep red, brown, yellow
EXTERIORS			
Doorways	russet, gray, burnt orange	brown, white, black, red	
Siding	platinum gray, ivory, buff, sand, federal blue, putty	white, brown, tan, beige, redwood	light green, yellow, pale blue, gold

Living Room

Area rugs, pillows, flowers, plants, draperies, slip covers, wall prints, wall hangings, louvered shutters, and window blinds can bring color to this room.

Entryways

Area rugs, upholstered chairs, wallpaper, framed prints, flowers, and plants add color here, too.

CONCLUSION

Recognize the impact color can have in improving the perception of your home and how inexpensive the use of color can be. By doing so, you will find it to be one of the most effective packaging tools you can use.

Color cannot be fully appreciated without proper light, however. In fact, certain colors can look entirely different under different lighting.

The following chapter will focus on the effect of light in the home and how it, too, can color the perception of your property.

CHAPTER HIGHLIGHTS

1. Color can be one of the least expensive and most effective packaging tools.

2. The right colors can suggest newness in those areas where newness is an asset and can imply Old World charm where it is appropriate.

3. Light colors make areas seem more expansive, while dark colors make spaces close in.

4. Strong personal color statements can cause territorial anxiety and make it more difficult for the buyer to visualize the home as his or her own.

5. To avoid territorial anxiety, stick with "safe" neutral colors like whites, beiges, and soft pastels and use special caution when selecting wallpaper.

6. Use light-reflecting colors to add brightness to a room.

7. Use dark colors to correct cosmetic flaws in walls or ceilings.

8. Add bold colors through accent features like fabrics, flowers, and trim, but keep the background neutral.

9. It is easy to become desensitized to dull or faded paint. Consider repainting if your focus groups indicate it is needed.

10. When repainting, choose premium-quality paint because the difference in results will far exceed the difference in cost.

4

The Most Favorable Light

Lighting can be an effective and inexpensive tool in enhancing the packaging appeal of your home. It can make a house or condominium seem larger and more dramatic and can actually improve the buyer's attitude toward the property.

A naturally bright home is a highly desirable feature, which explains why so many real estate ads boast "bright and sunny." But while most people realize that bright, sunny homes have more buyer appeal than do dark, dimly lit ones, few sellers understand how much control they can have over creating a bright environment.

Sellers often assume that a dark home is something you simply have to accept. But assumptions can be costly, and we will dispel this particular one by showing you how to improve the appearance of any home through proper lighting strategies.

The five steps in our system will help you understand the power of light and how to put it to best advantage in marketing your home.

THE FIVE-STEP SYSTEM
Step 1. Consider the Competition

Competitive homes are likely to vary widely in how much natural light they offer, how effective their artificial lighting is, and how attractive their light fixtures are.

Because lighting can have a major impact on how a buyer feels about your home, do all you can to assure that yours outshines the competition.

Additionally, the fixtures you use to provide light should be as attractive as possible. When touring other properties, take note of what types of lights are included, and apply any ideas that seem especially attractive and would suit your property.

Step 2. Consider the Buyer

Light is something that almost all buyers respond to, but it may have special significance to certain groups.

Older empty nesters and single women, for example, are most sensitive to the need for outdoor lighting for security purposes and for negotiating stairs and walkways at night. Young trade-up buyers look carefully at the fixtures themselves, which can make an important statement about the property in general.

But most important of all is the physiological and emotional effect light has on all buyers. We will explain the subliminal power of light on purchase behavior and demonstrate why it is so important.

Step 3. Evaluate Your Product

It's very easy to become desensitized to the lighting in your home. You can grow accustomed to a burned-out bulb or inappropriately low wattage, for example. But what you may no longer notice, a buyer easily might, so get a fresh perspective on your lights, as well as objective opinions on the appearance of your light fixtures, from your focus group.

Step 4. Eliminate Territorial Anxiety

While you cannot create territorial anxiety with light itself, you certainly can with certain light fixtures. Fixtures come in such a wide variety of designs and styles that they accommodate strong personal expression. Use your focus group to evaluate the light fixtures in your home.

Since fixtures are attached to the ceilings and walls of a home, they are often viewed as part of it, unlike personal property such as furniture. For this reason, light fixtures should be as neutral as possible, and not a vehicle for self-expression.

If your home is traditional, simple brass and glass lights designed for your decor are much less likely to generate territorial anxiety than, for example, ornate Mediterranean-inspired pendant lamps. If your home is contemporary, clean and simply designed fixtures are your best choice.

If you have potentially offensive fixtures, either remove them and supplement the lost light with a floor or table lamp, or purchase neutral replacements. This is especially important in critical rooms like the entryway, kitchen, and living room.

You don't have to buy top-of-the-line fixtures, but you should select ones that will add to the appeal of the rooms in which they are located. And whatever you do, don't use colored light bulbs or the simulated flickering-flame variety because both look contrived and will detract from your home.

Step 5. Maximize Packaging Appeal

Lighting is a powerful packaging tool that can affect the perception of your entire home. It can help establish a focal point in every room, assist in differentiating your home from the competition, and increase the perceived value of your property.

You can highlight particularly attractive features in your home, increase the perception of size of any room, and help minimize the appearance of cosmetic flaws. We will show you how to accomplish these and other effects through easy and inexpensive lighting techniques.

Beyond the impact of light itself, be aware of the statements made by the light fixtures. New or high-quality fixtures suggest the quality of the rooms they illuminate. Additionally, the quality and condition of the fixtures suggest the state of the wiring or electrical service within the walls.

Whenever I see cheap or antiquated fixtures. I immediately wonder about the quality of the wires feeding them. Don't provide buyers with unwarranted concerns about the state of your electrical service, and don't short-change the perception of your home by keeping old or unattractive lights. They are the jewelry of your house or condo and can really make it glow.

UNDERSTANDING THE POWER OF LIGHT

Light does far more than enable us to see; light is essential to our health. Studies conducted at the Massachusetts Institute of Technology show that 80 to 90 percent of the vitamin D our bodies take in comes from our exposure to sunlight. Lack of sunlight can affect calcium absorption, our ability to fight illness, and our growth rate during childhood.

How does this relate to selling your home? People are naturally drawn to light and feel physically and emotionally better when they have enough of it. Of course, a few hours in dim light won't hurt anyone, but we all feel happier in a bright rather than a dark environment.

The proof comes from hundreds of studies on human behavior. Dr. P. C. Hughes of the General Electric Company, for example, conducted an extensive study on light in the workplace. He proved that when light levels were increased, productivity jumped by as much as 9 percent.

Mr. Frank F. LaGuisa, an application engineer also with General Electric, conducted a consumer package study that has particular relevance to the presentation of your home. Mr. LaGuisa demonstrated that proper lighting increased the sale of packaged goods by up to 15 percent. Retailers have known for years that highlighting products will make them sell faster and that consumers have better attitudes on sunny days than on rainy ones.

Proper lighting has a powerful, though subliminal, effect on attitude that should not be taken for granted when marketing your home.

LIGHTING GROUND RULES

Whether your home is naturally bright because large windows and good sun exposure or tends toward the dark side, there are certain rules that always apply.

Let the Sun Shine In

While you can't control the weather, you can determine when to schedule tours. Whenever possible, plan showings with some thought to the weather report. If the forecast includes a 90 percent chance of heavy rain on Tuesday with clearing on Thursday, try to book your prospect accordingly.

This, of course, can't be done all the time, and you're far better off showing your home on a rainy day than letting the prospect slip away. But given the option, aim for the good weather.

I've found that the difference in perception of your home between the two types of days can be dramatic. A property toured under the sun will leave a far more positive impression.

Keep It Clean

Windows should be clean before any showing. Dirty windows can reduce light penetration and detract from the view outside.

Always assume they are dirty before you begin marketing your home. This is such a small detail that many homeowners don't bother to address it, and the difference between clean and dirty windows can change the perception of an entire room.

Try a trick used by the pros. Clean your windows with ammonia and vinegar added to a bucket of water. Add a half-cup of each to the water, and use newspaper to wipe the windows because it leaves almost no lint. To eliminate streaks, follow up with a clean blackboard eraser.

Also make sure the glass around light fixtures is clean. A bright bulb in a dusty fixture will only highlight the dust.

Clear the View

To allow as much light in as possible, move large objects that may be sitting on your windowsills. Pull draperies away and secure them with tiebacks, if necessary.

If you have bushes, hedges, or branches that have grown in front of your windows, trim them to let the sun shine in. (If your view happens to be particularly unattractive, however, obscuring it may be the best course of action.)

Show with the Lights On

If your home has rooms that are dark during the day, always make sure the lights are on *before* the buyer sees them.

Avoid walking into a dark room with a prospect. Even if you turn on the light immediately afterward, the first impression may stick in his or her mind. Similarly, don't shut the lights off after you leave, in case the buyer wants to return to the room. You'll waste a little electricity, but when you are showing a home it is no time to be concerned about saving small amounts of money.

Even if every room in your home is blessed with a good supply of natural light, leave some lights on in each room. They can fill areas that may be in shadow and can provide warm pools of light that can be an effective supplement to the sun.

LIGHTING ALTERNATIVES

Think of light as a decorating tool that can achieve a certain look or overcome a specific problem. There are a dizzying array of fixtures you can purchase to accomplish one or more of these goals.

To simplify matters, we will cover the three basic lighting categories and provide some basic suggestions. We will limit our discussion to lighting that requires minimal electrical installation or expense. In some cases, certain fixtures will be mentioned several times because of their versatility.

General Lighting

This refers to the background light that fills a room and is intended to reduce contrasts between light and dark areas. The hallmark of good general lighting is that you don't notice it, since it is intended to provide overall illumination, much like natural light.

Hanging Fixtures

Hanging fixtures that provide general lighting are most often found in an entryway, living room, or dining room and can range from chandeliers to pendant lights.

Remember two basic points. First, since hanging lights are most often decorative in design, the appearance of the fixture itself makes an important statement. The fixture should communicate quality, especially in the entryway.

Second, make sure hanging fixtures are perfectly clean and the bulbs have sufficient wattage.

Ceiling-mounted Fixtures

These lights tend to call less attention to themselves. They are typically shallow, light-diffusing fixtures with flat, semiopaque glass or plastic covers.

These lights are primarily functional, so make sure they are clean and have the proper bulbs. Since ceiling-mounted fixtures in the kitchen and bath, for example, are often fluorescent, always use the soft white bulbs so they don't cast an unpleasant green tint.

And always avoid uncovered fluorescent fixtures anywhere but the basement or garage. They create a harsh effect, and the fixtures themselves do little to increase the perception of newness or value of a room.

Accent Lighting

These lights help create visual excitement in a room by highlighting specific objects or features. They are usually directional and can be especially effective in establishing a focal point in a given area of your home.

Can Lights

These canlike cylinders come in ceiling-mounted or freestanding floor varieties. They cast a cone of light that flares out from the can.

Installing these in the ceiling can be costly, but purchasing one or two for the floor will provide a dramatic effect at little cost. Place one behind a large floor plant in a moderately lit living room, for example, or behind a bureau in the bedroom, and you'll create an exciting look. I can think of few more economical techniques for producing a dramatic feeling in a room.

You can also achieve an interesting look by placing a can light on top of a high shelf or piece of furniture. This will illuminate the ceiling and create an airy effect.

Plug-in can lights cost from $15 to $30.

Track Lights

Track lights are both versatile lighting tools and high-perceived-value items. They can be used in virtually any room in the home and are appropriate in a wide range of home decors. Track lights come in a wide variety of lengths and head designs to fit virtually any spot or accent lighting needed. They also suggest newness and sophistication.

Track lights can be expensive, however, ranging between $75 and $150 for a three-foot, three-head system, and installation will cost another $50. For this reason, consider installing track lights in parts of your home that need specific dramatic help.

Picture Lights

If you have an especially attractive print or painting in your home, a clip-on frame light can add a sense of drama and formality. This might be considered a little pretentious, but if the picture is worth calling attention to, it can make the kind of statement that appeals to a trade-up buyer.

Floor Spots

Installing ceiling-mounted spotlights can be expensive, but freestanding, plug-in floor spots can highlight objects on walls. These spots, which can be hidden next to pieces of furniture, or behind plants, are designed to call attention to a particular object or feature in a room. Aiming a spot at a fabric wall hanging or even an empty brick wall can create an interesting effect.

The cost of a floor spot will range between $20 and $40, depending on how large it is and what type you buy. If you do use one, make sure to hide the cord, and also be careful that the light is positioned so that it won't create an unpleasant glare.

Valance Lighting

This refers to lighting from behind a shield to produce both upward and downward lighting. Typically, valance lights are fluorescent and are placed over a kitchen sink or above a window.

These lights can be expensive if custom-made, but you can make your own by building a simple enclosure and attaching a plug-in General Electric Light Stick inside. For about $25, you can assemble a valance light that could fit over a small window.

Task Lighting

As the name suggests, this functional lighting is designed to assist a specific activity like reading, working over the stove, or shaving. It provides illumination without glare or shadows and is particularly important in rooms like the kitchen. Task lighting can also add to the aesthetics of a room.

Floor Lamps

This lighting provides an opportunity to define particular areas of a large open room. By creating warm pools of light within furniture groupings, like a desk and bookshelves, you can help the buyer visualize how a large area could be utilized. And floor lamps with fabric shades can generate warm light that adds coziness to a room.

Light Sticks

These plug-in fluorescent fixtures can be placed beneath overhead cabinets or shelves to illuminate a work surface below. This effect is particularly valued in the kitchen. Each light stick costs about $12 for an eighteen-inch fixture and can be easily installed.

Hanging Lamps

Fixtures over work or eating areas suggest definition and utility. You might install a hanging fixture to help sell a home if you have an open area that serves several functions. In a studio condominium, for example, where one room serves as the dining room, living room, and bedroom, a hanging light over an eating area will help set it apart.

It will cost between $50 and $75 to install a light if no receptacle is available, and you should plan on taking the fixture when you move.

Track Lights

In addition to working well as accent lights, tracks can also direct illumination to a specific spot like a reading table, piano, or cooking area. Track lights aren't cheap, but they can convey a level of utility and value that can easily exceed their cost. Always use a dimmer with track lights, since dimmers cost only about $5 to $10 and suggest a very up-to-date feature.

SOLVING LIGHTING PROBLEMS

The beauty of artificial lighting is that it can help solve costly problems in your home inexpensively. For example, if your home has a design weakness — a hallway that is too long or a room that is too small — certain lighting techniques can minimize the problem. A contractor may solve the problem more completely, but our goal is a positive return on investment, which is where good lighting can really shine.

Long Hallways

A long hallway, especially a dark one, can be viewed as wasted space. In condominiums and cooperatives, where prices are often determined according to square footage, a wasted hallway can be particularly unfortunate.

You can convert this liability into an asset with proper lighting. By hanging pictures along either side of the wall and illuminating them with track lights, you can create an art-gallery effect. This will not only help divert attention from the fact that the hall is not especially useful, but will actually make it a focal point.

Low Ceilings

Proper illumination in rooms with low ceilings will help minimize a feeling of claustrophobia. Lights that wash up walls — floor can lights, wall-mounted valance lights, or swing-arm lamps — will create a vertical effect that helps increase the feeling of height.

Avoid hanging pendant lights, since they will only dramatize the low ceiling.

High or Uneven Ceilings

There may be two reasons why you don't want buyers to focus on the ceilings. First, the ceilings may be too high in relation to the size of the room. Second, they may be old or in less than perfect condition, and you don't want to call attention to them.

The approach here is the exact opposite from the steps adopted for low ceilings. Focus as little light on the ceiling as possible, so you will cast as much light downward as you can. Hanging pendant lights, wall-mounted tracks, or valance lights sealed off at the top will help create this look.

Small Rooms

To maximize the feeling of light and size in room, nothing is more effective than mirrors. A mirror that covers an entire wall, for example, will appear to double the size of a room. While you may not want to go this far, there are many ways to use mirrors — closet or cabinet doors, over fireplaces or above a table — that discreetly enhance the feeling of spaciousness. A mirrored wall section can also be very attractive. Expect to pay between $2 and $4 each for mirrored squares; and for sheet mirror, plan on spending about $6 per square foot.

Placing mirrors across from windows can increase the light in a room and the feeling of spaciousness by reflecting the depth of the outdoor view.

A skylight is another, more expensive, remedy for a small or claustrophobic room, and is a feature to which buyers respond very favorably. Depending upon the design of your home and the style of window, skylights can cost anywhere from $150 to $450 each and several hundred dollars to install.

This improvement can be justified only if the small room happens to be a critical one, like a master bedroom, or if you have a very small studio condo and the skylight will dramatically influence the perception of the entire unit, or if the house is very expensive and this feature will significantly help justify your asking price.

Narrow Rooms

By illuminating the shorter walls and minimizing light on the longer ones, you can make any room feel wider. You can do this with various light sources, including valance or track lights or floor lamps placed along the wall.

Uneven Walls

The walls of older homes may exhibit bowing or unevenness that is a natural part of the settling process. Lights that wash up or down the surface of a wall will only exaggerate this problem.

Make sure table and floor lamps are placed away from uneven walls so the direct column of light coming from the top of the shade does not wash the wall.

Dark Windows

There are steps you can take to increase the light from otherwise dark windows. I once toured a home that had a room with poor sun exposure and large deep-set windows. To get the most out of the light that came in, the owner had applied mirrors to the walls of the window enclosure. These acted like the reflector inside a flashlight and magnified the amount of light entering through the windows.

Placing a valance light enclosure over a window and covering the enclosure with a fabric that matches drapes can also throw light on the subject.

CONCLUSION

Proper lighting can set the stage for a successful tour and should never be taken for granted when marketing your home. Too many buyers assume that a lack of light in a home or a particular room is an unalterable characteristic of their property. By using creative lighting techniques and employing the proper lighting strategy during showings, you can offset the disadvantages of a dark home. And even if your home is naturally bright, don't assume you can't make it even brighter.

As powerful as light can be in influencing the outcome of your tour, there are more subtle sensory clues that can also have significant impact. As surprising as it may seem, sound and smell can also affect the buyer's attitude toward your house or condo, as we will reveal in the chapter that follows.

CHAPTER HIGHLIGHTS

1. Light makes spaces appear larger and can have a significant effect on the buyer's emotional response to a room.

2. Sun is the most effective light source in improving purchase attitudes toward a home.

3. Try to schedule tours on sunny days because the difference in buyer attitude may be significant.

4. On dark days or in dark rooms, make sure the lights are on before the tour.

5. Not only is the quality of artificial light important but so are the quality and look of the fixtures themselves.

6. Use light to mask cosmetic flaws and to create focal points in a room.

7. Take advantage of mirrors to maximize the feeling of light and size in a room.

8. Make certain that all windows are clean and that all bulbs are working and are of adequate wattage.

5

Smell and Sound: The Sensory Side of Selling

How much would you learn about a home by walking through it with your eyes closed? Your answer is probably "Not much," because we generally think of sight as providing the type of information necessary to evaluate a home.

But besides our eyes, we have other sensory receptors at work that provide us with a tremendous amount of information about a home on both a conscious and subconscious level.

Think about the dynamics that take place when you are shopping for a new car. You may be drawn to a particular model on the showroom floor by the way it looks, but when you sit inside, you may become influenced by the way it smells. The aroma of the new seats, carpet, and upholstery surrounds you as you begin to imagine how this sparkling new machine will look in your driveway.

Similarly, when you shut the door and take it out for a test drive, you may be influenced by the way it sounds. The solid thud of the door closing, the reassuring quiet of tight-fitting parts, and the smooth purr of a powerful new engine create a symphony of positive messages.

And if you think all this is an accident, guess again. The way a new car smells and sounds can be as deliberately planned as its name and color. International Flavors and Fragrances, the world's largest manufacturer of scents and flavors for consumer and industrial products, makes what is generically known as the "new-car smell," which is actually applied to the interior of many automobiles. I.F.F. reports that this scent, which is similar to that of new leather, has been proven to increase the sale of both new and used cars. You can even buy this product in aerosol cans at auto supply stores.

As far as sound is concerned, automobile manufacturers have gone to great lengths to figure out how to deaden road noises and engine vibrations through various types of insulation. And some industry observers even suggest that the solid thud of a car door closing is deliberately engineered.

These auditory and olfactory messages supply the consumer with much of the information about the quality, condition, age, and appeal of the objects we buy. From the smell of automobile interiors, to "scratch 'n' sniff" strips on advertisements, to the background music we hear in supermarkets and department stores, the advertising experts on Madison Avenue have for years been using smells and sounds to influence consumers. Through our research, we have determined ways in which you can apply these same proven principles to marketing your home.

Not only can smell and sound make your home more appealing, they can also be used to correct certain weaknesses in your house or condo. And, best of all, taking advantage of sound and smell in marketing your home requires spending little or no money.

I. THE SMELL OF SUCCESS

Smell is rarely considered a conventional home marketing tool, but the right smell can have a real effect in improving the buyer's overall feeling about the your home.

The wrong smells, of course, can be of equal significance when it comes to selling your home, and knowing what they are and how to avoid them is essential.

THE FIVE-STEP SYSTEM
Step 1. Consider the Competition

Smell is not a feature of a home but a part of a home's environment. The objective is not to duplicate the smell of any home you are competing with but to make sure your house or condo has the right smell.

Step 2. Consider the Buyer

The right smell in a home cuts across all categories of buyers. Our research has shown that smells perceived negatively disturb almost all buyers. Similarly, the right smells are appropriate for the vast majority of prospects. Remember, despite ethnic preferences, the cardinal rule of neutrality should prevail.

Step 3. Evaluate Your Product

One important scientific finding about smells is that people have an ability to adjust to them, no matter how unpleasant. For example, did you ever notice how, after being in an environment that smelled terrible at first, you begin not to notice it after a while?

Studies have shown that the olfactory system, more than any other system, is highly adaptable. Your eyes, for example, cannot adjust to light that is much too bright, and your ears can't adjust to sounds that are far too loud. But your nose can adjust to smells that are offensive. It may take a while, but it will happen.

So don't let a bad smell deliver a knockout punch to your prospect, just because it doesn't bother you anymore. Use your focus group's evaluation, because it may take an objective source to pick up what you no longer notice.

Step 4. Eliminate Territorial Anxiety

In the same way that a strong personal color statement can generate buyer discomfort, so too can smells. Smells can create barriers that prevent a prospect from visualizing him- or herself living in your home. Imagine an ardent nonsmoker walking into a home filled with the stale odor of cigarettes. Not only is the smell unpleasant, it can also suggest a life-style that he or she disagrees with.

According to Professor Pierre van den Berghe of the University of Washington, dominant personal smells related to one's ethnic background, personal habits or manner in which a home is kept can act very much like the effect of animals marking territory with scents. These smells provide a clear statement that a particular environment is in control of a certain individual or group of individuals, and anyone else is an outsider.

Whether or not you intended to make a statement of this kind, the result is the same. And, by doing so, you run the risk of alienating the prospective buyer of your property.

Americans as a whole have a particular fixation on cleanliness. Madison Avenue even coined the term "housatosis" in an advertising campaign for Lysol disinfectants. The campaign was developed from the American phobia of personal smells.

Given our sensitivity to smell, it is important that you recognize which ones are considered bad and which can be introduced into a home to overcome potential territorial anxiety.

Step 5. Maximize Packaging Appeal

The smell of newness can suggest that no one has put a mark on a home or that the home is in mint condition.

Even old historic or vintage homes can benefit from a "new" smell because it can alleviate some of the fears about antiquated plumbing and wiring systems. We are conditioned to associate new smells with objects that are in their ideal working state, and, by applying new smells to old items, you can achieve this same effect.

UNDERSTANDING THE POWER OF SMELL

The power of smell is more significant than most of us realize, according to Dr. Morley Care at the Monell Chemical Senses Center at the University of Pennsylvania: the ability to smell allows us to appreciate the taste of food and quickly enables us to detect danger like the presence of smoke or gas in our environment. It may also influence our decisions to buy certain products.

Smell can bring back memories that are either positive or negative, and, depending upon the smell of your home, this can affect the buyer's attitude. How many times, for example, have you caught wind of a certain smell that vividly reminded you of a particular experience?

According to Marina Munteneau, Director of Technical Services at International Flavors and Fragrances, "The olfactory bulb is linked with the same region of the brain that controls emotion and memory. That's the reason smell triggers both of these functions so quickly."

You can harness this powerful sense to enhance the perception of your home and help increase its selling appeal.

SMELLS TO AVOID

Smells that can either create territorial anxiety or make negative statements about the condition of your property fall into some specific categories. We will show you what they are and how to eliminate them.

Ethnic Cooking

We all tend to be "ethnocentric," for we seem to feel more comfortable with people who have similar backgrounds. So when confronted with evidence that someone may be very different from us, we can feel uneasy, especially in something as personal as a home.

An example of this was cited by Toni Reuter, national sales director of Century 21. While a broker in upstate New York, she encountered a large and prosperous ethnic population whose homes often smelled of ethnic cooking.

This group was well respected and integrated into the community as a whole. Yet she found that when buyers who were not from the same background were shown similar homes with and without the smell of ethnic cooking, they invariably selected the latter.

Indian or Italian, Szechuan or Spanish, the particular ethnic origin is irrelevant; the objective is to keep the odor in the home neutral.

One way to eliminate cooking smells is to put a small saucepan of vinegar on the stove at low heat and let it simmer for fifteen minutes. If the smell has already pervaded the whole house, start by opening the windows and doors for as long a period as possible, and let it air out. Then go through the kitchen and give it a thorough cleaning with a conventional liquid detergent like Tob Job. Your kitchen should be spotless, anyway, so don't feel that you are wasting your time.

Then use a lemon-based furniture wax or polish around the house and on wood surfaces in the kitchen. Pay particular attention to the entryway, because that is where the buyer will first encounter a potentially discomforting smell.

Cooking Smells

As a general rule, the smell of any cooking is best avoided, because you never know what people object to. Most "how to sell your home" books recommend introducing the aroma of freshly baked bread or cookies, but I feel that this simply adds to territorial anxiety.

Bread and cookies are far less threatening than curry or souvlaki, but there is no correlation between home purchase behavior and the aroma of rising bread. Though this may work in a restaurant or a supermarket, there are other smells to choose from that can say more about the quality of your home.

Smoking Smells

Smokers represent a significant part of our population, but those who don't approve of smoking tend to be vehement about it. There are few smells more objectionable and obvious to a nonsmoker than cigarette or cigar smoke. Even many smokers object to the smell of other people's smoke, so you may lose on all counts if your home smells like a smokers' lounge.

To eliminate the smell of stale smoke, try filling small dishes with activated charcoal and leaving them around the room for a few days. As strange as it may sound, burning a few candles will also help eliminate smoke residue. Another measure is to fill a small dish half-full of vinegar and let it sit on a table for several days. Then throw out the vinegar so that it does not produce its own unpleasant smell.

You may have seen some of the high-tech air fresheners that introduce electrically charged ions into the air. These can be effective, but they also tend to give negative charges to the surfaces of objects near them and can cause dust and soot to settle on walls, for example. If you buy one, be sure you get the kind that has its own dust collector.

Pet Smells

Pet odors can elicit reactions that range from tolerance from those who love animals to sneezing and watery eyes from those who are allergic to them. Pet-related smells can also include pet food, Kitty Litter, birdcages, and playthings.

While pet smell isn't personal in the same sense as ethnic cooking, it contributes to the overall statement about the home. If the smell is unpleasant to the buyer, he or she won't care where it came from.

If your pet is actually causing the smell, either keep the pet out of the house or give it a bath. To eliminate the smell of "accidents," use vinegar to neutralize them and apply lemon oil on nearby furniture to freshen the air.

Medicinal Smells

If someone in your home is ill and using a particularly strong-smelling medicine, try to eliminate the source of the odor or cover it up as much as possible.

The heavy smell of disinfectants can make a home smell like a hospital. This aroma might suggest cleanliness, but it is generally not appealing. Again, lemon is a much more pleasant and universally accepted smell of cleanliness.

SMELLS LIKE TROUBLE

There are smells that can suggest defects or mechanical problems in your home. These smells may be benign and easy to eliminate but, if left unattended, they can cost you the buyer's confidence.

Mildew

The smell of mildew is not only unpleasant but can hint at potential problems in your home. It can be caused by something as innocent as a wet rug or damp laundry, but may be associated with a problem as serious as a leaky roof, a damp basement, or seepage between bricks.

To eliminate mildew, first eliminate the problem. If it is serious, it may require bringing in a plumber, a mason, or a roofer. But once the underlying problem is fixed, mildew can be killed with chlorine bleach or hydrogen peroxide.

A dehumidifier can eliminate moisture from the air, which the mildew fungus thrives on, and help remove some of the smell. But do not have it running when prospects tour your home, or they will suspect a problem that no longer exists.

Fresh air and sunshine will not only help remove mildew odor but will actually help kill it. Apply lemon-scented products to cover up the smell. If the odor is especially persistent, try dabbing wintergreen oil on the affected area; the aroma will last for weeks.

Mustiness

This may result from some of the problems covered above but it tends to be less serious. Musty-smelling homes are generally old and have had windows shut for long periods of time. An "airing-out" may solve the problem, along with the introduction of plants, flowers, or lemon-scented furniture polish.

Fuel Oil or Gas

The smell of oil or gas is both unpleasant and worrisome to buyers. The problem must be checked at the source and, once it has been corrected, any residual smell should be eliminated by airing out the house.

The smell of oil in particular tends to attach itself to everything in the home from curtains to carpeting. A professional cleaning job may be necessary, if this aroma pervades your home.

Traffic Fumes

Houses or condos located at busy intersections or on lower levels in urban buildings may occasionally suffer from the effects of traffic fumes.

This odor can kill a sale, and you should schedule your tours during periods of low traffic so as to avoid or minimize it. Traffic fumes are not a common problem, but where they do exist they should not become an issue when showing the property.

Pesticides

If you are planning to do some minor spraying — or major fumigating — around your home, do it well before you put your home on the market. The smell of pesticides can indicate a definite problem, and the astute buyer will notice it immediately.

Septic Tank

After a soaking rain, many septic tanks seem to want to make their presence felt. There are few smells as unpleasant, difficult to disguise, and tough to eliminate.

Beyond doing work to the tank itself or not showing the home after heavy rainstorms, keep windows closed on the side of the home where the tank is located.

Do not try to mask septic tank smells with heavy spray deodorizers because the smells may become apparent later in the tour when the person walks around your yard. There is, however, a liquid septic cleaner called Alumin-Nu Power, which contains bacteria that eat organic waste matter. It is sold in quart or gallon containers and may be found in large hardware stores.

Fireplace

Fireplaces smell great when they contain a blazing fire, but, after the fire is out, the smell can become stale and unpleasant. If your fireplace is efficient and does not cause a heavy odor, its smell can suggest warmth and coziness in the winter months. But making your home smell like the day after a forest fire will not help your sale. The best way to remove this smell is to open the windows and replace it with fresh air.

Wood Rot

Any odor of wood rot is a definite sign of trouble. Although it is relatively rare, a basement can suffer from this problem because of rotting windowsills or decaying wood lying on top of a foundation.

One solution is to try to dry it out with a heat gun and then scrape away the loose pieces. Next, apply a urethane sealer that will cover the surface and provide a smell of newness. Be careful you don't seal in the moisture so that the wood rots from within.

CREATING THE "MODEL" SMELL

Few homes smell newer and cleaner than model units, so the model unit smell is ideal for your home. It suggests that the property is in optimal condition and may include fresh paint, new carpeting, recently applied polyurethane, new kitchen cabinets, and furniture polishes and waxes.

What's so great about all these smells, and how do we know that most people like them?

To start with, new smells can trigger positive imagery in our brains because "new" generally has pleasing connotations. A new wall-to-wall carpet is likely to be more attractive than an old one, a new stove is apt to work better than one that's been around for a long time, and so on.

Because we associate the smells of products with their condition, a new-car smell in an old car subconsciously makes us feel better about the automobile. We equate this smell with a new engine, low maintenance, and high status.

What could eliminate territorial anxiety more effectively than knowing that you are the first owner of a home? If no one else has put their mark on it, the buyer does not have to mentally remove the previous owners before projecting his or her family in their place.

The smell of "newness" is likely to be chemical, such as the smell of a new floor covering or the latex smell of paint or the resin of a countertop adhesive. Of course, the buyer does not want to be surrounded by these smells all the time. In fact, some people develop irritations from certain chemical aromas. But generally speaking, new smells are less threatening or potentially alienating than a strong personal smell.

How do you go about creating a smell that sells? Is there a "new home" spray that you can fill your home with like "Essence de Model Unit" or "Eau de Renovation"? The answer is no, but there are many ways to suggest newness through certain very effective products. Let's review some of these materials and suggest ways to apply them.

Sealants

Clear petroleum-based sealants are most often used to coat hardwood floors and natural wood trim. When you are marketing your home, sealants can perform a second function. They can produce a smell that is often associated with newness.

There are many areas of the home where you can use polyurethane for small touch-ups. These include oak trim, thresholds, wooden kitchen cabinet doors, and wooden knobs.

Polyurethane is one of my favorite products because even a small application will do the trick. And chances are, whatever wood surface you're working on will benefit from several coats, anyway. Polyurethane dries in 6 to 8 hours; make sure it's not wet when your prospect arrives, because you never want to appear to be in the middle of a project when your home is shown.

Val-Oil is a brand of all-purpose sealant. It can be applied to anything from cement and masonry floors to wooden table tops.

Val-Oil produces a relatively long-lasting but mild petroleum-based smell and a highly reflective surface that can make the dullest ceramic bathroom floors come to life. It is quite thin, a quality that will help in applying an even coat to tired-looking kitchen-cabinet door fronts. Val-Oil looks especially good on a quarry tile floor, since it helps bring out the color.

If ever there was a generic "new" smell, this is it. Val-Oil dries in about 6 hours and is available at local hardware stores.

Paint

The smell of interior latex paint, together with the look of a freshly painted surface, suggests newness. Paint companies are working very hard to develop odor-free latex paints, so you may soon discover that they have no smell at all. But for now, new paint does produce a new smell, and the closer you apply it to the time you show the property, the stronger it will be.

I do not recommend oil-based paints for the interior, especially on large surfaces, because the smell can be overpowering. You don't want your prospect passing out before the tour is over!

The only surfaces I recommend for oil-based paints are wood trim and, for reasons of durability and shine, the basement or garage floor.

Carpet

New carpet is frequently the dominant aroma in model units. While you wouldn't purchase new carpet just for the smell, if you do need new carpet, the smell is an added bonus. In smaller areas like bathrooms, you can create the same effect inexpensively with latex-backed throw rugs.

Carpet Treatments

Shampooing a carpet can eliminate stale odors and help restore the look of newness to your rugs. I do not recommend using powdered rug deodorizers because their smell is often too strong. A professional rug cleaning will, in most cases, yield the best results and will generally be worth the expense.

Lemon Oils, Waxes, Polishes, and Deodorizers

"Lemon," according to Marina Munteneau of International Flavors and Fragrances, "is a universally accepted smell of cleanliness." Its wide appeal is evidenced by its use in a variety of products ranging from dishwashing liquids to laundry detergents to furniture polishes and even to scented garbage bags.

People generally like lemon, so it can be safely used as an all-around smell. In my experience, the most effective lemon smells are produced by natural lemon furniture polishes, like Old English Lemon Oil or Hopes Lemon Oil. There are some man-made lemon-scented spray wax products like Endust that are also reasonably good facsimiles.

While you don't want to make your home smell like a Florida citrus grove, in potential trouble spots like bathrooms and kitchens, lemon scents can provide a great cover-up. One trick to eliminate the unpleasant smell that sometimes wafts out from a garbage disposal unit is to quarter a lemon and throw a piece in. Turn on the disposal and in a matter of seconds the smell of fresh lemon will replace any bad odor.

On the other hand, room deodorizers can suggest that you are trying to cover up something. They can be very strong and artificial and may draw attention to themselves. For this reason, it is best to use a natural scent if possible.

Sunlight and Fresh Air

The sun is a natural air freshener. Research conducted at the international consulting firm of Arthur D. Little has shown that sunlight kills many of the bacteria and fungi that cause unpleasant smells.

The more sunlight gets into your home, the more difficult it is for these bacteria to survive.

Finishing Touches

There are many aromatic flowers that can improve the smell of a room. People seldom object to any of them, so most choices are safe.

In large, formal rooms, like the living room or dining room, try hyacinth or gardenia, which look elegant but are far too aromatic for small enclosed areas like bathrooms. More sublte smells can be generated by tuberoses and freesia.

Because it can be expensive to keep replacing flowers, add an aspirin and sugar to their water to make them last longer. Be absolutely sure that the flowers look healthy, because a wilting arrangement will have a negative effect.

The same region of the brain that is influenced by smell also responds to taste. Odd as it may sound, you can use taste to add to the sales appeal of your home.

By placing chocolates or other candies in a bowl on a coffee table and offering them to prospects, you may accomplish two goals.

First, the friendliness of this gesture will help break down the discomfort that the buyer may experience in being with a stranger. Secondly, there is a chemical effect that sugar can have that may improve the way the buyer feels.

According to research scientist Judith J. Wurtman at the Department of Applied Biology at M.I.T., "A tense or nervous person often craves carbohydrates. When consumed, these can have a measurably relaxing effect." Dr. Wurtman indicates that sweets are ideal for this because the relaxing effect occurs almost instantly.

II. SOUNDS TO SELL BY

Who would think that sound could influence the outcome of a house tour? The prospect has so much information to absorb that it would seem as if sounds would be the last thing to be noticed.

But imagine yourself walking into a home with kids screaming, the dog barking, and a vacuum cleaner going at full tilt. Your first reaction would probably be "Maybe I should come back a little later" rather than "What a great looking entryway!" And if you do complete a tour against a background of unpleasant noises, it is likely to affect your total impression of the home.

Sounds can help set the right—or wrong—tone for a tour. Go through the five steps of the system to gain an understanding of how to apply sound to your benefit.

THE FIVE-STEP SYSTEM
Step 1. Consider the Competition

Like smell, sound is a part of a home's overall environment and is not the kind of feature you set out to duplicate from the competition. The goal is simply to use sound as a way of enhancing the overall feeling of your home. In so doing, if you succeed in making it more desirable than the competition's, all the better.

Step 2. Consider the Buyer

Consumer surveys show that privacy is a high priority among all buyers. The desire for privacy has been cited as one of the primary reasons why people move. Sound can suggest how much or little privacy a home has.

We will discuss what kinds of sounds you should be particularly sensitive to and how either to eliminate them or to minimize the impact.

There are also certain types of sound that we recommend introducing into your home. Music, for example, can be very effective but must be catered to the audience.

Step 3. Evaluate Your Product

Every home has its own peculiar sounds. Some have odd noises from the heating systems, others have squeaky floors, while others may have plumbing that occasionally acts up.

When you have lived in an environment for several years, you can adjust to sounds like these and not even notice them. But when a prospect tours your home and hears one or more of these, it may generate unwarranted concerns about hidden defects.

To avoid having this happen, use your focus groups to point out potential problem sounds that you may no longer notice.

Step 4. Eliminate Territorial Anxiety

Walking into homes that make strong personal statements through sound can make the prospect feel like an intruder.

If a prospect enters a home that is "marked" by ethnic music, screaming children, or noisy pets, it makes it difficult for the buyer to imagine occupying it. On the other hand, when a person walks into a model unit of a new housing development, the relative hush or sound of unobtrusive music creates the opposite effect.

Your objective is to make the environment as nonthreatening as possible.

Step 5. Maximize Packaging Appeal

Experts in merchandising and consumer behavior have long known that certain sounds can either work for or against the selling process.

Muzak, for example—the canned music that is piped into stores, offices, and supermarkets—has been around for fifty years. And the only reason the company continues to grow is that Muzak helps shape people's purchasing behavior. You can apply the same principles used by Muzak to help increase the packaging appeal of your home.

UNDERSTANDING THE EFFECT OF SOUND

It is important to understand that sound can have a psychological and physiological effect on us. It is known, for example, that sound can affect emotions, pulse rate, and blood pressure.

Studies at the University of California at Irvine have been aimed at pinpointing some of these effects. Children in schools located near noisy airports, for example, do not perform as well as those in quiet areas. Some sounds create anxiety and produce adrenaline.

It is also recognized that positive sounds can influence consumer behavior. For example, research conducted by Gerald J. Gorn, Associate Professor of Management at McGill University in Montreal, concludes that positive music in advertising can subconsciously influence product choice. The most striking aspect of the research shows that consumers did not realize that the music had had any effect on their decision to select a particular product, even though it clearly had.

Companies like Muzak specialize in broadcasting music designed to increase store sales. Let's first take a look at areas in which sound can be a problem and then at those where sounds can be introduced to enhance the marketing environment.

One of the sweetest sounds in a home is silence. Most homeowners crave peace and serenity, and knowing that they can have it if they want it is a big plus. Quiet suggests privacy, and privacy can mean higher resale value. Silence also lets the buyer focus on what you or the broker is saying. Research shows that a person's power of retention is lowered under noisy conditions, so you want to prevent excessive noise.

SOUNDS TO AVOID

Some homes are noisy by virtue of their proximity to the street, loud neighbors, or thin walls. While it is not always possible to eliminate all of these problems, some solutions may help.

Children

Children can be delightful, but they can also distract the buyer. Whether they are crying or just having a good time, children can create a disturbance that makes it difficult for people to imagine themselves in your home. This may be particularly disconcerting for the empty nester who may not have been around children for some time.

Children may be candid to a fault and make remarks that can unduly concern the prospective buyer. Likewise, they can ask probing questions that the buyer may consider nosy.

So, depending upon your prospects, and the predictability of your children's behavior, consider sending your children to the neighbors' or to a friend's house during a house tour.

Pets

Again, pets can be great, but a chorus of barking dogs or fighting cats marks space with sounds that the buyer does not necessarily want to hear. It can also create an unwanted distraction during the tour.

If at all possible, pets should be out of the house during a tour. Some people don't like pets, quiet or not, so play it safe.

Vocal and Ethnic Music

Musical taste, like color preferences, can be highly subjective and personal. For example, some people may think Willie Nelson wonderful while others may feel the opposite. If you walk into a home and hear a recording by someone you don't like, it reinforces the differences between you and the owner of the home.

According to the experts at Muzak, taste in vocal music is more subjective than taste in instrumental music and, therefore, vocal recordings are not generally recommended.

The same rules apply to ethnic music. Distinctly ethnic sounds that have not become popular, and especially songs in foreign languages, may reinforce the differences in background between the buyer and the seller and potentially create territorial anxiety.

Work Noise

Work noise includes the sounds of the lawn mower, washing machine, clothes dryer, dishwasher, and vacuum cleaner, because it reminds the buyer of the more mundane aspects of life. Work noise should be avoided.

Also, keep your television turned off while showing your home. Not only is it distracting, it does little to enhance the impression of elegance and sophistication you are trying to create.

SOUNDS LIKE TROUBLE

There are sounds that suggest mechanical problems in a home. While they may just be peculiar to your particular house or condo and are perfectly innocent, they may be of real concern to the prospective purchaser.

Noisy Pipes

Heating and plumbing systems often cause banging noises in pipes. In a forced hot water heating system, it is not uncommon for pipes to bang when they have air in them. Bleeding the system until a little water also escapes can easily remove this noise by releasing the trapped air.

Sometimes when the water is shut off, there can be a loud, shuddering noise as though someone is hitting your pipes with a hammer. One way to eliminate this is to close the water valve to the house slightly, which in turn will lower the water pressure. Another way is to replace a spring-loaded faucet with a manual one because it will shut off more slowly. If the problem appears to be limited to the hot water pipes, try reducing the temperature slightly.

If at all in doubt, consult a plumber.

Squeaky Floors and Doors

Squeaky floors can be disconcerting and may suggest a lack of overall maintenance. In very old houses, squeaks may be expected and may even be a part of the charm of the home. This is not true in newer ones.

By hammering nails into the floor at roughly 90 degree angles to each other, you can "toe" the floor in place and prevent the movement that causes the squeaking. If you know where the noise is occurring, try a product called Lub-A-Lite from Panef Manufacturing Company. It is a dry white powder that works like graphite but does not leave dark stains on wood. Pour some of this dry lubricant between the pieces of wood that are rubbing together, and you may solve the problem.

Squeaky doors should also be corrected. Put powdered graphite into the hinges or spray a silicone lubricant in that area, and the noise should disappear.

For a good, all-purpose spray lubricant, try WD-40, which happens to generate a "new" smell.

Dripping Faucets

The sound of a dripping faucet can be annoying and also suggest plumbing problems that do not exist. Solutions to this problem can range from a ten-cent washer to a new faucet. If replacing the washer does not work, there is a kit manufactured by O'Malley Valve Company, St. Petersburg, Florida, that is designed for the do-it-yourselfer.

Minimizing Street Noise

There are several ways to prevent street noise from interfering with your tour. The first and easiest is to schedule tours at off-peak periods like Sundays or evenings. You probably know your area well enough to be able to anticipate low traffic times.

A second and more costly approach is to use a sound-absorbent ceiling tile. This is specially designed to deaden noise within a room and minimize noise from other sources. Gold Bond Building Products makes a wide variety of these ceiling tiles.

A third approach, one that takes a certain amount of forward planning, is plantings. Trees and shrubs can reduce sound by nearly 25 percent by breaking up or absorbing noise. This can be a costly measure, but may also be one of the most effective ways to block both the sound of traffic and the view of a busy street.

Eliminating Echoes

Echoes can create a cold feeling in a room. In the world of acoustics, rooms that have primarily hard surfaces are called "live" because sounds bounce off them. To eliminate echoes, you want to create a "dead" room that has soft surfaces and absorbs sounds.

Quilted insulating window shades will absorb sound and minimize echoes, as will heavy draperies. Placing additional padding underneath area rugs or wall-to-wall carpeting will have an even more noticeable effect. Large house plants can absorb sound, as can a simple tablecloth and pad placed on a table. Large, overstuffed pillows on a couch and fabric wall hangings will drink up some noise and minimize echoes.

Quieting the Neighbors

Noisy neighbors can be a real problem, especially if they happen to be acting up when your home is being shown. This can deliver an instant, and perhaps fatal, blow to a sale, because the prospect might feel that the peace and quiet of the property will be compromised.

If your neighbors' children are particularly noisy after they come home from school, consider scheduling the tours around them. If you can't, talk with the kids in advance and attempt to gain their cooperation.

If you live in a co-op or condo and the noise from your neighbors comes through the walls or ceiling, you may have a more difficult problem. The impact of someone simply walking around above can make some condos sound like the interior of a bass drum. The noise level of footsteps can depend on the quality of the construction or the size of your upstairs neighbors.

One solution is simply to explain the problem to your neighbors and ask them to tread lightly after you call to warn them about an impending tour.

I once had this problem and my upstairs neighbor was not cooperative. One day I became so aggravated that I asked him to come downstairs to my unit and wait while I went up to his. I proceeded to stomp around on his floor so he could listen to what I had been putting up with. He was so apologetic, I thought he would go around on his hands and knees for the next month.

Asking neighbors to put carpeting on the floor above you is a reasonable request, especially in condos and co-ops, where people have to learn to respect each other's rights. At the very least, you could offer to split the price of an area rug with them. You may think is an unnecessary expense, but it's a small price to pay for peace and quiet — and a home sale.

If the problem is severe, consider sound-absorbent ceiling tile.

SOUNDS TO SELL BY

When it comes to selling your home, the right music is a close runner-up to peace and quiet. Music can not only mask sounds that you don't want but add sounds that sell through a variety of positive effects.

According to research conducted by Muzak, music significantly improves the way employees feel on their jobs by reducing boredom, increasing relaxation, and creating a friendlier atmosphere. Research conducted on the effect of Muzak on purchase behavior shows that consumers purchase up to 8 percent more in supermarkets with Muzak than in those without because it also makes shoppers spend more time in the store. Music has also been shown to put consumers in a better frame of mind in which to make purchases.

How can you take advantage of the effects of Muzak or similar packaged music when it comes to selling your home? The right music will help to relax the buyer, put him or her in a more positive frame of mind, and make a positive life-style statement about the home.

Keep It Neutral

Muzak's research suggests that the right music to use is instrumental because it is less subject than vocal music to personal taste. Additionally, they advise that "minor modes"—church or other "heavy" music, for example—should be avoided because they can be depressing. The music you choose should be positive and upbeat, yet subtle. No matter what you decide on, keep the volume relatively low because it should serve as background support only.

Different buyers will respond differently to certain music. This is where your research on who is likely to buy your home will come into play. The following is a breakdown of the different groups of buyers we have discussed and the type of background music we recommend in each case.

First-Time Buyers

Contemporary soft rock, jazz, or light classical music can provide the upbeat atmosphere that appeals to this category. The following might be appropriate: Spyro Gyra, Chuck Mangione, James Taylor, Daryl Hall and John Oates, Al Jarreau, Boston Pops, classical "Greatest Hits" albums.

Trade-up Buyers

Classical and subdued contemporary instrumental music make the kind of life-style statement sought by this group. The right music is part of the package you are presenting, so be careful to project the right image. Suggestions include Mozart, Vivaldi, J. S. Bach, Pachelbel, Jean-Pierre Rampal, George Winston. Check for records under the Windham Hill label, since these are often pleasing instrumentals, yet sophisticated enough for the trade-up buyer.

Empty Nesters/Trade-down Buyers

This group tends to enjoy traditional instrumental music featuring familiar tunes of the 1940s, 1950s, and 1960s, pop, and "beautiful music." These include the following: Henry Mancini, Burt Bacharach, Boston Pops, Frank Sinatra instrumentals, Glenn Miller, Ames Brothers, Herb Alpert and the Tijuana Brass.

HOW TO CHOREOGRAPH A TOUR

The way to use music is as important as what you select. Muzak programs their music in cycles so that there are peaks of excitement. Ideally the peak of excitement should coincide with the conclusion of the tour, so the buyer will leave with an upbeat feeling.

Unfortunately, you can't always gauge how long your tour will last, so the safest bet is to have music that is upbeat or positive at reasonably close intervals. It is very important to remember that the volume should be kept down to a "background" level.

When showing your home, it is helpful if you have a cassette machine because the tape will last twice as long as a record. If you do not have one, put the record on before the person walks through the door. When one album side has finished, don't disrupt the tour by flipping it over. Simply let it end.

CONCLUSION

Sound and smell are subleties you should consider when marketing your home. Small details can often become major issues if they suggest underlying problems or make the buyer uncomfortable.

Be aware of potential negative messages your home may project through sound and smell, and take the time to correct them. In the chapters that follow, we will discuss smells and sounds with respect to individual rooms in your home.

CHAPTER HIGHLIGHTS

1. Sounds and smells can "mark" space and create territorial anxiety.

2. Silence is one of the best sounds of all.

3. Noise from the surrounding environment and neighbors can threaten the feeling of privacy in a home.

4. Sounds from mechanical systems like plumbing or heating can generate unwarranted concerns in the buyer's mind.

5. Music can be an effective mood enhancer and improve the selling environment.

6. People have the ability to adapt to unpleasant smells, so enlist the help of focus groups to alert you to negative odors in your home.

7. Smell is a powerful trigger mechanism to memory and can be harnessed to create positive associations with your home.

8. The smell of newness, the "model smell," is one of the most positive selling smells.

9. The fragrance of cleanliness is another positive smell, and lemon is one of the most universally accepted smells of freshness.

10. Smells of mildew and mustiness suggest problems with your home.

6

Packaging the Exterior of Your Home

"The effect of the first impression in influencing the outcome of a property tour is nothing short of powerful," says Allen Sabbag, president of Better Homes and Gardens Real Estate Service. And nothing creates a more lasting first impression than the exterior of your home.

The color and condition of the paint, the quality of your lawn, shrubs, and trees, the appearance of the shutters, light fixtures, and the doorway to your house or condo are all part of the exterior packaging. How effective this packaging is will have enormous impact on how much you sell your home for and how quickly you sell it.

The reason exterior packaging is so critical is that it influences a buyer's perception of the interior, too.

Think about the judgments you make when you meet a person for the first time. Chances are, the person's appearance will have a significant impact on your overall impression. Your conclusions may ultimately be wrong, but at first, a person's "packaging" is all you have to go on.

If you make snap judgments like this, you are not alone. It has been shown, for example, that a well-dressed person is often perceived as more intelligent than one who is only moderately well dressed. This may seem totally unjust, but what appears on the surface undeniably affects our perceptions of what lies within. The same holds true for your home.

Let's say you are in the market for a suburban ranch house and have set up a tour based on an interesting ad you saw in the classified section of the paper. With a sense of anticipation, you drive up to the property and park in front of the house. As you get out of the car, you note that some of the pickets in the fence lining the property are broken and some old newspapers have been blown between them. You also notice that the lawn looks as if it could do with a good cutting and that weeds are growing between the cracks in the walkway.

Although these points may be minor, you begin developing a certain wariness about the property. You unconsciously begin looking for problems, and the more you look, the more you find. Joe Hanauer, president of Coldwell Banker, the nation's largest residential real estate brokerage firm, comments, "A jaundiced eye, created by a negative first impression, can easily ruin the rest of the tour."

Given enough time and contradictory information, you can overcome a prospective buyer's negative first impression, if it is incorrect. But when you are selling your home, time is the enemy. Your first shot may be your only shot, and if you don't score with the buyer immediately, the opportunity to impress him or her later may never come.

In the world of consumer packaged goods, a product's success in getting attention and selling on looks alone is called "shelf presence." In the world of residential real estate, the equivalent term is "curb appeal." It refers to the total impression created by color, landscaping, features, and overall condition.

Without sufficient curb appeal, selling your home can be a slow process and less profitable than it should be. If, for example, you are selling your house by using a sign out front, the prospect may just drive by. If you are selling by appointment or through a broker, the negative first impression may dampen or eliminate the buyer's excitement when it comes time to see the interior of your home.

To make certain this does not happen to you, follow the five-step system.

THE FIVE-STEP SYSTEM
Step 1. Consider the Competition

To determine how much work you should consider doing on your home, scout the market. Locate your top competition and use it as a benchmark to make your home even more marketable.

Check to see if the homes competing against yours have lawns that look healthier, recently painted exteriors, or other noticeable cosmetic packaging that make them highly attractive. If the competition's overall curb appeal is better than yours, determine why.

Focus your attention on improvements that will help your home stand out against the competition.

Step 2. Consider the Buyer

There are certain aspects of the exterior that will appeal to all segments of the market, including features that suggest privacy and security. But there are also many characteristics of your home's exterior that have specific appeal to different segments of the market.

First-Time Buyers

These buyers are the most cost-conscious and least sophisticated of the market groups. The appearance of cosmetic flaws that may be perceived as significant problems can scare the first-time buyer, who is often seeking a home that will not require additional fix-up expenses.

Although starter homes are usually modest, first-time buyers do appreciate features which suggest an improved life-style. There are steps you can take to make even the most unassuming home seem more valuable by packaging it effectively.

Trade-up Buyers

The first impression the exterior gives the trade-up buyer can make or break a sale. According to research conducted by SRI International, a highly respected California-based think tank, the trade-up buyer wants a home that makes an impressive statement to others. While this generalization may not apply to all buyers in this category, it's clear that one of the prime motivations for trading up is to acquire a home with a more substantial look and feeling than the buyer's present one.

SRI's research indicates that the front of the home is especially important in communicating the stature of a property, so most improvement dollars spent on the exterior should be focused here.

Because trade-up buyers often have expensive possessions, the appearance of a safe home is very important. Later, we will take up steps you can take to reinforce this security message.

Empty Nesters/Trade-down Buyers

Ease of maintenance and security are two primary concerns of this segment of the market. By showing visible forms of security, without making your home look like a fortress, you will give comfort to many of the older couples and single women in this group.

Showing care about the condition of your home will also appeal to these buyers, since it will indicate little or no need for constant upkeep.

Step 3. Evaluate Your Product

Once you've looked at the competition and developed an understanding of the specific needs of your target market, turn your sights to evaluating your home.

Because it's easy to grow accustomed to the small flaws that may have developed in the front of your home, seek a fresh perspective. Feedback from focus groups can be particularly useful here.

Escort two or three friends around the front of your property and to the front door as if they were seeing the home for the first time. Ask them the following questions:

Does the home have any obvious flaws that suggest a lack of care or potential problems?

What do they like the most and the least about the landscaping?

If they had $1,000 to spend to improve the home's curb appeal, what would they spend it on?

After friends or neighbors have given you their comments, you might repeat this with your broker, if you're using one.

Step 4. Eliminate Territorial Anxiety

The first impression of your home should enable the prospect to imagine it as his or her own. To make this as easy as possible, remove objects or statements that either clearly mark the territory as belonging to you alone or suggest potentially conflicting values.

Political signs in windows or bumper stickers on your cars should be removed. Collect toys scattered on the lawn, and minimize strong ethnic or religious identifications.

Step 5. Maximize Packaging Appeal

The proper packaging of your home's exterior can make thousands of dollars of difference in the selling price.

From details as small as making sure the street and sidewalk in front of your home are clean, to dressing up your doorway, to totally repainting your home, there are many ways to increase significantly the marketing appeal and perceived value of your property.

Of all home improvements, the ideas discussed in this chapter can yield some of the best returns on investment.

CREATING THE SUPERIOR EXTERIOR

Like a great symphony, the first impression of your home is created by many factors working in concert. And all it takes is one flaw to destroy the harmony of your home's exterior.

You can't expect, for example, to have a fresh paint job maximize the value of your home if the lawn is poorly kept. And you can't expect to get the full resale value out of landscaping work if the driveway is in disrepair.

Each aspect of your home should complement the others. And by showing attention to detail in all areas of the exterior, you will maximize the curb appeal of the property. Curb appeal starts with the street in front of your home and includes everything up to the front door. We will address each of these components, focusing on the elements that require the least investment and offer the highest return.

The Street

Just because you don't have a deed to the street in front of your home doesn't mean you can't assume some responsibility for its appearance. The buyer is not only purchasing your house or condominium, he or she is also buying into your neighborhood. So if your city or town hasn't done its job to make your street attractive, you should at least make it look clean and well cared for.

If, especially after a windy day, papers have accumulated by the curb or along the street in front of your property, by all means grab a broom and sweep them up. If you have to get down on your hands and knees to weed the area between the curb and the road, don't think twice about what your neighbors might think. It might even inspire them to do the same.

The Sidewalk

Though you are not likely to own your sidewalk, because it is so close to your property, it should be of concern to you.

Make sure your sidewalk is clean and weed-free, then evaluate its overall condition. A badly cracked, pitched, or heaved sidewalk diminishes the crisp feeling of a well-maintained property. Conversely, a newly installed sidewalk is an attractive frame to the property behind it.

Unless the mayor is a close friend or lives next door, however, it may be difficult to snap your fingers and have a new sidewalk installed. But if the sidewalk needs repair, call your local government to inform them of this safety hazard and the resulting liability problem. Think about this early in the home marketing process because it's likely to take some time to get it done.

Beyond this, you can make your own sidewalk more attractive by planting flowers or grass around the base of a tree if there is a dirt area surrounding it. Digging several holes and planting potted geraniums can be ideal. Spreading crushed stone around the circumference of the tree also adds an attractive finishing touch.

The Fence

As Robert Frost said, "Good fences make good neighbors." Good fences also make good investments, because they can be attractive and project a sense of security.

The need for security is common among most buyers and is one of the top considerations in purchasing a home. Research conducted by professors Barbara Brown at Texas Christian University and Irwin Altman at the University of Utah has shown that territorial symbols like fences can have a real effect in deterring burglars.

Although most front fences are cosmetic rather than functional, they also give a feeling of security that even burglars respond to. And for the purpose of selling your home, they offer assurance to the buyer.

Another general requirement that a fence fulfills is privacy. Fences that provide privacy are generally found in a backyard or alongside a home, blocking the view of neighbors and outsiders. If your yard is edged by a chain-link fence that does not provide much privacy, consider attaching a canvas cloth to it. This cloth can be ordered in any size from speciality stores listed in the Yellow Pages under "Canvas Goods." Canvas cloth comes in a variety of colors and gives a fresh, contemporary look to an otherwise conventional fence. Windscreen material for tennis courts can also be purchased for chain-link fences, and a call to a local fence supplier will probably lead you to a reliable source.

The cost of canvas will run about $1 per square foot, while nylon windscreen will cost less than half as much. Either should be ordered with grommets so it can be easily tied to the fence.

Fences can also be used to block an unpleasant view, which might hurt the value of a property.

I recently toured a house located near a railroad line. Although the track was seldom used, the view was unsightly. Though I did not buy the property for a number of reasons, I advised the seller to spend $400 and put in a fence and plant a few small evergreen trees to block the view.

The change was dramatic and more than paid him back on his investment when the house was sold. My rule is, the uglier the view, the higher the return on this sort of investment, so determine how much of a liability you have and spend accordingly.

Upgrading a Fence

Fences can either be aesthetically pleasing or a liability to your landscape. If you have a fence in the front of your property, it will be one of the first things people see, so it should either complement your curb appeal or be removed. Before you act too quickly, though, there are steps you can take to bring new life to an old fence.

If you have rust on an old chain-link fence, use a wire brush to remove it. Then repaint the fence with dark green rather than silver. Silver repainting jobs never look new and are a telltale sign that the fence has undergone an inexpensive, do-it-yourself repair.

To save time and money, use a paint roller with canned paint rather than a spray, because the bulk of the spray will end everywhere but on your fence. A painter's mitten, which allows you to dip your hand into a paint can, is another option and can be used like a brush. And if specific parts of the fence, like a rusted bar or post, are beyond repair, replace them individually rather than installing new sections.

Repackaging a Fence with Flowers

If you have a natural-color stockade fence that is beginning to look tired, or you want to enhance further a chain-link fence, add some plants. They will add color to the area and draw attention away from the fence itself.

A perennial vine called silver lace, for example, is exceptionally fast growing and quite attractive. It can be planted in the spring and will bloom throughout the summer. Another option is the American bittersweet, which will grow very quickly and flower in a matter of months. There are also annual vines like morning glory and the scarlet runner bean, which will grow from seed in about six weeks.

The best way to place vibrant color in front of a fence is to use annuals. They will bloom in about three weeks after the last frost and will continue until the first frost in the fall. Annuals are the least expensive of this variety of plant and will give you the burst of color that you need. If you want to sell your house in July, for example, plant annuals in May or June.

Specific plants to consider are the spider plant, the amaranthus, both of which grow quite tall or, of the low-lying varieties, alyssum, verbena, or portulaca. Intermediate-sized plants to consider are snapdragons, marigolds, and petunias. If you really want to put on a show, plant these in rows, starting with the low-growing plants in front, the intermediate plants in the middle, and the tallest ones right up against the fence.

If the fence is tired looking, freshly painted latticework with flowers growing on it can be placed in front to bring new life. Roses make the most impact here. If you have a sunny area, climbing roses spread along a white or natural-color lattice can be exceptionally attractive. Buy two-year old plants that will bloom for you the first summer.

Mailboxes and Lampposts

If you own a mailbox or a lamppost, make sure it looks like new. If the mailbox is rusted or dented, either repaint it or consider purchasing a new one. This is one of those small cosmetic improvements that can catch the buyer's eye and help contribute to a positive purchase attitude. If the lamp is broken or the post needs touch-up painting, take care of it. Clean the glass if it's dirty, and replace the light bulb if it has burned out.

Front Wall and Hedges

If the first thing a buyer sees when pulling up to your property is a high wall or hedge, be sure that it makes a positive statement. As a general rule, a hedge should be neatly trimmed and a high wall meticulously maintained to set the tone for the rest of the tour.

Flowers can add color and interest here, too. If you have a high or imposing stone wall, plants will create a more personal and inviting appearance.

The Front Walkway

Because this is where the seller is first likely to set foot on what could ultimately be his or her property, the walkway should give the reassurance of quality and care that the buyer is looking for.

Your walkway should match the style of your home. A contemporary walkway, for example, only detracts from a colonial house.

You'll want the walkway and the lawn or landscape abutting it to appear immaculate. There should be a clean border between the grass and the adjacent walkway, rather than the ragged look of an encroaching lawn.

No weeds should be creeping through the mortar, nor should there be highly visible stains from fruit trees or bird droppings. Wash down the walk to remove these and, if necessary, try vinegar and water with a bristle brush. For more stubborn problems, dilute muriatic acid with three parts water, and scrub. As with any acid, it is wise to use gloves; be careful not to splash any on your skin.

Next, make sure that the paving material itself is in sound order. Cracked bricks should be replaced, deteriorating mortar regrouted, loose flagstones secured, and cracked asphalt or cement should be professionally patched. Unless you are having the entire walk regrouted, try to have the mason tone down the color of the grout so it will not call attention to the area that has been repaired.

Replacing or Upgrading a Walkway

If your walkway is on the danger list or if you have no walkway at all, seriously consider putting in a new one. There are many creative and relatively simple ways to turn a beaten path into a selling point.

Used brick set in a herringbone pattern and gently curving toward the front door can be dramatic and inexpensive. Bedding the brick in sand provides excellent drainage and you don't have to hire a mason to do it. Using timbers as a border can be inexpensive and attractive, and installation is easy. Go one step farther and plant low-lying flowers along the walkway, and you will have a handsome approach to your home. Hosta, also known as plantain lily, is a good plant for this purpose.

Expect to use 450 bricks for a 20-foot walkway at about 40 cents per brick. The timbers will cost about $20 each for 8-foot lengths. If you spend $350, the perceived value will far exceed the investment and help establish an attractive focal point for the landscape of your home.

Another approach is to use square flagstones or bluestone slabs divided by pressure-treated oak beams. This can be appropriate for a contemporary home. You'll need anywhere from 150 to 300 flagstones or bluestones; they cost about 50 cents apiece.

Concrete rounds used in an S pattern climbing up a hill to a front door or on a winding horizontal path can be graceful and distinctive. These are very easy to install and cost about $4.50 apiece. A 25-foot path would require about 50 concrete rounds.

Use plants and flowers to create interest along a walkway. For example, a small dogwood tree surrounded by a ground cover of pachysandra can be very attractive.

Each approach has its own benefits, and your choice would, of course, depend on the style of your home. Because brick is the most popular, it is probably your safest bet.

LANDSCAPING

According to Toni Reuter of Century 21, "Landscaping is second only to your house or condominium itself in influencing the first impression of your property."

We will not cover major landscape projects because they do not have a good record of acceptable returns on investment, except for homes in very high-priced categories ($300,000 plus). Custom landscaping jobs can range between $5,000 and $10,000 but will generally return far less than this on the sale of average-priced homes.

Statistics on exactly how much landscaping will add to the value of a home are quite subjective and vary from case to case. I've seen figures that range from 5 to 20 percent. But despite the range of opinion, one thing is very clear: an attractive landscape improves the marketability of your property. If you can enhance your landscape without spending a great deal of money, it's worth doing so. Since spring is the optimal time to sell your home, the following recommendations are designed for early spring planting. Always check with a local agriculture college or garden expert to determine the best planting times in your area, because they vary in different parts of the country.

The Lawn

Generally speaking, lawns are important to most home buyers in establishing the right landscape look and feeling. Lawns are more important to suburban buyers than urban ones and have more appeal to younger trade-up buyers than to older empty nesters. But as a rule, a good lawn is an asset that can be an integral part of the exterior packaging of your home.

If you are lucky enough to have a healthy lawn, you have little to concern yourself with. All that is needed is reasonable care.

Cut it on a regular basis, and fertilize it at least twice a year if you have a common blend of bluegrass and fescue. If you have primarily bluegrass, fertilize it five times a year, and watch for fungus disease. The minute you see any fungus disease, treat it with broad-spectrum fungicide. And, as with any lawn, always be on the lookout for chinch bugs and sod webworm, which can be easily controlled with Diazinon.

After you cut your lawn, make sure you rake up any grass your mower did not catch. If you don't, it will quickly turn brown and detract from an otherwise attractive lawn. Also, be especially careful to keep crisp edging lines between the lawn and the sidewalk, as they add to the overall tidiness of the property.

Common Lawn Problems

There is a wide range of causes for lawn problems. Some are easily diagnosed and cured, others are hard to pinpoint and expensive to solve.

One common problem is the lawn that is essentially healthy but has been damaged by either children who have played on it too hard or dogs who have torn it up. The easiest solution, depending upon how extensive the damage is, is sod. To resod specific areas, remove the damaged grass, roots and all. Buy some loam to build up the area to nearly the height of the adjacent turf, and add nutrients — like superphosphate, a starter fertilizer — to the soil so the sod will thrive. Then rototill or rake it all together. Now you're ready to put the sod down.

The cost of sod depends on how much you buy. It may cost as little as fifteen to twenty cents per square foot for a bluegrass mixture if you order 4,000 square feet or more, or as much as sixty cents a foot if you purchase considerably less. But no matter what you pay, all will be lost if you don't adequately prepare the soil.

Seeding is a less expensive alternative, but it will not produce grass overnight. If you need a great-looking quick fix, sod can't be beat.

Another common lawn problem is a lack of adequate sunlight. If you have a large shady area, it can be difficult to grow grass. Trees, which compete with grass for sunlight, usually win, and leave unattractive bald areas on your lawn.

Removing what remains of your lawn in these areas and replacing it with ground cover can provide an attractive solution. You can either follow a free-form shape dictated by the shaded area or you can cut a large circle or oval, depending on your preference.

Pachysandra is ideal for ground cover because it grows quickly, has a pleasing texture, and is very hardy. *Vinca Bowlesii*, or periwinkle, is another good ground cover that provides a long-blooming flower. Ivies are fine as well, but they will eventually climb up the tree.

If you don't have time to grow anything, consider replacing the grass with crushed stone. You can introduce a little color with potted geraniums, but make sure there is enough light for them to survive.

If you have an especially large tree, consider replacing the grass with brick, then add a birdbath or an outdoor chair to create a little seating area. This will provide an interesting focal point to your landscape at little cost.

The Suburban Dilemma

For the owner of an urban condominium or brownstone building, it is quite acceptable to replace a sickly lawn with ground cover — like pachysandra, periwinkle, Baltic ivy, English ivy, or some type of herb like pennyroyal. Unlike grass, ground cover is easy to care for, which happens to be a strong motivation behind the purchase of urban condominiums. Ground cover also provides an interesting texture, and many types actually bloom in the spring and summer.

But ground cover is not a practical alternative for a large suburban lawn of 5,000 to 10,000 feet. In this case, ground cover will become a real trash collector, trapping papers and debris, and it can't stand up to children or dogs tramping through it.

So, if your front lawn is downright disastrous, what do you do? Should you spend $1,000 or more to sod the lawn or simply hold your breath and hope the buyer is not a grass fan?

Even if you spend a great deal of money installing a new lawn, chances are you will not recover your expenses, because buyers expect a good lawn. But if you don't touch your lawn and the competition has grass that looks like a putting green, you will be at a distinct disadvantage.

The answer depends on the price of your home and the time of year you sell it. If you have a property that is considered expensive in your area, it will be difficult to sell if the lawn looks poorly. You would be well advised to either resod or reseed your lawn. My advice is to resod only the area visible from the street and reseed the rest.

You may be able to avoid all this if you sell during the late fall or winter. All brown lawns look equally undesirable and yours may not look much different from the best of the rest. If you have the good fortune to be selling under a blanket of snow, the entire issue will be moot.

Trees and Shrubs

More than any other single aspect of your landscape, trees can have a significant and quantifiable effect on your property value.

Trees have both an aesthetic and a practical function. They increase the feeling of privacy, reduce noise by acting as an acoustical buffer, help create a sense of security by defining property lines, and can increase energy efficiency by screening wind in the winter and providing shade in the summer. And beyond this, they add color and richness to the landscape and can lend a feeling of substance to the property.

In fact, trees are considered such assets that, if they are suddenly destroyed by lightning, you may be able to collect from your insurance company or deduct the loss on your federal income tax. Check the details with your insurance agent or accountant and take pictures of your trees now to prove their size if you should need to.

Dr. Brian R. Payne of the U.S. Forest Service has done extensive research in this area. According to Dr. Payne, "Trees can contribute 7 percent to property values if they are planted in sufficient quantity and are of sufficient size." Unfortunately, the cost of planting large trees on your land can be prohibitive.

Unless your home is extremely high-priced and has an evident lack of trees that significantly lowers your resale value, purchasing large trees will not pay off. For example, a 15-foot maple will cost $200. And you will need quite a few to make a difference. There are, however, other measures you can take.

High hedges may be a wise investment. A bad view can be screened out by a 4-foot hedge or arborvitae, which grows at the rate of a foot per year. Each 4-foot arborvitae costs about $40.

Foundation Coverings

A bare foundation and a lack of trees in front of a home or condo can seriously diminish its curb appeal. To soften this, plant trees or shrubs at either corner of the front of the house. To determine proper placement, draw a line out from the corner of the foundation, bisecting the corner angle. This will position a plant or tree in such a way that it will improve not only the appearance of the front of the house but the side as well. A dogwood tree might be ideal, as would a flowering crabapple tree. Then fill the gaps between the trees or bushes with low-lying plants to hide the concrete foundation from view.

Plants which are particularly suitable for this are the Japanese yew, rhododendrons, cotoneaster, or burning bush. To create a lush effect in the front of an otherwise barren home, expect to spend at least $500, although this amount will vary with the length of the area to be covered.

Flowers and Occasional Plantings

Almost everyone likes flowers. According to a *Better Homes and Gardens* consumer panel, more than 80 percent of home owners grow them, mostly outdoors. In the front yard of your home or condominium, flowers can have a positive effect on buyers.

But plant flowers in moderation. Busy dual-career couples and empty nesters might consider flowers a source of additional work.

If you like, select some plants that will be in full bloom during the time when you sell your home. You want them to be hardy so you won't have a garden full of wilting plants. Geraniums, marigolds, and African violets are ideal.

Lighting

Outdoor lighting can be a dramatic way to make your landscape distinctive. Spotlights aiming up a large tree can create a spectacular effect in both summer and winter. Low-lying path lights or "Malibu lamps" lining a walkway can impress the trade-up buyer. There is a product called Moodliter made by Electripak, Inc., that can be installed by the do-it-yourselfer.

Spotlights placed adjacent to a house or condo, washing up the face of urban townhouses or condominiums, will create a striking effect. I recently sold a home that featured lighting of this variety. It was unique to the street, setting the home apart from others in the neighborhood. The buyer was a single woman who appreciated the lighting for both aesthetic and safety reasons.

Crime prevention experts agree that the brighter the home, the less likely it is that a burglar will attempt a break-in. The police departments recommend at least one spotlight placed over a garage aiming at the driveway and one placed up against the home illuminating walkways. Intruders, not surprisingly, do not want to be seen milling around your property.

But before you do any of this, first determine what the chances are of showing your home when it's dark enough to use outdoor lights. If you are a working single or a couple selling the home yourselves and are likely to have scheduling problems during the day, exterior lighting might be worthwhile. If you are using a broker or plan to show the home mainly on weekends, this investment will probably not be necessary.

The Driveway

Because of its size and generally dark color, the driveway tends to be a focal point of your landscape, like it or not. Since the driveway may take up 20 percent or more of the property in front of a home, it has the potential to influence a great deal of a buyer's first impression.

If your driveway is in good condition, you have nothing to fear. Just sweep or wash it down and keep the grass neatly trimmed along the sides. But if your driveway is noticeably cracked, heaved, oil-stained, or broken up, fix it.

The most common problem to driveways is surface cracks, particularly if you have a concrete driveway, for concrete tends to be more brittle than asphalt or tar. Concrete will require patching, which is generally quite noticeable because the colors seldom match. If the cracking or damage is small, fixing it is likely to draw more attention to the problem. If the area that needs work is large, do it in sections that are square or rectangular, which create a neater appearance.

If the driveway is tar or asphalt, the patches are much easier to match. There is a product called Tamp 'N Set Driveway Patch, by HMJ Industries, which is designed to allow you to fix holes on your own. Driveway sealants can be used, but be very careful because they tend to leave a quick-fix look. Be sure to use the highest-quality sealers, for only they will produce adequate results. If the sealant is too thin, part of it will be absorbed into the surface and a portion will actually evaporate.

Another telltale sign of a poor sealing job are traces of tar or asphalt along the grass. Before you attempt to seal a tar or asphalt driveway, put an edge guard along the sides — a roll of galvanized garden edging material will work particularly well — then pull it up when you are done. Also, be careful not to leave spreader marks, which will be another clue to a do-it-yourself project. If you have oil stains on a concrete or asphalt driveway, it's worth the effort to remove them. Try Mechanics brand degreaser, made by Blue Coral.

If you are lucky enough to have a circular driveway in the front of your house, take advantage of it. Consider placing attractive plantings or rock gardens in the center.

An element that affects the appearance of the driveway but is seldom considered is the one or more vehicles parked on it. Whenever your car is sitting on your property, it becomes a part of the landscape. And, like the lawn and sidewalk, your car should be immaculate. A newly cleaned or waxed car makes an important statment about how you take care of your property. Keep the interior neat in the event that the prospect walks by.

The kind of car you drive and the condition you keep it in says a lot about you and your life-style. If you drive a rust bucket, consider parking it around the corner.

John T. Molloy, author of *Dress for Success* and consultant to the real estate brokerage industry, once conducted an experiment to determine the impact of automobiles on the resale value of homes.

Molloy selected a home that was for sale and had both buyers and professional appraisers assign a value to the property. He then rented several Mercedes-Benzes and Cadillacs, and had them parked around the neighborhood and in front of the home. Once again, he asked both buyers and appraisers for their opinion.

The results showed that not only did the buyers perceive the homes with the expensive automobiles as being more valuable, but so, too, did the professional appraisers.

I am not advising you to go to the expense of renting cars to market your home, but I do urge you to recognize the importance of your automobile as part of your landscape.

The Service Areas

There are certain aspects of your landscape that are inherently unattractive and under no circumstances should they be visible from the front of the house. They include clotheslines, trash cans, and outdoor storage for an old trailer.

The best strategy is to move these items out of sight, if possible; if not, consider adding a visual barrier, such as an inexpensive wooden lattice screen that you can cover with plants or ivy.

In any case, it's important not to have clothes on the line when prospects view the home, because they suggest the mundane aspects of home life that run counter to the upbeat life-style statements you want to make. If you have a very noticeable clotheslines or outdoor hanger, consider putting it away until after the tour.

Make sure all lawn furniture is neatly arranged or stored out of sight. Also, children's toys, lawn mowers, garden tools, and playthings for your pet should all be hidden.

The Neighbors

Although you did not hand-pick your neighbors, they are an important visual part of your surrounding landscape. Sellers should take an active role in making sure that their neighbors at least don't hurt the resale value of their home.

If your neighbor's home desperately needs a painting job, a major landscape overhaul or serious structural work, there is little you can do about it. But if the work is cosmetic, and you are on good terms with him or her, there are certain steps you can take. Even if you and your

---

Do-It-Yourself Improvements
under $100

1.   Repaint the doorway ($10).

2.   Install brass door knocker and kick plate ($80).

3.   Buy high-quality house numbers ($10).

4.   Install door molding ($30).

5.   Install new front-door light fixtures ($100).

6.   Put potted plants by the front door ($25).

7.   Repaint the fence ($75).

8.   Put flower boxes beneath windows ($100).

9.   Plant flowers along the walkway ($30).

10. Reseal the driveway ($100).

11. Paint the fire hydrant, lamppost, or mailbox in front of your home if needed ($5 each).

12. Replace dead grass around the base of a shade tree with crushed stone ($40).

---

neighbor do not get along, the prospect of your imminent move might motivate him or her to help!

In cases of neighbors' dirty front yards, suggest that materials from your clean-up efforts may have blown over to their property. This way you are not accusing anyone of being sloppy but are blaming yourself. Then offer to help spruce up the area if they will work with you. Even though you may feel that you have enough to do on your own home, never mind someone else's, remember that people are buying more than just a home, they are buying a life-style, and the neighbor's unkempt property will work against you.

Another approach to consider before you begin your cleanup is to tell your neighbors about your plan of action in advance and suggest that you pool resources to do it together on a given weekend. This will imply that you are all equally guilty of being less than meticulous when it comes to property upkeep. A good line to use might be "I keep thinking about cleaning up the yard but keep putting it off. Our doing it at the same time will let us share our misery." Offer to have a cookout afterward or supply the beer.

Municipal Property

Beyond the street and sidewalk, which are not owned by you but which affect the perception of your home, there are city or town properties that you should also look after, if the municipal government does less than a perfect job.

If there is a fire hydrant in front of your home that is rusty or unattractive, get permission from the city or fire department to paint it. A shiny red or yellow hydrant suggests good working order, care, and upkeep.

The same holds true for a municipal lamppost if it is located in front of your home. In older big cities like Manhattan, Philadelphia, Boston, and San Francisco, black wrought-iron lampposts are quite common. If you happen to live in a brownstone house or condominium with an old lamppost in front, buy a can of glossy black rust-inhibiting paint and turn public property into a private asset.

No matter what style of lamppost, it's very important that the lamp be operating so as not to make your home look unsafe at night. Call the city or town you live in and insist that they replace a burned-out bulb immediately.

THE HOME FRONT

The front of your home is the focal point of the first impression. While the landscape sets the tone and can influence the overall perception of the house or condominium, it is easier for the buyer to imagine making necessary improvements to the landscape than to the house. The home is viewed as much more tangible than plants or grass and therefore should leave little to the imagination.

Because of the lasting impact of first impressions, the front of the home is where you should put the most effort. If you have only enough time or money to fix a part of the exterior, the front is your best bet.

Studies conducted by the California-based Stanford Research Institute, now known as SRI, on purchase behavior of home buyers confirm this. Their research has concluded that among the largest segment of the market, the front of the home has the biggest impact because most buyers are concerned that their home make a big enough statement to others. A buyer's need for esteem and peer approval is an important purchase motivator that you should act upon.

One California developer did just that by using this information to design units targeted toward young professional buyers. The developer spent a substantial amount of money placing expensive features — like elaborate window frames — in the front of each home, while installing inexpensive ones in the rear. By the time most people got to the back of the home, they were so impressed with the property, they either didn't notice or didn't care about the less expensive windows. All that truly counted was the first impression.

While your home should not be thought of as a facade on a Hollywood set, you will want to put your best foot forward. We all want to spend as little as possible when selling our homes, and concentrating on one section can be cheaper and more effective than spreading our dollars thinly all over the house or condo.

First, decide what components make up the front of your home, what can be done to maximize the impact of each, and then set your priorities. The following list offers items in order of their impact on the buyer's first impression.

Treating the Face of Your Home

Because the facing material is generally the most dominant visual feature of the front of your home, it should be your top priority.

Wood

There are few investments that can yield a higher return than repainting or restaining. Conversely, there are few conditions as detrimental to the sale of your home as peeling, blistering, or badly faded paint or stain.

Most brokers cringe at the prospect of showing a home that needs painting because it makes such a poor statement about the overall property and is so difficult for buyers to visualize as their own.

If your home only needs light painting, consider limiting your dollars or efforts to the front. If the home needs more substantial work, you'll need to consider the entire exterior.

When painting, don't scrimp on high-quality paint, especially if you are doing only the front. The real expense is in the labor, and any money saved on cheaper paint will be lost in the diminished appeal of your home.

Selecting Colors

Choosing the right paint color should not be based on what you like but rather on what the buyer is most likely to respond to. A bold color statement can create territorial anxiety and make it very difficult for the prospect to imagine the home as he or she would like it.

The general rule for selecting exterior colors is to keep them neutral. Whites, beiges, tans, and grays are far less risky than reds, greens, or bright yellows.

If your home is an authentic colonial or a reproduction period house, historic colors like Farmhouse red, Federal blue, Richmond bisque, Hancock gray, or Tudor brown, can be very appropriate. While these may include less neutral colors than whites or beiges, if it means making your home historically correct, go right ahead.

Benjamin Moore Paints offers a Historic Color Collection designed for eighteenth- and nineteenth-century-style homes. These colors can enhance the authentic look of a home.

Solving Common Painting Problems

There are a variety of common painting problems that should be corrected before you repaint. Nothing looks shabbier than a fresh coat of paint applied over a badly cracked, blistered, or peeling surface. The following are suggestions about how to address these problems so you can prepare your wood surface properly.

Cracking or Alligatoring This condition reveals paint that looks like the surface of an expensive pocketbook, and is caused by the topcoat's not bonding properly to the undercoat. To get a smooth surface, scrape down to the bare wood, reprime, and paint again. Always let the primer dry for at least 48 hours before repainting.

Blistering This is caused by moisture and is evidenced by long bubbles of paint that will eventually peel off. You will have to remove the paint on affected areas and start over. Before you repaint, call in a professional to determine where the moisture is coming from and so prevent the problem from recurring.

Wrinkling In this case, the paint looks as if it had shrunk after it dried. This is often caused by do-it-yourselfers who apply paint too thickly. Because it looks unprofessional, the surface should be stripped down and repainted.

Flaking Evidence of flaking can include horizontal or vertical rows of cracks, which lead to chipping. This is caused by the paint's inability to expand or contract as the wood reacts to environmental changes. Lack of proper priming is one common reason for this condition, as is a buildup from numerous repaintings. Sand or scrape down the affected areas, then reprime and paint.

Mildew This may look like soot or grime, but it is actually a living fungus. Mildew thrives on moisture, so try to eliminate the source of the problem. To remove mildew, mix a solution of one part bleach to three parts water, and use it like a detergent. Protect your hands and eyes with gloves and goggles. If you plan to repaint this area, make sure you have rinsed off the chlorine before you proceed.

Nailhead Stains These are spots that occur around a nailhead. Sand down the affected areas and apply a rust-inhibiting primer, then repaint.

Bleeding Stains Woods like redwood and cedar can bleed tannic acids and cause blotchy stains through a painted or stained surface. To eliminate this, sand and apply a stain-blocking primer before repainting.

Brick

Brick is far easier to maintain than wood, a fact that may explain why consumer surveys report it as the preferred building material. But brick can also have its problems, and we will address the most common ones that should be eliminated before marketing your house or condo.

Repointing

Pointing refers to the mortar between bricks. Over time, this mortar deteriorates, causing leaks in your walls and detracting from the look of your home.

If the problem is highly visible, have the bricks repointed in the front of your home at least. This will give the masonry work a fresh look and is a sure sign of a well-maintained home.

Peeling or Chipping Paint

The mortar between bricks and on other masonry usually contains alkali, which diminishes the adhesiveness of the paint. Especially on new brick, use paints and primers that have built-in resistance to alkali.

If your paint is chipping or peeling because of age, you can use either a wire brush or a paint scraper to remove it.

Pollution Stains

Especially in urban areas, soot and various forms of pollution considerably darken brick. If a home is very old, this darkening may actually add to the property's character. But, if the home is contemporary, cleaning the brick may be called for.

You can hire a professional to use a high-pressure detergent spray on your home or have some type of sandblasting done, depending on how stubborn the problem is. Look under "Sandblasting" in the Yellow Pages, but avoid using sandblasting itself because it will leave an unnatural, pitted look to the brick.

Check several contractors to get their opinion on which option is best for you.

Cracking

Bricks can crack for reasons which range from age to structural problems. If a series of cracked bricks is plainly visible on the exterior of your home, fix it.

If your home has structural problems, they should be addressed before you put it on the market. Seasoned buyers will immediately perceive this as a potential problem, even if it turns out to be merely cosmetic. Try to have the mason match the color of the new mortar with the old so the repair does not call attention to itself.

Vinyl or Aluminum Siding

These are the easiest surfaces to revamp if they are not dented, cut, or so old that the surfaces have faded. Common household detergents like Top Job or Mr. Clean may be all you need. For more stubborn problems, there's a product called P-Tackle from Aminco, which is designed to restore the color to faded siding.

When painting aluminum, make sure the surface is clean of peeling, chalking, or oxidized paint. Use a zinc chromate primer and a topcoat of exterior latex, oil-based, or alkyd paint.

You should be aware that the popularity of vinyl or aluminum siding can vary significantly from region to region. New siding is quite expensive to install and thus not recommended.

Some think of vinyl or aluminum siding as an asset because it significantly cuts long-term maintenance costs and can be an energy saver. Others find the look unattractive or feel it raises suspicions about what's underneath. If your siding was applied on top of another surface material, be prepared to answer questions from prospects about this. I had once considered purchasing a vinyl-sided two-family home and was more concerned about what dark secret lurked beneath the siding than the benefits of never having to paint again.

When the owner brought out before, during, and after pictures of the installation process, he dispelled my fears that he was trying to cover up some major flaw. In areas where siding is commonplace, this question is less likely to come up, but in places where it is not as common, it's best to be prepared with answers.

The Doorway

Cosmetic improvements to the front doorway have been the device I have used most often to help sell a property more quickly and for more money without spending a great deal. If there is one marketing device that can affect the buyer in so many ways so inexpensively, this is it.

The very first property I owned had a doorway that would have sent an encyclopedia salesperson back to his or her car. The door itself was a dull gray and had thirty years' worth of old paint caked on it. The doorbell and house number were painted over, and the entire frame hadn't been washed in years. The building was in otherwise reasonably good condition, except for similar maintenance problems with the windows.

I decided to strip the paint from the frame, and I purchased a new raised-panel door for $100. I painted the frame white and used clear polyurethane on the door. After I was finished, I put on a brass door knocker and a brass kick plate. The total cost of the project was under $200.

The visual change was dramatic. It transformed the entire look of the building and helped me sell it within 24 hours.

Repainting

The first statement your doorway should make is of care and maintenance.

If it needs even light painting, start with fine sandpaper and smooth out any imperfections that may exist. Painting over old drip marks only makes them more visible.

If the doorway has a buildup of paint, remove the door and use a stripping compound like Strypeeze. If you choose to do it your :lf, don't plan to have a lot of fun. It's tedious work and the chemicals are highly caustic. Be careful.

As an alternative, use a heat gun, which actually melts the paint, enabling you to scrape it off with a putty knife. The best idea is to try this first and then use a stripping compound to remove what remains. Black & Decker makes a heat gun that sells for about $35, or you may be able to rent one. Check the listings under "Rental Service Stores" in the Yellow Pages.

Keep an Eye on the Details

The framing around your door may range from simple flat-surfaced uprights, with a plain cap molding on top, to ornate columns capped with a Greek-style pediment. Whatever the amount of detail surrounding your door, go over it fully to make sure it looks as if you care.

Also, make sure your doorbell works and that the fixture itself is attractive. If it isn't, replacing it with a new one may be worth it. Because the prospective buyer will try the doorbell in order to get into your home, don't start off the tour with a sign of an electrical problem, small as it may be.

The same holds true for the light fixture(s) alongside or above the door. They should be clean, or repainted if necessary, and must work properly. Attractive, high-quality light fixtures can be high "perceived value" items and add charm and a feeling of quality to the entire doorway area. Avoid using yellow "bug light" bulbs in fixtures because they do little to enhance the appearance of your home if a buyer tours it in the evening.

Many doorways have brass fixtures, including door knockers, mail slots, kick plates, doorknobs, and nameplates. Because brass polishes up so well, there is no excuse not to have the hardware glistening at all times. If you hate to polish, there are some brass-wax products like Brass Wax by J. P. Products, that are supposed to maintain a shine up to ten times longer than usual.

If the brass fixtures are in bad condition or you don't have any at all, consider replacing them or buying some. You should not have to spend a fortune, but buy quality because people will be close enough to tell the difference.

Dressing Up a Door

Some front doors are simply uninspiring, and over and beyond adding brass fixtures, there are certain measures you can take. If you have a traditional six-panel door, try painting in an accent color in the in-dented area framing each rectangular panel. This will highlight the detail on the door and create visual interest. An attractive set of brass numbers, a brass kick plate, or a nicely crafted mail slot can also add to this sense of quality and differentiation.

If you have a flat-surfaced door and your home is traditional, adding molding to create a paneled effect is an inexpensive and easy way to turn an uninteresting door into something special. If you do it yourself, it shouldn't cost you more than $20 to achieve a look that appears to cost many times that amount. You can purchase "picture frame" molding at any lumberyard and ask them to show you a six-panel door to model yours after.

Chances are good that if you are selling your home in the spring, you may have a screen door, or, if selling in the winter, a storm door. Seldom are these as attractive as a nicely appointed entry door, and they can actually diminish the effect of all the work you may have done. For these reasons, remove the screen or storm door for showing purposes. If you'd rather not, make sure they are in as good condition as possible, including not only the surface of the door but the closing mechanism as well. There is something annoying about a screen door that is either set so tightly that it acts like a mousetrap for humans when you get behind it or is set so loosely that it flies open at the slightest touch.

Attractively potted plants like geraniums, located on the steps at either side of the door, can create an inviting look and reinforce the doorway as a focal point.

Windows

There are four components that make up the visual effect of windows: the glass, the frame, the shutters, and the view inside.

Glass

The first one is easy. There is little that can enhance glass more than cleaning it, unless of course a pane is broken (it must be fixed immediately). A cleaning trick we've mentioned is to rub windows with newspaper dabbed in ammonia, rather than paper towels or rags, because it won't leave lint or streak as easily.

The Frame

Frames tend to be the first part of a home to suffer from peeling paint because of constant heat reflection during the summer and dripping from condensation or melting snow in the winter.

If you need to repaint, preparing the frame can be tedious, but effort up front will pay off. The key is to remove all chipped, cracked, or blistering paint so the new coat will be even. Sanding, scraping, or the use of a wire brush should do it, or you can try a heat gun to melt it off.

You might also consider highlighting the window frame by installing flower boxes. There are few accents that can spruce up a window more than the sight of brightly colored geraniums or marigolds planted in an attractive window box. This is a high-perceived-value improvement that can add to the packaging appeal of your house or condo.

Shutters

Shutters are a very effective way to highlight a window frame. They can, it seems to me, be compared to attractive eye shadow that enhances a woman's eyes. A shutter sets off a window and directs attention to it.

Wooden shutters are preferable to vinyl or metal but are also two to three times more expensive. However, you may be able to find used wooden shutters at a local home-salvage company that specializes in saving pieces from demolished houses. A little elbow grease and fresh paint can make the shutters look new at a fraction of the cost.

Since the front of your home is most important in forming the first impression, you may well consider limiting shutters to this area. You could also put wooden shutters on the front and less expensive shutters on the sides and rear. A company called Cellwood makes very convincing polystyrene shutters that clip on the siding for easy hanging. They cost between $28 and $83 a pair, depending on the size.

The View Inside

The fourth item is the view inside. The cardinal rule is to keep the shades and drapes always open. The home should look open and inviting when toured during the day. Keep large objects off the sills so that you don't block the view into the home.

To avoid causing territorial anxiety, remove any stickers supporting political candidates. The only decal you should leave on a window is one from a professional alarm company alerting potential intruders that the home is protected.

Avoid leaving portable air conditioners in your front windows, if possible. They are unattractive and immediately signal a lack of central air-conditioning. If you can't or don't want to remove them completely, move them to windows along the side or rear of your home.

And seriously consider securing any window air conditioners located on the ground or first floor. Otherwise they offer easy access to your home.

Window Security

Other aspects of window security can be important, especially if your home is an urban condominium or co-op located on a first floor or at the ground level. Consider installing window grates if your area is prone to break-ins, because a significant percentage of your market will be concerned about this issue. Women and older empty nesters are particularly sensitive to security.

My advice is to install the grate on the inside of the window, if possible, and paint it a light color so it doesn't call attention to itself. There is a product called Burglar Bars by Sterling that costs under $30 and can be very effective.

The Roof

Few people consider the roof from a visual point of view, but it is usually prominent, especially from the street.

Unless your roof happens to be flat or you are in a high-rise building, be aware that missing shingles or a badly pointed chimney can be of concern to the more observant or seasoned buyer. If the problems are minor — such as a gutter section requiring replacement or a few missing shingles — take care of them so your roof will not mistakenly suggest that it is in need of major repair.

As discussed earlier, if your resources are running low, focus your efforts on the front of the home. But if you do have serious roof problems, you have an obligation to tell the buyer about this potentially major problem.

The Downspouts

Dented, weathered, or missing downspouts can detract from the crisp appearance of your home. Since aluminum or vinyl downspouts are not very expensive, there is little reason not to have them in order.

Aluminum downspouts run about $1 per foot, while vinyl ones cost a little less. At least have them replaced on the front of your house, if need be.

The Foundation

There are very few interesting things you can do for the part of the foundation that may be exposed in front of your home. You can either hide it with plantings, as discussed on page 79, or leave it exposed. The most important thing is to make sure it is in sound condition.

Often an old home may have a crumbling stucco or skim coat of cement covering the above-ground portion of the foundation. While the foundation itself may be sound, surface decay may wrongly suggest that a larger problem exists. Don't let the buyer jump to conclusions. There are few areas that warrant more concern than a condition of the foundation. Therefore, by fixing any damage and applying a fresh coat of paint, you can help reinforce the appearance of newness or structural integrity of the foundation.

THE C.U.M.E. EFFECT

The Common-Area Upgrade Multiplier Effect has significant implications for the exterior of condominiums and cooperatives. Because the exterior plays such a key role in establishing the first impression, it should reflect positively on your individual unit. But exterior common areas often are the first to show signs of neglect in a condo or co-op, hurting the value of all units within.

First, it is not uncommon for developers to cut corners on the quality of materials in mailboxes, exterior lighting, or landscaping, leaving the unit owners to decide whether or not to make cosmetic improvements. Since developer-installed items may be functional, at least the natural tendency of condo or co-op associations is to delay replacements.

Second, because common areas get many times more foot traffic than a single-family house, they tend to show wear more quickly.

Last, since condo and co-op inhabitants so often have difficulty in deciding on exactly what improvements to make and what styles to select, it's often easier to do nothing at all.

But in some ways, the appearance of the exterior of your building or complex can even be more important than it is for single-family detached homes. If a sophisticated buyer looks at your condo and sees a building that needs work in the common areas, he or she will know that there is no assurance that the problem will soon be corrected.

Furthermore, a condominium that has shabby common areas makes a negative statement about the unit owners. A prospect may wonder whether they don't care about appearances or can't afford to make the changes. Either way, each unit owner will have to live with the problem when it comes time to sell his or her unit.

From creating a sensational doorway to putting a fresh coat of paint around peeling window trim, the exterior improvements discussed in this chapter can pay off handsomely when applied to common areas of condos or co-ops.

CONCLUSION

I can't emphasize enough how important the first impression of the exterior of your home can be in influencing the outcome of your tour. If the buyer does not like the exterior, it is unlikely that the interior will change his or her mind.

Remember, curb appeal includes everything from the condition of the sidewalk to the cleanliness of the neighbors' front lawns to the look of the car parked in your driveway. Don't let any one weakness detract from the main attraction of your property, your home itself.

Once the buyer has seen the exterior of the home, the next critical impression will be made by the entry. This room should help reinforce the buyer's first impression of your property. For this reason, the entry is of key importance in creating a successful showing and will be discussed at length in the chapter that follows.

CHAPTER HIGHLIGHTS

1. Curb appeal starts with the street in front of your home, so make sure it and all other city property look their best.

2. The look of your neighbors' property will also have an impact on the value of your home. Follow the steps outlined in this chapter to make sure the property next door will be an asset to you.

3. Repainting the exterior of a tired-looking home, although costly, can be one of the most profitable packaging steps.

4. If you are trying to determine the best way to allocate a limited improvement budget, spend your money on the front of the home only and exclude the sides and back.

5. Recognize the power of the doorway as a low-cost, high-impact packaging tool.

6. Be sensitive to strong design, political, or ethnic statements made by the exterior of your home.

7. Take the necessary steps to make your home look secure from the exterior, especially if it is in an urban area.

8. Make sure your lawn and landscape enhance the overall look of your home but try to limit improvements to the low-cost methods discussed.

9. Be aware that an automobile parked in the driveway is part of the landscape. Make sure it makes the right statement about you and your home.

10. If your home is a condo or co-op, take advantage of the Common-Area Upgrade Multiplier Effect to improve its value.

7

A Grand
Entrance

The look and feeling of your entry plays a critical role in setting the right tone for the rest of your home. The first impression of your home's interior is established here, and you want it to be favorable.

Brooke Warrick of SRI International, the California-based think tank, states, "The entryway establishes the social contract with outsiders and clearly communicates the position and status of those owning the home."

If the prospect did not seem excited by the exterior of your property, this is your chance to make up ground quickly. And if the buyer was impressed with the exterior, here's the opportunity to begin cementing a sale, whether your entry consists of a separate room or a small hallway or is simply the first stopping point before walking into an open layout.

The National Association of Home Builders reports that over 74 percent of home buyers want and expect a formal entry hall to be a feature of their next home. When three quarters of your market speaks, it pays to listen.

THE FIVE-STEP SYSTEM
Step 1. Consider the Competition

Entryways vary considerably from home to home, and there is no single right or wrong look. Even if you find your competition has more dramatic or impressive entries than yours, we do not recommend wholesale changes. But knowing what you're up against should give you the incentive to upgrade what you already have.

There are a number of inexpensive packaging techniques that will make your entry stand up to or above the competition.

Step 2. Consider the Buyer

As always, understanding your buyer is important when marketing your entryway. By considering the specific needs of different segments of the market, you will strengthen its appeal.

First-Time Buyers

Young first-time buyers, who are just beginning to earn enough to buy certain trappings that higher-income groups already enjoy, want the entryway to speak of their new position in life. Research indicates, for example, that mirrored surfaces are quite popular with this group, as are plush carpeting and expensive-looking light fixtures.

Trade-up Buyers

For the more sophisticated trade-up buyer, the entry should be understated but suggest success. Research conducted by SRI International reveals that to this group art objects and oriental carpets can help project the right message. The entry as a whole is particularly important to the trade-up buyer in terms of the signal it sends to visitors and friends.

Empty Nesters/Trade-down Buyers

Many empty nesters and trade-down buyers moving to smaller homes may be resigned to losing a separate and formal entry. But there are many ways to create a feeling of a separate entry where none exists.

Because older buyers are particularly sensitive about security, your entryway should suggest how secure your home is and help satisfy their safety needs. We will cover ways to increase the feeling of security in your entry and to add to the perception of value in the process.

Step 3. Evaluate Your Product

When you bring your focus groups through the entryway, pause to get their first impressions. Because their reactions are likely to reflect those of prospective buyers, you will want to listen attentively.

Ask them what they like the most and least about your entry and what first pops into their minds when they first step into your home. Be particularly sensitive to comments relating to sources of territorial anxiety.

Step 4. Eliminate Territorial Anxiety

Because people are on their guard when first setting foot in a stranger's home, it's particularly important to avoid personal statements that create territorial anxiety in the entry.

Eliminate strong personal color, ethnic, or design statements. For example, if your focus group testing or your own research concludes that the violet-patterned wallpaper gracing your entry may not have general appeal, we would certainly recommend stripping it and painting the wall a neutral shade that complements your furnishings.

Remember, no detail is too small as far as the entry is concerned, because this is where the buyers' impressions of the exterior will either be reinforced or contradicted. A few points scored one way or the other at this stage of the tour will influence the final outcome.

Step 5. Maximize Packaging Appeal

Since the entryway is usually small, each feature of the room can make a significant impact. For this reason, use small details to make big impressions, and we will show you how.

SETTING THE STAGE

You want your entry to set the right tone immediately. The entry should clearly suggest that your house or condo is in excellent condition, and that your home offers a positive life-style.

Walls

The dominant visual influence of your entry is likely to be the walls and the items hanging on them.

Wall Colors and Covers

There are two basic rules we've already discussed about the use of color in areas like the entry. First, in small spaces, use light colors to avoid making the area seem even smaller. Second, colors should be neutral so as to avoid causing territorial anxiety.

Whites, beiges, and light pastels are the safest. Stronger colors should be limited to accents like prints, flowers, or upholstery.

Wallpaper in the entry can be especially tricky since it can overwhelm a room. Neutral colors and small prints might be acceptable, but large prints and strong colors can definitely work against you.

Use your focus groups to determine if your wallpaper is too personal and, if so, strip it and paint the walls.

Pictures

Use pictures to add color and interest to neutral walls. But if you have very expressive or abstract art that people either love or hate, move it elsewhere. You would do better opting for more reserved paintings and photographs. Always avoid religious art since it can cause territorial anxiety.

Mirrors

A mirror can be a big help to a small or dark entry. It will enhance the perception of light and size in this all-important area of the home. Of course, the mirror should be spotless and the objects it reflects should be attractive.

Depending upon the layout of your entryway, you can choose a single-framed mirror, a large mirror above a counter, or a full-length wall mirror. Don't place large mirrors directly across from the door, however, because you want prospects to focus on your home, not how they themselves look.

Wall Molding

If your house or condominium is traditional in design, molding can transform a nondescript surface into a focal point. Molding is one of the least expensive ways to set your house apart from the competition, increase perceived value, and compensate for design flaws.

I've applied wall molding to traditional properties with excellent results. The look of the molding reinforces the charm of the home and invariably elicits comments like "They just don't build homes like this anymore." Seldom do buyers consider that the marvelous detail work so common in authentic colonial and Georgian homes can be bought by the carload at the local lumberyard.

Molding can make an impressive statement in the entry and in other formal areas of the home. The ideas we will discuss apply not only to formal entryways but will later be applied to other rooms in the home.

There are also a number of manufacturers who make some handsome wood molding and precast plaster products. These are usually much more elaborate than any you could produce on your own and can create a dramatic focal point to any room, especially one as small as the entry. Precast or wood molding products cost between $1 and $9 per foot, depending on how elaborate they are, and can be installed by any handy person.

One manufacturer of precast moldings is Dovetail, Inc. This company makes a wide range of products using gypsum cement or plaster reinforced with fiberglass. For a copy of their catalogue, send $3 to Dovetail, Inc., P.O. Box 1569, Lowell, MA 01853. Another manufacturer of molding is Driwood. They produce a detailed catalogue that costs $6 and can be obtained by sending a check to P.O. Box 1729, Florence, SC 29503.

If you decide to use conventional wooden molding from a lumberyard or home-improvement retailer, you can be assured that an amateur can install it. You need a few tools, including a miter box and saw, a tape measure, level, hammer and nails, a drill, and some spackle.

There are many good books on home restoration, including *Old House Woodwork Restoration* by Ed Johnson (Prentice-Hall), that provide ideas on how and where to put up molding. Magazines like *Colonial Homes* or *Better Homes and Gardens* also provide interesting suggestions.

Molding Alternatives

There are three types of molding that are especially effective in enhancing the look of your walls. They are chair-rail, picture-frame, and cornice.

Chair-rail molding was originally designed to prevent the tops of chair backs from denting or marring walls. For this reason, they are traditionally located about 30 to 33 inches above the floor and wrap around the perimeter of a room.

Considered decorative by today's standards, chair-rail molding adds a feeling of detail and charm to walls and lends continuity to a room by unifying it. Plan to spend about 80 cents per linear foot on basic chair-rail molding, more if you choose an elaborate style.

Picture-frame molding looks like a large empty frame, and is similar to designs on the walls of old colonial or Georgian homes. The placement of picture-frame molding should be above chair-rail height and about 10 to 12 inches down from the ceiling, depending upon the height of your walls.

Picture-frame molding is usually delicate in design, measures about one half-inch in width and is characterized by a fluted surface. Like chair-rail molding, picture-frame molding adds a feeling of charm and detail to a room. It can also be used to break up large empty expanses of wall. Picture-frame molding is easy to install and costs only about 40 cents a linear foot.

Cornice molding is designed to dress up the point at which the wall and ceiling meet. This molding can range from the very simplest design to elaborate carved surfaces. By combining several different types of cornice molding, you can reproduce the feeling of detailed molding at a fraction of the cost. However, this kind of work is just beyond most casual do-it-yourselfers.

You can use even a single piece of cornice molding to add an entirely new dimension to a room. A 5-inch-wide piece of crown-cornice molding costs about $1.75 a linear foot. This molding, as well as most other varieties, is generally available in lengths from 3 to 20 feet, although most of your home's requirements can be met by lengths of 8 feet or less.

If you don't feel you are enough of a handyman to do the job yourself, hire a carpenter. I advise against the plastic moldings sometimes available at home-improvement stores. If the buyer recognizes they are fake, the perceived value of the molding itself and the room in general will be diminished, and the buyer will take a harder look at other aspects of your house or condo.

Of the three moldings, my choice would be chair-rail. Applying it requires very little work and it is highly visible. To make moldings even more visible, painting can be very effective. If your walls are any color but bright white, consider painting the molding a lighter color to accentuate it. This will also help to make the room appear larger.

Ceilings

The ceiling is not generally thought of as a major selling point, but it can have a real impact on the buyer's perception of your entry. If the ceiling has cosmetic defects or design flaws, you can use a number of inexpensive packaging improvements to correct it.

Paint

Remember, if the ceiling is disproportionately high for the size of the room, a darker color will make it seem lower. The darker color will reflect less light and will also effectively minimize surface defects.

Ceiling Moldings

There are a range of interesting products available that can transform a conventional ceiling into a focal point of the room. Precast ceiling medallions or rosettes are one such product. They are circular plaster reliefs that were common in old, elegant homes but are rarely seen in today's reproduction colonial homes.

Dovetail manufactures these and indicates that they can be easily installed with adhesive. The prices range from $35 to over $200.

Major Defects

If your ceiling has major cosmetic problems — surface cracks, bulges, or visible tape-joint marks from sloppy plasterboard installation — consider applying moldings, replacing the ceiling, or installing a textured ceiling.

You can purchase decorative metal ceilings, featuring turn-of-the-century designs. A company called W. F. Norman in Nevada, Missouri, offers this product. It costs about $2 per square foot and can be installed by most do-it-yourselfers. This is an ideal way to cover up a cosmetically flawed ceiling and turn it into an asset.

A textured ceiling covers minor defects and is available in a product called Textone Ready-Mixed Texture from U.S. Gypsum. It comes in a variety of textures, depending on how coarse you want it to be. To achieve an even, professional look, apply this product with a roller.

Floors

When your prospect first steps into your home, the floor that greets him or her should project a feeling of quality and care.

If the floor is wood, wax it or give it a new coat of urethane. This will not only make it look better but will also add a smell of newness. If the floor is carpeted, cleaning or vacuuming is a must.

With either type of floor, an area rug will add a look of richness; it can also be a great cover-up. Use a thick pad beneath the rug to provide an added feeling of luxury.

If you need a new floor for this small area, consider using a high-quality material like marble or flagstone. You may be able to put down a new floor yourself by, for example, applying a self-stick solid oak parquet designed for the do-it-yourselfer. Bruce Parquet floor sells an oak parquet product for $2 per square foot.

Installing a more luxurious floor in the entry may well be worthwhile, because it will suggest overall quality. When it comes time to advertise the property and you state, "Features marble entry," you can be sure people will take notice.

Lighting

An attractive light fixture can be the centerpiece of your entryway. It can help set the tone of the tour by suggesting quality. Proper lighting of the entryway is also essential in helping to establish the warmth and cheeriness of your house or condominium.

If you have a ceiling fixture that is clearly not up to the standards of the rest of your entryway, consider replacing it with one that can provide a true focal point. You may find that, depending on the size of your entryway, one general overhead light is sufficient, or it may be that a second accent light is needed. Because the ceiling is likely to cover a small area only, there is probably no room for a second ceiling fixture. On the other hand, the area might accommodate a large table lamp. If your entry does not currently have one, simply borrow a table lamp from another room.

Furniture

If the area is large enough, consider providing an attractive furniture grouping. For example, you might borrow a small side table with a favorite lamp or a pair of candlesticks from the living room. Only you are likely to notice their absence from the larger room; on the other hand, most prospects are sure to notice them in the entryway.

The Front Door

The front door is the first and last part of your home that buyers encounter. For this reason, it should reinforce the positive impression made by your property.

Any glass in the door should sparkle, and so should the hardware. Take a moment to consider the hardware because it can offer a telling detail about the quality of your property in general. A reproduction cut-glass, brass, hardwood, or porcelain knob placed on an otherwise conventional hollow-core door can increase the perception of value.

These knobs cost $5 and up and they can be found at large home-improvement stores or by writing to Renovator's Supply in Millers Falls,

Massachusetts, for a catalogue. I don't advise replacing the knobs in every room, but installing them in the entryway helps to establish a special tone for your home.

Door Security

The lock and handle should have the look and feeling of quality and provide reassurance about the property. If you have worn or flimsy hardware, fix or upgrade it.

Eliminate any sign of burglary attempts — such as pry marks on the wood or hardware. Plastic wood, a wood filler, should be used to fill any gouge marks. Damaged metal parts should be replaced.

Placing an attractive brass peephole in the door for screening visitors is a good idea, but don't buy the small, inexpensive kind since it will cheapen the look of the door. Baldwin Hardware in Reading, Pennsylvania, makes a variety of quality peepholes, including "Observ-O-Scope," which provides 175-degree visibility.

There are a variety of attractive surface-mounted brass deadbolt

---

Do-It-Yourself Improvements
under $100

1. Apply chair-rail or cornice molding ($50).

2. Use a fresh cut-flower arrangement ($15).

3. Install brass, porcelain, or cut-glass doorknobs ($5 each).

4. Install brass or porcelain switchplate covers ($5 each).

5. Repaint the entry ($25).

6. Apply a new coat of polyurethane to a hardwood floor ($10).

7. Install a new central lighting fixture ($80).

8. Add raised-panel molding to a plain entry door ($20).

9. Mirror a wall or wall section ($70).

---

locks, spring-loaded latches, and chain locks available from Baldwin and Omnia Industries, Inc., of Montclair, New Jersey. Both functional and decorative, these products are high-perceived-value items but may cost no more than $15.

Door Molding

If the rest of your home features traditional architectural detail and if you have a plain flat door, it's easy to reproduce the look of a raised-panel door. Simply use picture-frame molding and affix four or six vertical rectangular panels. Go to a lumberyard and measure the size of the panels on doors so you can get the right dimensions for your door.

The Closet

When you offer to hang up your prospect's coat, he or she will get a first glimpse of the organization of your home. If your closet is packed with clothing, boxes, or other space robbers, clean it out. Move items down to the basement or up to the attic, but avoid giving the impression of a messy, inadequate closet.

Once you've done this, buy a set of the most attractive hangers you can find. Rather than having a collection of old wire, wooden, or padded hangers, use a set of chrome or brightly colored, heavy plastic hangers that add a feeling of quality to the closet.

The closet should also smell attractive. Replace the odor of shoes, mothballs, and mustiness with smells that sell. A product called SLA Cedar Scented Spray from Reefer-Galler Company, St. Louis, Missouri, will make your closet smell like a cedar chest. So will cedar bars from Eddie Bauer, a national retailer and mail order house specializing in outdoor products. If you need protection from moths, try Lavender Scented Moth Sachet by Reefer-Galler Company.

Details Make the Difference

The smaller an area is, the more impact small details will have. Your entryway provides an ideal opportunity to "impress for less."

One of my favorite nice touches is to replace the standard plastic or metal switchplates or outlet covers with more substantial ones. You can choose from brass, porcelain, or wood.

Brass plates cost about $5 apiece, so if you have to replace six covers, you'll spend $30. But this investment will immediately suggest a higher level of detail and value that will enhance the buyer's perception of the room as a whole.

Another nice touch is the addition of a small shelf or counter near the front door. Because the shelf will be small, you might consider making it from an expensive material like marble, or an attractive wood like walnut.

The shelf should look professional, but if you are not good with your hands, the cost of bringing someone in to do such a small job may not be economical. Remember, a job that looks amateur may actually cost you points.

DEFINING AN UNDEFINED ENTRY

Not all entryways are clearly defined square or rectangular rooms. Some are not true entries at all but part of an open-plan layout. These may be most common in small condominiums or co-ops — where space is at a premium — or in very contemporary homes with an open design. There are, however, many ways to create the feeling of an entry area in a studio co-op or a small condo.

The creative use of flooring can help. If your main room has either wall-to-wall carpeting or hardwood floors, replace a portion with a different surface material. For instance, cut out a rectangular area of your carpeting — one that's large enough to accommodate the sweep of your front door and a few extra feet to spare — and replace it with hardwood, ceramic tile, quarry tile, flagstone, or even marble. This will divide the space visually.

You may have to call in a professional to put down the floor, because it must be applied so that it doesn't interfere with the opening of the door. And since the area is small, it will pay to buy the best material you can find.

Erecting a half-height wall with a countertop of oak or other attractive wood can also help define an entry. You could also use a low bookcase. To add visual interest, place a vase with flowers or a decorative table lamp on the bookcase.

THE C.U.M.E. EFFECT

If you live in a condominium or cooperative apartment, you really have two entries, one to your building and one to your home. To maximize the value of your unit, pay close attention to both of these areas by applying the Common-Area Upgrade Multiplier Effect (C.U.M.E.).

The condo or co-op association, management, or trustees who fail to recognize the importance of an attractive common entry or lobby are doing a major disservice to all of the building's owners. An impressive lobby will improve the value of all units, while a shabby one will do just the opposite.

The same rules that apply to your own entry apply to the common area, with one significant difference. While you have to absorb 100 percent of the cost of your unit's improvements, you're responsible only for a fraction of the cost of common-entry improvements. For this reason, you may be able to afford to spend more on this part of the building, thereby greatly increasing its perceived value.

The lobby should look clean and smell fresh and suggest a well-managed property and a caring group of owners. Carpets should be shampooed regularly, pet odors eliminated, and hard-surfaced floors waxed. Old newspapers, magazines, and mail should be tidied up.

No detail is too small, because the entry is an integral part of the first impression of your property. The following is a checklist for improvements to the lobby or entryway in a condominium or cooperative building.

Walls

A neutral color scheme is important. Developers often leave behind a legacy of bad taste when they complete condominium or cooperative projects, but because the walls or wallpaper are new, unit owners learn to live with it. But becoming desensitized to potentially offensive colors or designs can be costly. Strong colors can create territorial anxiety and will hurt not only your unit but others as well.

Floors

If the carpet or other floor covering is worn or dated, have it replaced. Gold or deep red shag carpeting, for example, may suggest that other parts of the building are old.

The floor should say as much as possible about the quality of the property in general. If it looks tired, it should be refinished, upgraded, or replaced. Refinishing a wooden floor or coating a tile floor with Val-Oil will create a newer look and also introduce new smells. But a damaged or poorly maintained parquet floor, for example, can lead to questions about the maintenance of other parts of the property.

If replacement is in order, the condo or co-op should invest in the best possible quality. Individual unit owners will have to pay only a fraction of this cost, yet each will benefit fully from a more luxurious lobby.

Light Fixtures

The ceiling-mounted light fixture in the entry to the building can provide an exciting focal point. I'm always impressed when I walk into a condo or co-op building and see a very attractive hanging lamp in the entry. It suggests that the developer or the unit owners are doing something right and may be indicative of the quality of the rest of the property.

Whether you live in a thirty-unit or a three-hundred-unit building, it pays to put in an eye-catching light fixture. A polished-brass or cut-glass chandelier may cost several hundred dollars, but its impact will benefit all units.

Furniture

A lobby with a grouping of attractive furniture can add luxury and dignity to an entry. Making the entry look more like a suite than a utilitarian service area will help improve the ambience of the entire property.

Keep the furniture neutral and consistent with the design of the building. Don't let others impose their personal tastes on the selection of furniture.

Plants and Flowers

Plants and flowers can add color and fragrance to a common area and suggest that the unit owners are interested in its upkeep. Flowering plants will make even more of an impression.

Even if you have to supply the flowers yourself while your unit is on the market, it is well worth the small investment. When choosing plants, consider spathiphyllum, a Chinese evergreen, or a dracaena since they are durable and do not require much light. When buying flowers, hyacinths, tuberoses, or gardenias are appropriate.

Security

The feeling of security in a condominium or cooperative apartment building is very important, especially in urban areas. Break-ins can be quite common since unit owners are often well-paid professionals who work during the day, leaving their apartments unoccupied.

If there are any signs of attempted break-ins, like screwdriver marks around the door, make sure they are filled in. The locks on the door should be top-quality, and the latch should shut firmly.

Alarms can be impractical in buildings where people are going in and out all day. For this reason, secure doors and locks are about the best measures you can take.

CONCLUSION

Whether your property is a condo, a co-op, or a detached single-family home, the entry will make a lasting first impression that will remain with the buyer throughout the rest of the tour.

Because the entry is small and because the buyer will be looking at it so closely, make sure every detail is looked after. By perceiving quality and care in this room, the buyer will approach the rest of the home with a positive attitude.

Many of the techniques that work for the entry can also be applied to the living room. Consumer surveys indicate that this room is among the two most important rooms in the home. The next chapter will detail ways to make sure the living room becomes a key selling point in your home.

CHAPTER HIGHLIGHTS

1. The entry can help create a lasting first impression of your home.

2. Over 74 percent of home buyers want a formal entryway.

3. Be especially sensitive to strong personal color or design statements in the entry to avoid creating territorial anxiety when the prospect first enters your home.

4. Use quality details in the entry to suggest quality and attention to detail in the rest of your home.

5. The lighting and lighting fixtures are important in setting the right tone for the entry.

6. Mirrors can be used effectively to make this area seem larger.

7. In homes where there is no formal or separate entry, you can create this effect through several approaches, including furniture groupings or half-height dividers.

8. Move a small grouping of furniture or a prized antique from the living room to the entry, where it will have more impact.

9. The Common-Area Upgrade Multiplier Effect (C.U.M.E.) has important implications for common lobbies or entries in condos and co-ops.

8

The Lavish Living Room

According to the sociologist Irwin Altman, "The living room is more often a place to impress others than to enjoy ourselves." This may be one reason why, according to *Better Homes and Gardens*, consumers spend more money furnishing the living room than any other part of the home.

The importance of the living room as a status symbol ranks it among the most important selling rooms of any home. To sell your house or condo quickly and for more money, you must make every effort to make your living room as impressive as possible.

THE FIVE-STEP SYSTEM
Step 1. Consider the Competition

You are likely to encounter some strong competition when prospects compare living rooms, because homeowners focus so much attention on this room. After touring competitive properties on the market, you may well find some living rooms are larger, brighter, or have more attractive views than yours.

While we do not advocate making structural changes to your property, we do advise trying to close any gaps that may exist between your property and the competition's. We will show you inexpensive ways to achieve this, once you have determined your competition's strengths and which aspects of your living room need attention.

Step 2. Consider the Buyer

Consumer research conducted by the National Association of Home Builders, *Better Homes and Gardens,* and the Gallup Poll shows that home buyers respond strongly to certain features of the living room. But different buyer groups place different importance on these features.

First-Time Buyers

This group is likely to be the least demanding of all market segments since the intrinsic pleasure of simply owning a new home is their greatest reward. But first-time buyers still have certain requirements that influence their choice between one home and another.

They want a bright, upbeat atmosphere that makes the home as pleasant as possible. If your living room is dark, you can make it brighter, and if it's small you can increase the buyer's perception of size. And by purchasing flowers and plants, you can inexpensively add splashes of color.

This group also wants a quality carpet in the living room. Because carpet can be expensive, the thought of replacing it can add to the financial burden that the first-time buyer usually experiences. We will discuss ways to minimize buyer concerns by making your carpet seem as new as possible.

Trade-up Buyers

For young professionals and successful executives, the living room takes on special significance. It is often thought of as a place for entertaining, so its suitability for this purpose becomes a top priority.

The size of the room, condition of the carpet or flooring, and the look of the fireplace all take on increased importance. We will show you how to improve the perception of each of these features through inexpensive packaging techniques. We will also show you how to make the room more elegant and impressive by incorporating special features.

Empty Nesters/Trade-down Buyers

Because this group has probably been accustomed to a larger living room and must now come to terms with a smaller one, it's important to make the area look and feel as large as possible. By suggesting different ways of arranging furniture, for example, you can suggest the room's versatility. Lighting and mirrors can also help the room seem larger.

Again, the fireplace and carpet are important to these buyers. Empty nesters and trade-down buyers are also very responsive to small touches you can add that increase the feeling of security.

Step 3. Evaluate Your Product

Spend extra time in the living room with your focus group, and evaluate all of their comments. Although the living room is likely to be one of the best maintained rooms in the house, that doesn't mean it's above creating some of the more common marketing problems.

Your focus groups will help you identify features that may hinder the ability of prospects to visualize themselves enjoying "their" living room. If focus-group members comment about inappropriate pictures, ethnic statements, or your choice of wallpaper, listen and don't get defensive.

Also, small cosmetic flaws — wall cracks, soot stains around heating vents, musty smells, or even dirty windows — are other potential problems your focus group may point out that you should act upon.

Step 4. Eliminate Territorial Anxiety

Since the living room can make such strong statements about the homeowner, be careful that your living room doesn't provide personal messages that cause territorial anxiety in the buyer.

The colors of walls and carpets are two of the most common offenders. Other less frequent but equally important sources of territorial anxiety are ethnic, political, or social statements. We will discuss these in detail below and show you how to avoid them.

Step 5. Maximize Packaging Appeal

There are certain features and characteristics of the living room that most buyers respond to. Size and elegance are always appealing, as are a fireplace and quality carpet.

You can improve the perception of each of these through the proper use of lighting, color, sound, and smell. You can also increase the perceived value of your living room through small and inexpensive details.

THE SHOWCASE OF YOUR HOME

The living room is your showcase. To create the right feeling about the room, you'll want your walls, windows, ceilings, and floors to look as attractive as possible.

Walls

As with any room in the home, the walls can create a dominant visual effect. Let's start with the basics and address some common problems that are easy to correct but can make the wrong kind of statement if left unattended.

Preparing the Walls

No matter how new your home is, surface cracks on walls often appear. To the uninitiated, cracks of any kind may spell trouble even though most are perfectly benign.

The fact is, homes settle over time, surfaces expand and contract, and vibrations occur that can shake your house. Plaster does not flex with this movement and often develops hairline cracks. These frequently appear at the top corners of doors or window frames and run to the corners of the ceiling.

The cracks to be concerned about are those that are growing fast, going deep in walls, or running horizontally along them. These may suggest too much weight coming from above or unusual settling from below.

Filling cracks is a relatively simple procedure, but substantial painting may be necessary if you're unable to match your touch-ups with the rest of the wall. If you've never repaired a wall before, buy a small can of premixed spackle and a putty knife. Open up the crack so that enough spackle can be forced inside, and then apply it generously over the affected area. When it is dry, sand it smooth, and paint right over it.

If you have a problem of recurring surface cracks, try the vinyl sealing caulk that is used with caulking guns. Apply it to the area, wet it, then smooth it flat, using a tool or your finger. This material is more flexible than spackle and will not crack as easily.

Paint

Once the walls are free from cosmetic surface flaws, a fresh coat of paint can brighten up a room. It will not only suggest a high level of general maintenance and add a "new" smell to the living room, but it can also hide small, benign defects that may still remain on your walls.

As far as your choice of color is concerned, remember to use safe neutrals and pastels and avoid strong personal statements.

Also, spend a few extra dollars for higher-quality paints like Benjamin Moore or Martin Senour and avoid private-label bargain brands. The difference of $4 or $5 per gallon will be lost many times over if the coverage is poor and the finish inferior.

Wallpaper

Again, the key is to keep it neutral. Since the living room is much larger than the entry, wallpaper can be very risky.

Wallpaper can be useful in altering the perception of room size. Vertical patterns, for example, tend to make a room look taller, while horizontals make it look wider. A patterned wallpaper can also hide cosmetic irregularities.

But these patterns must be subtle enough not to be offensive. Therefore, I don't advise wallpapering if you have the chance to paint.

If your focus groups say the wallpaper you currently have is a potential risk, seriously consider stripping and repainting. If the paper is especially dark or dated or has an unusual pattern, be especially wary. If time is a problem, roll right over the wallpaper with a neutral-color paint rather than leaving this potential source of territorial anxiety unattended to.

Dressing Up the Walls

You can make conventional walls distinctive by using some of the methods we've discussed. Dressing up the walls in the living room is especially important because they play such a key role in shaping the buyer's first impression of this room.

Mirrors

The strategic use of mirrors is the most dramatic and economical way to increase the feeling of size in a room. Doing an entire wall with either mirrored squares or large sectional plates will maximize the impact and can actually increase the perception of size by 50 percent. An entire wall may not be necessary and, in fact, may be overdoing it. But mirrors can help compensate for a small living room.

By placing a mirror in a position that causes it to reflect a window, you add dimension and light to a room. As always, be careful to position the mirror so that it reflects attractive views, because the only thing worse than one unattractive view is two.

Another logical place to install a mirror is over a fireplace. Since this may already be a focal point of the room, people will certainly notice the effect.

Look for a defined section of wall that you can cover by the mirror. If the area around your fireplace juts out from the wall, placing a mirror above the mantel, covering the entire width of the wall, will give the mirror a custom look. The mirror should look as if it were an integral part of the house rather than a last-minute addition.

The cost of mirrors varies significantly depending upon the thickness, quality, and size. For a 4-by-6-foot mirror of average quality, expect to pay $125 and about $75 for mirror squares.

Your decision on how much wall to cover may be dictated by the available space. But if spending $100 can increase the perception of size in a small living room, you'll find this a worthwhile investment, given the significance buyers place on this area of the home.

Molding

Molding is an ideal packaging tool because it can add to the perceived value of the living room at relatively little cost. As mentioned in the section on entryways, molding comes in a variety of styles, including chair-rail, cornice, and picture-frame.

Because the living room is the room in which the most entertaining takes place for large segments of the home-buying public, formality is often appropriate. Molding gives a feeling of elegance and Old World charm, which many of today's buyers will pay a good deal of money for.

If you don't have the time or inclination to put up molding but feel the room needs a decorative touch, there is a wallpaper product called Flair Trim Decorative Borders that can achieve a similar effect for a fraction of the cost or effort. The paper strips are prepasted, so all you have to do is dip them in water and apply them to the wall. They can convert a boring wall into an attractive one, and they cover a small enough area so they will not make a powerful design statement. The trim costs about 25 cents a foot and should be available at wallpaper dealers.

Given the choice of molding or wallpaper trim, however, I'd put up the real thing. For about $100, you can really upgrade the feeling of the room with molding.

Decorative Wall Hardware

It's often the smallest of details that can suggest how special your home really is. There is a variety of attractive products that inexpensively upgrade your property.

Brass switchplates and outlet covers, for example, are ideal since they are quite visible. Brass or pewter wall sconces also add an impressive decorative touch.

Windows

Windows can alter the look of your entire living room. If they are bright and cheery, the rest of the room will be, too. If they are dull and drab, you'll have to compensate in other ways.

Solving Window Problems

Start by making sure the windows are clean and the view is as unobstructed as possible. Pull back the curtains and pull up the shades, unless you have a view you want blocked.

Fix any cracked panes and lubricate old or sticky window sashes so they will operate easily if a prospect takes a closer look. A product called Window Fixer, from Quaker City Manufacturing, is designed for this. And whatever you do, never show your home with windows that are covered with plastic shrink film. This suggests a lack of energy efficiency and a need for storm windows.

Install window locks in urban properties to enhance the feeling of security. Brass locks are the most attractive.

Coping with a Bad View

A bad view can hurt the appeal of a living room, but a window can help mask this. Hang plants over the center of the window and use them as the focal point. Make sure the pot is attractive and the plant looks as healthy as possible.

Sheer drapes or French café-style curtains can also be effective. They let light in but obscure a bad view. Using brass rods for café curtains can be appealing and add a look of formality to the room.

Dealing with Unattractive Windows

Windows that are simply unattractive because of uninspiring views or poor architectural design can be greatly helped by the installation of floor-to-ceiling vertical blinds. This approach will let light in but draw attention away from the windows themselves.

Avoid painting the window frame a darker color than the wall because it will break up the expanse, making the wall seem smaller, and will call attention to the window. The great attraction of windows should be the view outside and the curtains that frame them. If the view is not attractive, then a darker color will only call attention to the area.

Correcting Window Positioning

If your windows are narrow and separated by large amounts of wall space, place a wide panel of curtains on either side to cover up some of the dead area. This will suggest a larger enclosure.

If the windows are unusually low, install a shelf above them and display small collectibles or old books on it.

Dressing Up the Window

Once you've covered the basics, focus on dressing up the windows.

You can attractively frame a window by building a simple valance and covering it with a fabric that matches or accents your curtains. An amateur carpenter can build a valance for no more than $20 per window.

Louvered wooden shutters, instead of curtain fabrics of your choice, can help to avoid taste conflicts with the buyer. Shutters suggest substance and can be very attractive in certain decors. They are not cheap, though, for an average-size window, shutters cost about $100. When you sell your home, you may be able to charge extra for the shutters (on the other hand, rarely will people want to buy your curtains). If the buyer doesn't want to pay for the shutters, you may be able to take them with you.

Levolor-style venetian blinds can also be effective because they tie in nicely with the rest of the room and add a high perceived-value item. They have a crisp, clean look and are less subject to personal tastes than curtains or drapes.

If you do have curtains, make the most of the curtain rods. You can buy simulated brass traverse rods that look quite elegant for surprisingly little cost. Kirsch makes a 48- to 84-inch simulated-brass-finish rod with decorative end caps that retails for around $25.

Ceilings

The look and condition of the ceiling can make a statement about the living room in much the same way as the walls do. Common surface problems like cracks, unevenness, and small water stains can worry the buyer and should be corrected.

Apply polyurethane or varnish to the spots and then paint over them so they do not recur, as discussed in Chapter Three. You may need to repaint an entire ceiling if the paint does not match, so proceed carefully.

Darker paint will draw attention away from a damaged surface, but it will also make the ceiling seem lower. Decide which is the greater drawback before taking any action.

Special Ceiling Features

Ceiling fans offer both practical and visual appeal. While not quite as fashionable as they used to be, fans are clearly a high-value feature to which buyers in warmer climates are attracted.

The cost of these fans starts at about $100; installation can amount to the same, if your ceiling needs to be reinforced to hold the weight. Ceiling fans save energy by forcing hot air down from the ceiling in winter and reducing the need for air conditioning in summer.

If you live in a market where these items are essential and your home is in the luxury category, consider buying ceiling fans. If your competition has air conditioning and you don't, you suddenly have an even more compelling reason to install them. Ceiling fans offer a way of bridging this gap.

As discussed, ceiling medallions and friezes add detail and elegance to the living room and differentiate it from the competition's. These are definitely a frill that should not top your list of priorities. But if your home is in the higher-price range and otherwise needs very little work, this feature provides that added touch of elegance that upscale buyers definitely look for in traditional homes.

The Floor

The lowly floor is considered by consumers to be a very important feature of the living room. For example, according to *Builder* magazine, 98.2 percent of all new home buyers consider the quality of carpeting a very important part of the basic purchase price.

There are steps you can take either on your own or through a professional to improve the look of the flooring in your living area.

Carpet

If your living room carpet is badly worn or stained, it will immediately devalue the room. You'll want to do whatever you can to make it look as good as possible.

Of course, you're not anxious to replace carpeting just to sell your home, so start by cleaning it. If the carpet needs only a light cleaning, try a store-bought carpet cleaner that requires you to wet-sponge it into the rug. Woolite carpet cleaner is good for this. Many supermarkets also rent out rug shampooers and special cleaners for under $15 for 24 hours. After the cleaning solution has been applied and the carpet is dry, vacuum it, and bring back the original nap by using a light bamboo rake.

For especially tough stains, make up a solution of Tide and warm

---

Do-It-Yourself Improvements under $100

1. Shampoo the carpet ($10).

2. Put out fresh cut flowers ($5).

3. Install brass switchplates ($5 each).

4. Install brass, porcelain, or cut-glass doorknobs ($5 each).

5. Use floor can lights ($20).

6. Repaint the room ($50).

7. Add fresh polyurethane to the floor ($15).

8. Install track lights ($100).

9. Add large floor plants ($50 each).

10. Install chair-rail molding ($100).

---

water and brush it into the affected area. Dab the area with a towel to soak up the excess moisture.

If your rug needs more extensive help, it's hard to match the work of professional cleaners. Expect to pay around 25 to 30 cents per square foot.

If your carpet is beyond help, you are faced with some tough decisions. Do you just leave it alone and hope it won't devalue your home too much in the mind of the buyer, or do you go out and buy new carpeting?

You could always put a large area rug over your carpet and cover up the problem. This may be an acceptable, low-cost alternative. It is unlikely to leave a negative impression in the mind of the buyer after the tour is over, and you can take the area rug with you after you sell the home. But you should be honest about the condition of the carpeting.

There is an argument for buying new carpeting, especially in trade-up homes. New carpet can dramatically change the feeling of a room by making it look more crisp and by introducing a very effective "new" smell. Given the weight the living room carries in the marketing of your home, a new carpet could be a wise investment.

Shop around for large remnants, which are often high in quality but much lower in price than wall-to-wall. The carpet, pad, and installation will cost a minimum of $15 per square yard. If you buy from a retail carpet store, you can just about double this. Incidentally, it pays to spend extra for a thick pad, since this will make a less expensive carpet feel more luxurious.

Wood Floors

Hardwood floors and parquet are very popular and can look handsome if properly maintained. But they also show wear quite readily, so give them a critical appraisal.

If your floor needs to shine, Preen is a very effective product that's widely available. For floors that need more attention and don't have a wax buildup, a fresh coat of polyurethane will make them look newer and offer a "new" smell. A thick layer of wax, however, will prevent the polyurethane from bonding.

Refinishing might be necessary if the floor has lost its sheen and hasn't been refinished for ten years or so. Refinishing by yourself, using either an electric sander or chemical floor stripper, can be messy at best and disastrous at worst. Neither method is recommended for the amateur. A floor-restoring kit by Gillespie produces quality results without sanding. It is not designed for floors with serious surface damage but for those that have either dulled or become worn in certain areas. The kit costs $15 and can restore up to 500 feet of floor area.

If all else fails, call in a professional, who will charge about 50 cents per square foot. Although it can be expensive, a newly refinished hardwood floor can make all the difference in the first impression of a room.

THE SHOWPIECES OF THE LIVING ROOM

The features and accessories of your living room can make the kind of life-style statements your buyer is looking for, help establish your living room's focal point, and differentiate it from the competition's.

Lighting

The living room provides great opportunities to use light to its best advantage. Light can focus on special features or accessories in the room, or it can add to the overall ambience.

Natural light is best, and you should do all you can to maximize it. Mirrors and light colors are the most efficient ways to do this. But if your house or condo is on the dark side or is being shown at night, artificial lighting will have to take over.

General Lighting

The most common sources of artificial light for general illumination are either ceiling-mounted fixtures or floor lamps. Be sure ceiling fixtures are clean and their bulbs are in working order. If the fixture is unattractive because of age or condition, remove it and cap the receptacle with a metal cover that can be purchased in a lighting store.

Replace the lost light with floor lamps. Make sure that the lamps are clean, the shades in good order, and the bulbs are working.

Spot Lighting

Here you can have some fun with light. Track lights, for example, are an ideal way to create an art-gallery effect with a grouping of pictures you might have along a wall. The fireplace is another feature which lends itself to spot lighting, or a piano if you have one, or a particularly attractive piece of furniture, or simply an exposed brick wall.

If you've got something special in your living room, let lighting help it sell the rest of the area.

Accent Lighting

These are the mood lights that create drama and excitement in your living room. Let's start with effective and inexpensive ways of generating the right mood.

For about $20, you can purchase floor can lights or floor spotlights that simply plug into the wall. By placing one or more of these behind a large floor plant, in back of a sofa, or simply in an open corner, you can create a truly dramatic effect.

A more common approach to accent lighting is to use small table lamps. If you want to establish a feeling of separate groupings in the living room — like a conversation area, a writing or reading area, separate light sources will provide a sense of definition.

If you want to compensate for dark window enclosures, consider placing a light stick behind a valance above the window.

But remember, don't go to the expense without having a specific objective. If you want to highlight a special object, compensate for a dark room, or draw attention away from a curtain, light can be useful.

The Fireplace

The fireplace ranks near the top of consumer preferences in the living room. The National Association of Home Builders reports that nearly 90 percent of new home buyers consider fireplaces extremely important.

The reasons behind this are varied. A fireplace can be an attractive focal point in a room. It is also thought of as an energy saver even though many actually are not. The fireplace has symbolic appeal and can suggest warmth, family, and togetherness. It can be the heart of the home, and the more attractive you make it, the better for your home sale.

So conditioned are we to having fireplaces in our homes that developers report nearly 70 percent of the upscale new homes built — even in Florida — have fireplaces. Obviously, the appeal goes beyond function. A roaring fire on an 80-degree winter day doesn't make much sense, but the presence of the fireplace, even if it is unused, is aesthetically pleasing.

Accessorizing the Cold Fireplace

To improve upon what you have, start with the accessories. Do you have an attractive fireplace screen to draw attention to the fireplace itself?

How about a brass-framed glass enclosure or a set of attractive fireplace tools? Is there a neat pile of wood near the fireplace to create visions of a roaring fire on a cool fall night? All of these items help draw attention to this focal point. And if you don't have any, borrow them from friends or neighbors. When it comes to something as influential as the fireplace, my rule is "If you've got it, flaunt it!"

Frame It with a Mantel

If your fireplace is simply uninspiring, try covering the brick area around the hearth opening with an attractive ceramic tile. There are some very appealing tiles—like Delft-style, Mexican, or marble—that make an impressive statement for little cost.

If you have a fireplace without any mantel, consider buying one. Mantels can be found at home salvage stores. If none of these stores is near you, pick up a copy of *The Old Home Journal* or *Colonial Homes*, and check their ads and product listings.

The cost of an old mantel will vary widely depending on the size, material, and condition. Prices start at about $150 for one that needs some work, but refinishing it can be fun.

If the layout of your living room makes the fireplace the star attraction and you have little else to differentiate your home from the competition's, make it the focal point of your living room and perhaps your entire house.

Should You Use the Fireplace during a Tour?

A fireplace can be a hot selling tool, especially if a prospect walks into your home on a crisp winter day and the fireplace is crackling. There are few more appealing marketing devices.

It will not only show the buyer that the fireplace works, but it will also create an unbeatable ambience. Use caution, however, if you have a temperamental fireplace. Because of design or wind conditions, some fireplaces can be unpredictable, and you definitely want to avoid a tour of your home when it's filled with smoke.

If you can count on your fireplace, fine, but if you have any doubts about it, don't take the gamble.

Always leave logs in and around the fireplace, though, to help the buyer visualize how attractive it looks when there is a fire in it. Naturally, if the fireplace does not work, you should tell the buyer and provide an accurate answer about what can be done to make it usable.

Furniture

Too much furniture or clutter in a living room can make it appear smaller than it is. Consider relocating unnecessary chairs, tables, or occasional pieces, if removing them will increase the openness of the room.

Once you've done this, make sure every piece is waxed or dusted, using either Endust or a lemon oil product. This will suggest a high level of care and create a positive smell.

Minimize the impact of strong ethnic statements like crucifixes, menorahs, or religious art located on or around furniture by moving them to less obvious places. If your home happens to contain collectibles from different cultures, like Mexican artifacts, Oriental vases, or African wood carvings, this is fine since it is more a statement of a high life-style than a specific ethnic affiliation. Also be sensitive about articles that reveal strong social or political beliefs.

There are certain life-style clues that you will want to leave in open view. Glossy magazines placed on coffee tables, such as *Architectural Digest* or *Town & Country*, suggest the type of life-style that most buyers, particularly trade-ups, want to lead.

Plants and Flowers

Plants and flowers in the living room add color and life. If you have a healthy-looking floor plant, it will look attractive and suggest that there is enough natural light in the room to keep it thriving. If you have a corner that is in need of furniture, a large floor plant will fill the space nicely.

If you want to create a room-heightening effect, a tall plant can help. A tall palm or ficus plant will draw the eye toward the ceiling and make other objects in the room seem lower by comparison.

Fresh-cut flowers have a positive effect on just about all of us. They add color and positive smells and, especially in the dead of winter, can really brighten up a room. Hyacinths and freesia mixed with a bunch of flowers are good choices because they have scents pervasive enough for large areas.

When selecting flowers or flowering plants, always make sure their colors are brighter than the walls surrounding them. Flowers should add a spark to a room, and the brighter that spark, the better.

Doors

If you have a doorway leading into your living room, an effective way to set an elegant tone is to install glass french doors. This will help set off the room and establish a feeling of formality and value.

The cost of installing double doors is perhaps less than you think. If you have a conventional 30-inch opening, you can buy two 15-inch glass "sidelights," which are the glass frames often used at either side of a front entry door. The sidelight will work perfectly as a double door and give you the opportunity to install attractive brass or porcelain knobs to enhance further its perceived value.

The cost of the doors will be about $75 each, and the hardware should run about $10 to $15. The doors can be purchased through any large lumber supplier.

The expense of french doors makes them a luxury, not a necessity. They are desirable only if they add impact. A feature like this can have far more impact in a small condo or co-op than in a sprawling house, where it might get lost. A lot depends upon the configuration of the entry area to your living room, because double doors can slow the flow of traffic.

For any existing doors you have, consider replacing conventional knobs with either brass, porcelain, or cut glass. They add an expensive-looking cosmetic touch which will increase the perceived value of the entire door. I recommend this improvement in all cases.

Radiators

Steam radiators are a sure sign of an older heating system. Though they can be an eyesore in a room, they can actually be made to look attractive, if you're willing to spend a minimum of time and money.

Painting is the easiest step. Rather than opting for silver or another metallic color, consider painting the radiators the color of the wall, so they blend in as much as possible. In a child's room, a bright color like red or yellow might be fun. Use an oil-based or rust-inhibiting paint like Rustoleum, and make sure the radiator is off when you are painting.

Buying a radiator enclosure can be very effective, especially if you are trying to make an older home seem more contemporary. These range in price from $20 to $150 per unit, depending upon how large your radiator is. Look under "Radiator Covers and Enclosures" in the Yellow Pages for a local supplier.

Entertainment Features

Because entertaining plays such an important role in a living room, especially for the trade-up buyer, features that can make your living room seem better suited for entertainment will excite buyers. These can range from small luxury touches like a bottle of fine wine or a bowl of Godiva chocolates to more substantial additions.

Bars

A bar can suggest the entertainment possibilities of your living room. This can be accomplished in several ways without major expense, but should be incorporated only in homes that appeal to upscale buyers.

If you have a built-in bookcase with base cabinets or a base cabinet running along one wall, find an area on the top of the cabinet that you can clear, then install a dry sink. Simply cut a hole in the surface and drop in the sink. It should just sit in the opening so you can easily remove it to empty melted ice. You can purchase a small stainless sink for less than $30.

Hang a glass rack, a mixing-tool holder, and various accessories nearby to help define this as the bar area.

Stereo

A stereo should not be a focal point of the room, but it should be treated like an important piece of furniture

The components should be dust-free and the speakers waxed or wiped down. Hide the wires and organize the records carefully. Playing music during your house tour will inevitably draw attention to the sound system, so make sure it looks as good as it sounds.

The Piano

If you have a piano, it too should be treated like a piece of furniture. Not only does it suggest entertainment and family gatherings, it can also be a focal point of the room. If you're fortunate enough to have a grand or baby grand, prop up the top to make it look more dramatic.

CONCLUSION

Your living room is as much a statement as it is a place to live, and the more impressive it is, the better it will sell. The larger, more elegant, and better cared for it appears, the more influential it will be in shaping a prospective buyer's decision.

As indicated, the living room and the kitchen are regarded as the two most important rooms in the home. If you can make both these rooms winners, your chances of getting a premium price for your home will be greatly improved. The upcoming chapter on kitchens will discuss ways to achieve this goal.

CHAPTER HIGHLIGHTS

1. The living room and the kitchen are the most important rooms when it comes to selling a home.

2. The living room is often a vehicle for impressing others and should appear as stately as possible.

3. The suitability of the living room for entertaining is important, especially to trade-up buyers.

4. Take advantage of finishing touches like molding, brass switch covers, and cut-glass doorknobs to suggest the quality of your living room.

5. Highlight antiques, paintings, or favorite furniture pieces through spot lighting.

6. The fireplace can be the most appealing feature of your living room, so make sure it is a focal point.

7. The size of the living room and its appeal to buyers are directly related. Use proper color, lighting, and decorating strategies to maximize the perception of size.

8. Play down strong personal design, ethnic or religious statements.

9

Kitchens
That Cook

Your kitchen is one of the most influential rooms in determining the sale of your home. According to Robert Dyson, president of Red Carpet Real Estate, a national real estate brokerage company, "If ever there were a single deal maker or breaker about the interior of a home, the kitchen is it."

While people may be forgiving about specific weaknesses in other rooms, there is little tolerance for a worn or outdated kitchen. So make every effort to assure that your kitchen is a winner.

We'll show you how by applying the five steps in our system. It would be easy to recommend costly ways to upgrade your kitchen, but the ideas in this chapter will be limited to those that require low investment and yield a high return.

THE FIVE-STEP SYSTEM
Step 1. Consider the Competition

If two homes are basically alike except for the kitchen, the one with the superior kitchen is likely to come out on top. Your objective is to make sure your home is the winner.

To help gauge the level of improvements your kitchen may need, take a look at your competition's. Check to see what features they are offering — microwave ovens or the latest in kitchen cabinets — that you are not.

Step 2. Consider the Buyer

Different segments of the market have distinct preferences and needs as far as kitchens are concerned. By targeting your improvements, you will have a better chance of maximizing the appeal of this strategically important room.

Professor Emeritus Rose Steidl of Cornell University is one of many who argue that, despite "liberation," the kitchen still carries more weight with women. Others, including Toni Reuter of Century 21, suggest that men's and women's interest in the kitchen is nearly equal.

Of the many experts interviewed on this subject, it seems that the West Coast is more progressive than the rest of the country but that any generalization is dangerous. Play it safe when showing your home and assume that males and females share the same view about the importance of the kitchen.

First-Time Buyers

Because the kitchen is such a costly area of the home, first-time buyers want the assurance that they will not need additional cash to make it acceptable. Make sure the major appliances look their best even if they are not new. And demonstrate the efficiency of the kitchen if it's small.

Trade-up Buyers

The kitchen can be a showpiece for trade-up buyers, and the more impressive it seems, the better it will sell. This market segment is looking for upscale life-style statements, the most up-to-date appliances, and suitability for entertaining.

Timesaving features are also important since this group is so often on the run. According to Brooke Warrick of the California-based think tank SRI, "Young professionals are often speed eaters during the week and big entertainers on weekends. They appreciate a kitchen that can fill both needs."

Empty Nesters/Trade-down Buyers

The size of the kitchen is often a major concern because trade-down buyers may have grown accustomed to a larger room in the previous home. Make the kitchen seem as spacious and efficient as possible.

Older empty nesters also have a very relaxed attitude toward the kitchen because they may have more time to use it. For this reason, areas for sitting down and watching television or reading the paper are valued. Good lighting and safety features can also be of special importance to this group.

Step 3. Evaluate Your Product

After you have sized up your competition and decided on the type of person most likely to buy your home, take a hard look at the results of your focus group's evaluation. If all goes well, the bulk of your work will be limited to cosmetic improvements.

But if the feedback you receive suggests you have major work to do, consider making a more substantial investment. An inadequate kitchen can slow down a sale as well as reducing the sale price.

Of course, if you don't want to spend the money on major improvements, you could always lower the sale price, but you will still be at a disadvantage when compared to a slightly more expensive home with a strong kitchen. There are three reasons for this.

First, virtually all home buyers have difficulty imagining how exciting something might look after it has been upgraded. Even though they know that the price of the property has been discounted, they will still walk away with an image of an inferior kitchen.

Second, a smart buyer also knows what an inconvenience renovating a kitchen can be. He or she is likely to be unhappy about the idea of having to supervise a renovation and may be put off enough to rule out the home entirely.

Last, it is easier for a buyer to finance a kitchen through a first mortgage on the property than it is to get a separate loan or reach into a savings account. This is exactly what will happen if a person buys the property unimproved and decides to fix it up later.

There's one more piece of bad news.

Don't count on getting all your investment back. Buyers expect a reasonable kitchen to come with the home, and the fact that you had to spend a lot of money to bring it up to par is irrelevant to them. This is especially true if your competition has strong kitchens.

But, by upgrading one of the most important rooms in the house, you will enhance your property's marketability and sell it more quickly.

Step 4. Eliminate Territorial Anxiety

The kitchen can be a very personal room. Because it is part and parcel of family life, it can be difficult for the buyer to imagine someone else's kitchen as theirs.

Make every effort to remove anything that might contribute to territorial anxiety. Smells are among the more common offenders and should be eliminated. Strong color statements are another potential problem. Above all, the kitchen and its appliances should be absolutely spotless.

Step 5. Maximize Packaging Power

The general rule to follow in preparing your kitchen is "The newer, the better." Newness in the kitchen suggests low maintenance, efficiency, convenience, cleanliness, status, and value. Unlike an old fireplace mantel in the living room or original molding in the entryway, an antiquated kitchen has little appeal.

Through various cosmetic improvements, you can increase the perception of newness in your kitchen and suggest the kind of life-style statement trade-up buyers are looking for.

We will also show you how to make the room memorable by establishing a key focal point, as well as ways to differentiate your product by including one or more special features.

THE INGREDIENTS OF YOUR KITCHEN

There are many ways to make your kitchen a winner with low-cost, strategic improvements to high-impact areas. We will focus on what consumer research has shown to be the most important elements and discuss them in order of priority.

Major Appliances

One of the first things a prospect notices about your kitchen is the make, model, and appearance of your major appliances. These include the stove or range, refrigerator, dishwasher, and trash compactor.

Since all or several of these items put together can be the most expensive components of a kitchen, the buyer is obviously interested in how new they are. Additionally, new major appliances can make impressive statements about kitchens. These may be particularly meaningful to trade-up buyers.

Some people may feel that all appliances are essential. Life without a trash compactor, for example, might seem intolerable. But there is a clear order of priorities in even the most pampered buyer's mind.

The stove and refrigerator are at the top of the list. If either of these is in immediate need of replacement, it would probably pay to do so because the buyer is likely to deduct them from your asking price anyway.

The presence of a dishwasher is almost taken for granted today, although many homes are still sold without them. If you have an old dishwasher or do not have one at all, you could probably get away without one. We do not advise purchasing one just to sell your home, unless you are selling to a trade-up buyer and in the upper price ranges of your market.

Trash compactors are appliances we never thought we needed until they came out. There are more buyers than not who still feel this is the case. So unless you are selling an expensive home that is expected to offer every major convenience, our advice here is to save your money.

Generally speaking, as long as your major appliances are in good working order and appear to be well maintained, it will not pay to purchase new ones. But there are certain inexpensive cosmetic measures you can take to update their appearance, thereby increasing their perceived value.

Updating with Today's Colors

Like automobile manufacturers, the makers of major appliances periodically change model colors. Since they rarely make major changes in the actual design of the appliance, color is the big tip-off to the age of a product.

If a buyer walks into a home and sees the latest colors, he or she will presume the appliances are new. Conversely, when a buyer walks into a home and sees appliances with discontinued colors like avocado or harvest gold, it suggests the items are dated. But the same set of appliances in white, a color offered all the time, gives no hint of age.

If you have appliances with dated colors, you can have them repainted by specialists. To find a supplier, look under "Porcelain" or "Appliance Refinishing" in the Yellow Pages. The cost runs about $100 for a stove, $75 for a refrigerator, and $50 for a dishwasher. Some specialists will repaint appliances in your home; others charge $30 or more to transport the appliances to and from their workshop.

You can also paint appliances yourself with epoxy spray paint. A company called Illinois Bronze Paint Company manufactures spray paints designed to match those of both new and old appliances. The finish provides a durable, porcelain-like surface, which can duplicate the look of a professional job, if applied carefully.

White is the very safest color, but you can be a little more adventurous and pick some of the newest shades. The latest ones being offered by General Electric, for example, are "Sand" and "Platinum," while Frigidaire is showing similar colors called "Toast" and "Silver."

If the chrome handles or trim on your appliances are worn or damaged, you can purchase a product called Nybco chrome aluminum spray enamel, which produces a shiny, bright, chromelike finish.

To eliminate chips or scratch marks, either write to the manufacturer or contact the dealer you bought the appliance from and order some touch-up paint.

Keep Them Clean and Looking New

There is no excuse for a dirty stove or a pungent refrigerator. They not only cause territorial anxiety, they also suggest a lack of care, which the buyer may think applies to your home in general.

Clean the enamel with rubbing alcohol and bring back the original shine with car wax. Use a chrome polish like Brasso to make the chrome handles and trim sparkle like new.

If your white appliances have yellowed, mix ½ cup of bleach and ¼ cup of baking soda with 4 cups of warm water, then apply with a sponge. Let the mixture sit on the surface for ten minutes before rinsing it off.

Clean out the refrigerator if it smells stale. Remove any food or residue that is creating the odor. An open box of baking soda will absorb any new smells, as will a small bowl of planting charcoal. A cup of vinegar will also work to neutralize odors.

Cabinets

Like major appliances, kitchen cabinets can immediately reveal the age of your kitchen. And since they are such a dominant feature of a kitchen, they can affect the buyer's perception of the whole room.

Consumer research reveals that the three most important points to remember when appraising your kitchen cabinets are how new they look, how well they're made, and how much storage capacity they provide.

By looking at the competition's, you should have a good idea of how well your cabinets compare.

Updating Old Cabinets

There are different measures you can take to revive old cabinets. Let's start with minor packaging improvements and move up to more substantial remedies.

If your cabinet doors and drawers are basically in good shape but could benefit from a cosmetic upgrade, new hardware can be remarkably effective in repackaging them.

I have used this technique on doors that looked so uninspiring that I was going to replace them entirely. By making this small upgrade after simply repainting, I was able to sell the property without changing the cabinets and saved myself over $1,000.

The key is to use the best hardware you can buy, within reason, of course. Since this is all you are going to do, let the knobs and handles say as much as possible about the quality of the cabinets. Also, make sure the new knobs are large enough to cover up the marks left after removing the old ones.

Solid brass knobs may run from $2 to $4 each. Plated brass or chrome knobs will run about $2 each, and baked enamel knobs will cost about the same. To get an idea of what to choose, go to a home supply store or kitchen cabinet supplier and look at the type of fixtures being offered on top-of-the-line doors and drawers.

If your cabinets need more than just knobs and handles to bring them back to life, go one step farther by repainting or refinishing the doors and drawer fronts.

For painted cabinets, take off the doors and give them a light sanding with either fine-grade sandpaper or 00 grade steel wool. Then either spray them the desired color or use a polyurethane foam brush to avoid bristle marks. Remember, keep the colors neutral — use whites, beiges, or pale yellows — and stay away from bright reds, deep blues, and sharp greens.

To avoid painting the hardware, either cover it with masking tape or remove it. If you don't want to do either, cover the handles with petroleum jelly so that any paint that touches them will simply bead up.

If you want a more professional look, take the doors to a refinisher, who will do the job for about $15 per door.

For stained and urethaned doors, sand them down entirely, since new stain will not penetrate the old sealer. This can be a major job and might be best done by a pro, especially if the cabinets have a thin veneer which you could damage. The cost will be about $10 to $15 per door.

If you have old or worn kitchen cabinets that have obnoxious scratch marks, consider a product called Scratch Fix, made by K. J. Miller Corp. The product comes in a variety of wood tones and can be an inexpensive cover-up for damaged or tired cabinets.

Keeping Up with the Trends

As long as you are upgrading your doors, you should be aware of the latest trends in kitchen cabinetry so you will make the right changes.

The dark wood surfaces that were so popular in the seventies are now out of style. They have been replaced by light and medium wood tones like oak and maple.

As far as colors are concerned, the hottest trend in contemporary houses or older houses with modern kitchens is the "European" style of cabinets. These often feature a white or almond-color Formica-like surface with oak handles or trim. Once at the leading edge of kitchen fashion, these cabinets are experiencing much wider appeal and are a sure sign of a contemporary kitchen.

If you are repainting your doors, you can duplicate this contemporary "European" effect by painting them white and attaching natural oak knobs or bentwood handles. If you want to take this one step farther, you can have a plastic laminate like Formica applied to your flat-surfaced wooden doors. Then add the oak hardware. This will cost about $20 per door if done by a professional and will dramatically improve their appearance.

Another very popular style is the "country kitchen" look that includes the oak doors and drawers with porcelain knobs. The advantage of this style is that it is suitable for homes that are either modern or traditional in design.

Putting on a New Front

Depending on how much work your doors need, you may want to replace the doors entirely.

Look under "Kitchen Cabinets" in the Yellow Pages, and you will probably find several companies that specialize in them. If you can't find one, Sears offers this service and will come to your home to give you an estimate.

To replace 20 doors, expect to spend about $450, which is one third the cost of new cabinets.

Going All the Way

If the time, effort, and expense of a halfway measure do not seem worthwhile to you, consider buying new cabinets. Especially if you have older appliances or other weaknesses in the kitchen, there is no single improvement that I have found more effective than brand new cabinets.

In the case of a small "efficiency" kitchen, the cost may not be very significant, but it can change the entire perception of the room.

You can find reasonably priced closeouts if you do some shopping. Most cabinet stores or large home-supply companies have them. If you have to purchase cabinets at retail, the markup is usually very high, so don't be afraid to drive a hard bargain.

The More the Better

Consumer surveys repeatedly show that a large amount of kitchen cabinet and storage space is extremely important to buyers. If you are putting in new cabinets and have the opportunity to add more than you removed, it will make the kitchen more appealing to a larger number of buyers.

Beyond simply adding space, you can make your cabinets more efficient by throwing out what you don't need on your shelves.

Adding a few Rubbermaid lazy susans at about $5 each will also increase the perception of efficiency, as will plastic-laminated wire racks and bins that are attached to the inside of doors and broom closets. These range from $5 to $20 each, depending on their size, and can be found at hardware stores and the housewares section of department stores.

An inexpensive way to increase storage space in an especially small kitchen is to suspend a flat door about two feet from the ceiling. Finish the door to match the cabinets and hang it with hooks securely anchored to the ceiling. You will then have a surface to place items on or hang them from.

Counter Space

The counter space in your kitchen probably matches the condition and style of your cabinets, since both were probably installed at the same time. And as in the case of cabinets, consumers rank quantity of space and newness as their top priorities.

Since counters constitute a major surface area in your kitchen, don't let them detract from the overall look of the room. Remember it's also important that the color doesn't tip off the consumer to the age of your kitchen.

Fixing Flaws

If your counters are basically in good condition but have one or more cracks or burn marks in a particular area, try fastening a butcher-block cutting board over the flaws. This will hide them from view and add a valued built-in feature. A half-inch-thick, 2-foot square board will cost about $6. It can be secured from beneath by drilling four holes in the countertop and four starter holes in the bottom of the board, then securing it with short wood screws.

If you already have a built-in butcher block in your counter and it looks worn, you can easily bring it back to life. Scrape the surface with a wood scraper in the direction of the grain. Then sand the board with medium-grade sandpaper followed by fine-grade paper and 00 grade steel wool. Finish the surface with mineral oil, and it should look like new. If the flaw is minor, you can install a ceramic tile or series of tiles over the area and use them as a trivet for resting hot pots or frying pans.

If you are a do-it-yourselfer, you can apply ceramic tile right over an existing countertop and create the "country kitchen" look. The cost will vary significantly, depending upon the type of tile you select and how large your space is, but as a rule of thumb, figure on at least $4 per square foot.

If your counters are in very bad shape, consider purchasing new ones from a home-improvement store; they will run about $8 per linear foot. These can be ordered custom cut to include a hole for your sink or range top, but the installation may require a professional. A compromise measure between expensive retiling of an existing counter or total replacement of a countertop is to apply ceramic tiles against the wall behind the counter. This will also create a country-kitchen look and add a focal point which may draw attention away from an otherwise lackluster counter area.

A Pass-Through

If your cooking and eating areas are entirely separate and could benefit from appearing larger, consider cutting an opening in the wall and creating your own pass-through. Then put a small counter over the base of the opening to finish it off.

I have done this and found it makes both rooms feel more spacious. To give the opening an even more finished look, and to block the view into the kitchen when it is not presentable, consider installing wooden louvered shutters on either side.

A feature seen in more expensive kitchens is the freestanding work island. These islands often contain grill-top ranges, but they can also be used just to add another work surface and extra storage space.

An island provides an attractive focal point to a kitchen and differentiates it from the competition. The cost of a prefabricated island will run a minimum of $200.

An Eat-in Counter

A feature that is growing in popularity, particularly among single buyers and dual-career couples who often eat on the run, is the eat-in counter.

You can make one yourself by purchasing a long, 2-foot-wide laminated countertop and affixing it to an empty wall. Buying wooden stools to slide beneath the counter will add the finishing touch. This improve-

---

Do-It-Yourself Improvements
under $100

1. Install new cabinet knobs and drawer hardware ($40).

2. Buy colorful tablecloths and matching towels ($20).

3. Install a new central light fixture ($70).

4. Create a pass-through to an adjacent room ($100).

5. Tile the backsplash wall ($80).

6. Install a built-in butcher block in a countertop ($20).

7. Supplement the general lighting with fluorescent light sticks ($12 each).

8. Add laminated wire shelves ($40).

9. Mount a wine rack beneath an overhead cabinet ($30).

10. Repaint a major appliance ($100).

---

ment can convert wasted space into an asset or, in the case of a very small condo or co-op kitchen, add to its perceived value and utility.

Mistakes to Avoid

No matter what you do with counters, always remember that horizontal surfaces below eye level merge in a buyer's eye. This means that countertops should work in with the color or design of the floor, so that it appears that the kitchen was designed carefully.

Don't try to match them but make sure they don't clash. A white countertop will go with just about anything and is the least likely to create territorial anxiety. If you must have color, be safe and bring home a small sample to see how well it works with the room.

Floors

The floor is a dominant visual influence in the kitchen because it can take up nearly a quarter of the surface area. From a packaging standpoint, it provides a good opportunity to enhance the room's perceived value. Flooring can be relatively inexpensive yet suggest far more than its cost.

For this reason, I have found installing a new floor to be a particularly good investment in the kitchen, if the existing floor needs help.

In one kitchen I owned, the floor was so badly worn that only after it was replaced could the other improvements to the room be appreciated. Don't let an expenditure of $400 to $800 jeopardize the buyer's perception of the most important selling room of your home.

Vinyl Floors

Vinyl is by far the most popular surface because of its wide range of colors and prices and the ease with which it can be installed and cleaned. If you put in a new vinyl floor, buy the no-wax variety because this is what most consumers prefer.

Avoid simulated surfaces — like slate, flagstone, wood, or Mexican tile — because they invariably look like poor excuses for the real thing. Also, to avoid causing territorial anxiety, do not select strong colors and patterns.

The kitchen should be bright and upbeat, so try to keep the colors light and neutral.

Special Floors

There are ways to make your kitchen distinctive by installing unconventional flooring materials. According to industry experts, there is a trend in higher-priced homes toward natural materials like hardwood, quarry tile, ceramics, and stone.

These have much more appeal to the urban buyer or trade-up purchaser. And although these materials may sound expensive, some are not much pricier than high-quality sheet vinyl.

Quarry tile is about $2 per square foot, hardwood flooring is about $4 per square foot, and ceramics can go as high as $5 per square foot.

Our recommendation, if you are appealing to a more sophisticated market, is to try quarry tile. It is reasonably priced and gives a very substantial look. After it is installed, apply a thin coat of Val-Oil with a polyurethane brush to give it an attractive shine and a new smell. Val-Oil also makes the floor easier to clean. Keep a few extra tiles in case some become cracked or chipped.

If you are upgrading a very small kitchen, a high-priced floor can maximize packaging appeal at a reasonable cost.

Lighting Up the Kitchen

Proper lighting can greatly enhance the overall packaging appeal of your kitchen. It can make an important emotional impact by creating a room that seems happier, cleaner, larger, and newer. Additionally, the fixtures themselves can affect the perception of the room by introducing a relatively low-cost, high-perceived-value item.

The goal of lighting up the kitchen is threefold: to provide even and sufficient general illumination, useful task lighting, and attractive accent lighting. Each of these requires different fixtures.

General Illumination

For general illumination, a large, shallow diffusing fixture mounted on the ceiling is the most efficient and least expensive approach. These have translucent covers and hold fluorescent bulbs. Make sure you use the soft white fluorescents so you don't cast a green shade over the kitchen.

Fixtures like this can cost anywhere from $30 to $150 depending on how large and how elaborate they are. Whatever they cost, they are worth it if they replace a light that makes your kitchen look unattractive.

Some homes still have the old circular fluorescent fixtures, which are not only harsh on your eyes but immediately suggest that the kitchen is antiquated. Retaining this sort of fixture when marketing your home will work against you.

Task Lighting

There are many options available for task lighting. These lights can really differentiate the appearance of your kitchen by giving it a custom look.

Placing fluorescent "light sticks" that illuminate countertops beneath overhead kitchen cabinets can be both attractive and functional. They will highlight the work space and give the cabinets more dimension by creating a "floating" effect.

These lights can cost as little as $10 each for a 25-inch fixture, which can be plugged into a regular outlet.

Task lighting over work areas like the sink and range are a very useful aid to the utility of the kitchen.

Track lights are another way to provide effective task lighting and at the same time add a feature that suggests the newness and sophistication of your kitchen. A three-foot track with three heads will cost between $50 and $80 and at least another $60 to install.

This is not a small expense, but if track lighting can be used to highlight a specific focal point of your kitchen and give it that high-tech look that many urban professionals and trade-up buyers seek, it may be worthwhile. If you do install one, you should add a dimmer to complete the effect.

Hanging lights are most often used over eating areas. If you already have one, make sure the glass is clean and the bulbs are working. There should be no need to add a hanging fixture if you do not have one or to replace the one you already have. The only caveat is that if you have a highly stylized light — an elaborate Mediterranean lamp or something very specific to one's taste — it might be a good idea to take it down and cap the receptacle in the ceiling. This sort of decision can be made after reviewing the feedback from your focus groups.

Accent Lighting

The same light sticks used for task lighting can be placed above kitchen cabinets if there is at least an 18-inch clearance between them and the ceiling. This will create a dramatic wall-washing effect and will also assist in general illumination.

Accent lighting will help differentiate your kitchen but may be worth installing only if you have a convenient wall outlet. Otherwise, you will have to hire an electrician to provide additional wiring.

Natural Light

The more natural light you have in a kitchen the better. Unfortunately, increasing natural light can be very expensive.

If you feel the situation warrants it, you can install a skylight. This feature rates very highly with home buyers but may cost anywhere from $500 to $2,000 to install. Under most circumstances, it would be hard to expect a return from this investment unless the structure of your roof somehow enabled you to do this for much less.

A "punchout" greenhouse window behind a sink can add an unforgettable focal point to a kitchen that few homeowners can boast of. Filled with small plants yet affording a view outside, this can be a real seller. Prices start at about $300. It is an improvement that you should install right away so that you can enjoy it before you sell your home.

Mirrors are a much less costly way to maximize the perception of natural light in a room. Hanging one on a wall across from a window will act as another window and considerably brighten the room.

If you have a wooden outside door with only one or two panes of glass, consider replacing it with one that has more glass. A colonial-style door with small panes or a contemporary glass door will let in more light. The cost of this, however, will be about $200, exclusive of installation.

Small Appliances

Small appliances can make a big difference in imparting the value, convenience, and status of your kitchen. It is very important to consider your market and competition when determining what you should be offering with your home.

The Microwave

Microwave ovens are fast becoming a staple in the American kitchen. A survey conducted by *Professional Builder* magazine reports that over half of all new home buyers expect a microwave to be included with a kitchen, and the U.S. Census reports that nearly 20 percent of all households have one.

Obviously, some people consider the microwave not as a luxury but a necessity. Those who are most likely to expect a microwave are the trade-up buyers, urban condominium and co-op buyers, and retirees.

If the competition includes microwaves and your kitchen is weak in other areas, purchasing one may be an effective move. If you do buy one to increase the appeal of your kitchen, buy the kind that can be attached beneath an overhead cabinet. Litton has one, for example, that costs about $200. This will give it a built-in look, yet it can be removed if the buyer doesn't have his or her heart set on it.

The price of microwaves has come down so much that their perceived value to the consumer may actually exceed their cost. But don't offer the microwave as part of the sale price until the buyer asks for it. If and when that happens, don't say it's included but that it can be negotiated as part of the deal.

The Garbage Disposal Unit

Professional Builder magazine reports that more than 68 percent of new home buyers expect this feature to be included with their next home. It is extremely useful, and to a buyer accustomed to one, moving to a house without a garbage disposal unit is a step backward.

If your home is either a moderately priced starter, or your study of the competition shows that garbage disposal units are not very common, you can probably get away without one. But if you're promoting a premium-priced trade-up home, be prepared to spend around $150 to put one in.

Ceiling Fans

Depending on the height of your kitchen ceiling and how essential the need for ventilation is, a ceiling fan can be an effective way to differentiate your product and create an interesting focal point.

If your kitchen ceiling is less than 9 feet high, there will not be enough safe clearance for a fan nor will it be aesthetically pleasing. But if it is sufficiently high and your kitchen is not air-conditioned and tends to get hot, a ceiling fan can add an attractive feature.

The cost of a fan and installation will be about $200, so it is most appropriate for higher-priced homes targeted toward the trade-up buyer. But only include one to make an average kitchen more exciting. Ceiling fans are less effective in an already terrific kitchen.

And don't forget to point out the energy-saving features of a ceiling fan, because they can be significant.

Fire Extinguishers

A small fire extinguisher can be purchased for about $15 and make an effective statement to families with small children, to empty nesters, and to retirees, all of whom are particularly sensitive to safety.

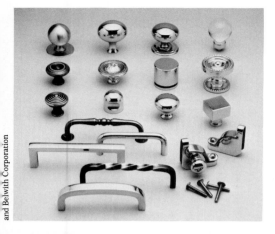

Replacing cabinet knobs and hardware can upgrade the look of the entire cabinet at a minimal cost.

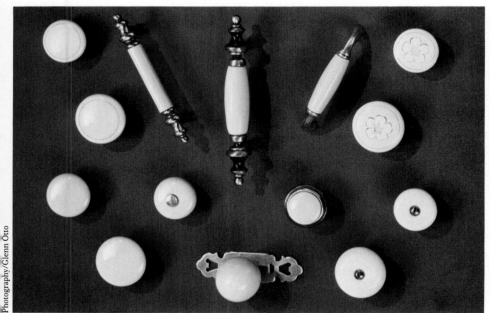

Upgrading door-knobs and handles can change the entire perception of a door. By spending little money, you can make an impression with quality hardware.

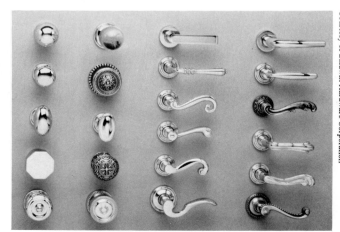

Without replacing the old cabinets this kitchen was made to look brand new. By installing new counters, cabinet doors, and drawer fronts but leaving the original

framework, several thousand dollars were saved over the cost of a total renovation.

The difference between a furnished and unfurnished home can be dramatic. Once the desk, pictures, and accessories were removed from this room, much of the appeal was lost. Remember, a furnished home will almost always sell for more than an empty one.

An organized closet will seem more spacious and will make a positive statement about how you care for your home. These modular plastic laminated shelving units are ideal for maximizing efficiency. And when you sell your home, you can take the shelves with you.

The first impression created by this entry will set a positive tone for the rest of the house tour. The brass knocker, hardware, and kickplate accents on this handsome raised panel door suggest quality and attention to detail in this home. The plants and oriental rug reinforce the life-style image that up-scale buyers will be looking for.

Moldings can turn an ordinary surface into something extraordinary without spending a great deal of money. From appliqués to a stairway to elaborate wall brackets, you can give your home a look of substance that will set it apart from the competition.

All it takes to make a badly worn tub look new is to have it professionally resurfaced. At a cost of about $250 this can save hundreds of dollars over the cost of ripping out an old tub and installing a new one.

Courtesy of Ortho Books

Creating a brick patio can add perceived value to your home without your spending a great deal of money. Lawn furniture demonstrates the usefulness of this area and helps the buyer visualize the enjoyment it will give.
A deck can add a new dimension of living space to a home at a fraction of the cost of an actual addition. You need not make it this elaborate to create a strong selling point for your home.

Photo by Michael Landis

Two identical entryways create two entirely different impressions. With $50 worth of molding and some attractive furnishings, one provides a feeling of richness and detail, while the other looks cold and empty.

The use of backlighting to illuminate accessories or decorative objects in a room can add to the overall ambience. Fluorescent light sticks are ideal for this purpose, since they are inexpensive and easy to install.

Backlighting provided by free-standing "can" lights give the wall behind this couch a warm and inviting look. This effect creates an interesting focal point for the room and helps give it an airy feeling.

Track lights and louvered shutters can give a sophisticated look to a room and compensate for weaknesses. An unattractive view combined with poor sun exposure can be overcome with creative lighting and window treatments.

You can add significantly to the value of your home by adding extra living space. This empty basement was dramatically transformed into a valuable living area through installation of wall paneling, ceiling tile, and carpeting.

While this is an ambitious job, if it means that your home can be sold as a three-bedroom rather than a two-bedroom house, it will be well worth the investment.

There is no easier way to increase the perception of the size of a room than through mirrors. By reflecting windows in a mirror, you can also increase the light in a room at minimal cost.

Dressing up the front door will help sell the rest of the home. There is a wide range of door knockers and attractive numbers that can help turn an ordinary door into the focal point of the exterior of your home.

The difference between an ordinary flat door and a six-panel door can be dramatic. You can either replace an existing door or upgrade it inexpensively by applying picture-frame molding.

Smoke Detectors

This is another low-cost feature that makes an effective statement about safety and attention to detail in your kitchen. A smoke detector costs less than $10 and can provide assurances to buyers that a home is safe and modern.

Some states require them before you can pass papers on a property. If this is the case, you may as well buy one now.

COLOR IT APPETIZING

The kitchen should be positive and upbeat, as well as bright. Color can help make this room attractive and easy to work in.

Walls

As always, we advise using a neutral backdrop as the color theme for the kitchen. This can range from pure white to pastel yellow. Avoid large areas of red since it is often equated with heat, of which there is usually more than enough in the kitchen. Also avoid expanses of dark green or blue, since they seldom make food more appetizing and absorb much needed light.

Be especially careful with wallpaper because it can make a personal statement in a room that must be neutral. If in doubt about your existing wallpaper, consider stripping it and repainting the room.

Accent Ideas

Rather than risk bold color statements in the kitchen, limit them to accent features. Because these are not an integral part of the room, the buyer will be able to look beyond them if he or she does not like their color. And chances are accents will add life to the room.

Start with color-coordinated canisters that might sit on a countertop. Then tie them in with matching towels on a wall rack.

Tablecloths can add flair to a room and may be especially appropriate if your table is not in good condition. Try matching the tablecloth with curtains of the same color for a more unified feeling.

A display of wicker baskets or polished copper pots can dress up a dull wall and lend a country look to the kitchen. Hanging plants and fresh flowers will add the final touch and provide a fresh smell at the same time.

LUXURY TOUCHES

There are a number of luxury touches you can add to a kitchen that can set it apart from the crowd and increase its packaging appeal. These items are best targeted toward the trade-up buyer who is seeking tangible evidence of an improved life-style.

Built-Ins

Built-ins are rated by consumers as a popular item especially if they increase storage, cabinet, or counter space.

In galley kitchens in condominiums or co-ops, space can be at a premium. You can install a drop-leaf counter that is hinged to a wall with a folding leg beneath. When you need the surface, just prop it up. This feature should be pointed out to the prospect by you or the broker, or the buyer may never see it.

Space is often wasted on walls beneath overhead cupboards and countertops. Narrow shelves along these walls can be ideal for storing spices or small objects.

Overhead racks with hooks to hang gourmet cookware on are another space saver and should appeal to those who see themselves as master chefs.

Take a look at the objects sitting on your counters. If you have a microwave oven taking up valuable space, consider building a shelf beneath a cabinet to hold it. If you have a coffee maker or a can opener and really want to create a designer kitchen, purchase the types of appliance that can be mounted beneath the cabinets and include them in the sale. This type of amenity will help differentiate your kitchen from its competition.

Lastly, consider buying a butcher-block cutting board that you can adapt to fit over one side of a double sink. This will increase the buyer's perception of the size of the counter and will provide extra space.

Sensational Ceilings

The kitchen ceiling rarely receives much attention although it has the potential to make a kitchen really stand out.

Installing 2-inch-wide wooden slats, 1 inch apart and running along the length of the ceiling, can create a contemporary and unique effect. Build a frame around the circumference of the ceiling using 2 by 4's, and nail the slats to this frame. The 2-inch gap between the slats and the ceiling will create a floating effect. Both the ceiling itself and the 2 by 4 frames should first be painted a matte black. This type of dropped ceiling has seen extensive use in offices and restaurants and is now being applied to expensive houses and condominiums.

There is a similar approach that uses chrome metal instead of wood. This creates a high-tech feeling that is likely to appeal to a younger market in an urban environment. The cost of this "Prestige System" is $4.50 per square foot. It is available from Donn Corporation in West Lake, Ohio. Because the cost of this product is quite high, it should be limited to very small kitchens in order for you to see a return on your investment.

Another approach is to wallpaper the ceiling. As long as the paper follows our rules about neutrality—a simple grid pattern or a muted print—it can add warmth and a custom look to the kitchen.

Super Sinks

Turn a conventional or tired sink into one that appears more expensive by putting in an elaborate faucet. There are some great products on the market that range from classic to twenty-first-century designs. These faucets can make even older sinks look like showpieces.

Wine Racks

The first sign of one who truly appreciates life's finer things is a well-stocked built-in wine rack. This can be added inexpensively by purchasing one and simply mounting it beneath a counter. A slightly more elaborate approach is to replace an overhead cabinet door with a glass one and fit a wine rack inside the cabinet. It is important that the rack be visible because you have to make as much of an impact as you can within a fairly short time.

Gourmet Library

Shelves that display a library of gourmet cookbooks and magazines suggest that you have a professional kitchen that can accommodate the extensive preparation necessary for lavish entertaining.

If you don't have a library of this sort, a well-placed copy of *Gourmet* magazine should do the trick.

Gourmet Appliances

If you have any trendy appliances—like pasta machines, electric coffee grinders, gelato machines, or espresso machines—put them on display. This will appeal to the sophisticated high achiever and chic city dweller. Two or three of these appliances are plenty because more will take up too much counter space.

CONCLUSION

Buyers know that the kitchen is one of the most expensive rooms in the home. Consequently, there are few more significant purchase deterrents than the thought of purchasing a home and then having to redo the kitchen.

By taking the necessary packaging steps, you can add life to a tired kitchen. You can also take an already acceptable kitchen and make it the star of your home. There are no rooms that carry more clout with the buyer, so take the time to make your kitchen a selling point of your home.

CHAPTER HIGHLIGHTS

1. The kitchen is generally considered one of the most influential rooms in determining the outcome of a home sale.

2. "Newness" is almost always viewed as a positive characteristic of major kitchen components like appliances and cabinets.

3. Ample cabinet and counter space is an important sales point.

4. Color can be the most cost-effective and least expensive packaging tool for suggesting newness.

5. The floor is a dominant visual influence in the kitchen and can improve the perception of the entire room.

6. Cooking smells can create territorial anxiety and should be replaced with smells of cleanliness and newness.

7. Quality light fixtures and bright lighting can make the kitchen seem more appealing and more valuable.

8. Stick with neutral colors as the basic theme for the kitchen and limit bolder colors to accent features — like tablecloths, canisters, and decorative objects.

9. Overall cleanliness and order in the kitchen are especially important in helping the buyer visualize him- or herself in it.

10. Subtly display high-life-style statements like gourmet cookbooks or cookware, European appliances, or special bottles of wine.

11. Repainting dated appliances can be one of the best investments you can make in an older kitchen.

10

The Dignified Dining Room

The dining area of a home can take on special meaning for many buyers. It can suggest family gatherings, lavish parties, or intimate candle-lit dinners.

In some homes, the dining area is a separate room, while in others it is an extension of the living room or kitchen. Consumer surveys report that the separate dining room is the more sought-after because it is usually more formal. But in some homes, a formal dining room can be a liability: for example, in small houses or condominiums it can draw usable space from the kitchen or living room.

The current trend in homes is toward smaller units, so developers are designing "great rooms," as opposed to separate dining rooms.

Whether you have an open or an enclosed dining area, we'll show you how to make the most of what you have.

THE FIVE-STEP SYSTEM
Step 1. Consider the Competition

If the homes you are competing with offer separate dining rooms and yours doesn't, there are certain steps you can take to make yours the most attractive.

Start by taking a look at homes in your area that lack separate dining rooms. They may give you ideas on ways to enhance the look of your open dining area and suggest how much work your room may require.

Step 2. Consider the Buyer

The dining room has a very different appeal to different segments of the market. Some buyers consider it relatively unimportant, while others consider it an integral part of the home.

First-Time Buyers

Functional space is a primary concern for first-time buyers, and a separate dining room may diminish that space. If your home is small but has a distinct dining room, you should suggest the versatility of this area. You can also make small structural changes that will open up a separate dining room and increase the feeling of size in the home.

Trade-up Buyers

Entertaining is an important consideration among all trade-up buyers, and the dining room can play a big part in this. A separate dining room is very important to this group. Whether or not you have a formal dining room, we'll show you how to make this area more elegant and attractive for entertaining.

Empty Nesters/Trade-down Buyers

Because this category of buyer often moves with large furniture, like dining room tables, separate dining areas are often needed. But because trade-down homes are usually smaller, there is a premium put on space and a separate dining room may be better used for other purposes.

We'll show you how to keep the feeling of a dining room but also suggest the versatility of this area.

Step 3. Evaluate Your Product

Be sure that your focus groups critique the overall appearance of your dining area. Because a dining room is one of the least occupied areas in the home, it can project a lifeless feeling. There are clues — plastic fruit, dusty table tops, and musty smells — that suggest a lack of use.

You may not notice these, but a person touring your home for the first time might. There are many other small cosmetic defects that may appear obvious to an objective eye but unobserved by you, so listen to your focus-group feedback.

Step 4. Eliminate Territorial Anxiety

The dining room can be a personal place because it is closely associated with family events and intimate dinners. The buyer wants to be able to picture his or her family sitting around the dining room table at Thanksgiving or Christmas. Strong personal statements will make this process more difficult.

While your favorite colors, art objects, or tablecloths make you feel comfortable, they may do little for the buyer. We'll cover the factors most likely to create territorial anxiety and show you how to eliminate them.

Step 5. Maximize Packaging Appeal

Because the dining room is often the scene of more formal events, adding a feeling of richness and elegance to the room can be an effective packaging strategy.

Color and light are also an important part of the dining room's overall packaging. Certain colors, for example, have been proven to increase people's appetites. And certain types of light enhance the atmosphere of the room, while others should be avoided.

SETTING THE SCENE

Each component of the dining room contributes to the overall atmosphere. We'll address each feature separately, addressing low-cost, high-return improvements.

The Walls

If you have a separate room, the walls will influence the total feel of the area.

There are some general considerations about walls to bear in mind and, later in this chapter, we'll show you how to use walls to give the impression of a separate room, if your dining room needs to be set apart.

Paint

Some homeowners paint their dining rooms a very dark color in hopes of creating a feeling of subdued elegance. But this same effect can be achieved by painting walls a lighter color and turning the lights down with a dimmer. The big difference is that, if you use a light shade, your room won't look claustrophobic.

Before deciding on a color for your dining room, you'll want to know that certain colors increase the appetite while others seem inconsistent with food. The renowned color expert Faber Birren says that peach is the most appetizing color of all. Subtle pastel shades of yellow, rose, and beige can also be appropriate because they make food look better. Deep blue and green, on the contrary, can make food appear less appetizing.

In any case, a fresh coat of paint will create a look and smell of newness and help the buyer visualize the space as his or her own.

Wallpaper

It's quite common for dining rooms to have wallpaper, which creates a feeling of formality in the room. The same rules that apply to paint also apply to wallpaper. Keep it relatively light and neutral and avoid strong personal design statements.

Molding

There are few cosmetic improvements that can add more of an impression of elegance than molding. As discussed extensively in Chapter 7, "A Grand Entrance," molding creates a look of detail and charm. Whether you choose simple chair-rail or the more elaborate cornice molding, it will make your dining room stand out and add a dramatic focal point.

Windows

Windows provide a good opportunity to express the elegance of your dining room. Draperies can make a room seem more luxurious and can be highlighted with tiebacks. By selecting a matching or accent fabric as the tieback and purchasing brass hardware designed for this, you can create a distinctive look.

If your room is more contemporary, louvered wooden shutters or Levolor-style blinds can be effective.

And, if you have an unattractive wall in the room that you would prefer to hide or if you want to offset a low ceiling, consider a floor-to-ceiling vertical blind made by Levolor Lorentzen, Inc., of Lyndhurst, New Jersey, which accentuates the vertical symmetry of the room.

The Ceiling

You can make the ceiling into a focal point of the room through the use of molding appliqués. But first you must make sure the ceiling doesn't show any signs of cosmetic flaws that can create concern in the minds of buyers. Take the necessary steps to eliminate evidence of old water stains and surface cracks, then repaint if necessary.

(If the ceiling is too high, remember that a dark color will seem to lower it and also draw attention away from any cosmetic flaws or irregularities.)

After repainting, you could consider adding a plaster medallion around a central hanging light fixture.

The Floor

The floor plays a different role depending upon whether you have a separate or open dining area. The following are general considerations for any type of dining area, to be followed later in the chapter by ideas on how to use the floor to help create the impression of a separate dining section.

Hardwood Floor

The dining room can often be a formal room, which is why area rugs on hardwood floors can be most appropriate here. A Chinese or oriental rug on a hardwood floor makes an effective statement, especially to the trade-up buyer. If you prefer a bare hardwood floor, make sure it looks its best by using the techniques described in Chapter 9.

Carpet

Wall-to-wall carpet adds warmth and comfort to the dining area. But, even if your carpet looks fine, give it an overall cleaning yourself with a carpet shampoo or have a professional come in and do it for you. This will help restore the carpet's original look and enhance its perceived value.

The Furniture

Furniture can provide a focal point. Because the dining room may not be in daily use, be sure that it looks as fresh and well maintained as possible. Lemon oil will help bring back life to a dusty dining room table and add an appealing smell.

A centerpiece of plastic fruit sitting in a bowl on the table will only reinforce the fact that the dining room is rarely used. You want to convey the opposite impression and should look for ways to add life to the room.

I once toured a home with a broker late in the afternoon while the owners were preparing for a large cocktail party. They had just set up an ice sculpture on the dining room table and helpers were scurrying around with champagne glasses and silverware. The preparations showed off the possibilities of the dining room and lent a feeling of excitement.

While I do not recommend going this far, you should set the table with your best china and silverware. Leaving an unopened bottle of wine and a pair of candlesticks on the table will add a finishing touch.

Lighting

Because most people tour homes during the day, the more natural light the better. But buyers also realize that dining rooms are used during the evening, so demonstrating the effectiveness of artificial lighting is also important.

Because the dining room requires bright light during holidays and large family gatherings and less light during romantic dinners or formal parties, a dimmer is essential; one costs about $5.

The most practical fixture to use is an attractive overhead chandelier. Keep it polished if it has a brass or silver-colored surface, and make sure all of the bulbs are working. If you have an especially prepossessing fixture, keep it on during a tour, even during the day. This will highlight it and add to the room's elegance.

You shouldn't have to include a dining room hanging light fixture with the sale of your home unless the buyer is either willing to pay extra for it or it becomes an essential last-minute negotiating point.

Do-It-Yourself Improvements under $100

1. Install a dimmer switch ($5).

2. Place a floral centerpiece on the dining room table ($15).

3. Add a chair-rail molding ($75).

4. Paint or wallpaper to define an open dining room ($75).

5. Set the table with your best china and silver (NC).

The Doors

If you liked the idea of installing french doors in the entryway or living room, but they would be more appropriate in the dining room, seriously consider them now. Of course you wouldn't want them in all three rooms because of their cost and the fact that they could be overwhelming.

French doors in the dining room will give it an added touch of elegance.

Mirrors

The perception of the dining area's size and grace can be enhanced through mirrors. By placing one along the wall at the far end of the dining room, you can create a dramatic effect by making the table appear twice as long. A mirrored ceiling creates a decidedly avant-garde atmosphere but would be appropriate for only the most sophisticated urban home.

Mirrors can be very effective to emphasize the feeling of light and size in a room, but just be sure that what the mirror reflects is attractive.

Flowers and Plants

Freshly cut flowers are very appropriate in the dining room. They make an ideal centerpiece and add a splash of color and fragrance. The same is true of many flowering plants, including large floor plants placed in any of the four corners of the room or leaf plants sitting on side tables.

DEFINING YOUR DINING ROOM

Home buyers fall into two categories: there are those who would do just about anything for a separate dining room and there are those who would wish the room could be converted into more useful space. Through creative repackaging, you can satisfy both groups.

Getting More out of the Separate Dining Room

Since formal entertaining or holiday gatherings may be relatively infrequent, a separate dining room is likely to sit empty more often than not. For this reason, the room lends itself to a variety of uses.

Furniture Strategies

By moving bookcases from one section of your home into the dining room, you can create the effect of a combination study and dining area. This will not detract from the formal air of the dining room and will free up space in another section of the home. Books and assorted collectibles on shelves might even enhance the atmosphere of the room.

If you have a large, sectioned dining room table, make it as small as possible and put a small grouping of furniture in the newly created space. A reading chair by a small desk can further reinforce the versatility of the room.

Removing Walls

A more serious approach to this dual-purpose problem involves taking down walls. This can make your home seem much larger and brighter and can provide numerous layout ideas for the buyer to visualize.

But you'll want to explore the consequences of this action before taking it. If the wall is a structural or bearing wall, it cannot be moved without introducing a support in its place. We recommend avoiding this type of alteration without the advice of an engineer or architect.

If the wall was put up after the home was built, you're in luck because it should come down quite easily. But if it was built as a part of the home, be prepared to spend some time patching gaps in the ceiling, floor, and adjacent wall. The return of all this depends on many variables. If it makes a small home seem larger and more efficient, it may be worth it. Ask your broker for a second opinion if in doubt.

Defining Undefined Spaces

There are ways to suggest a separate dining area in a house or condo if one does not exist. This can be done with color, lighting, furniture, or a modest amount of carpentry.

Walls

The easiest and least costly method is simply to paint or wallpaper the area around your dining area. Framing the paint or wallpaper with molding will help to define the area further.

Flooring

A change in flooring will also help create a separate eating area. If you have wall-to-wall carpeting in the living room and you dine in one corner of this area, consider replacing a section of carpet with hardwood squares or strip flooring. The cost will be roughly $18 per square yard, so if the area if 8 feet by 10 feet, it will cost approximately $170.

If your home is large, and comparable properties on the market have separate dining rooms, this may be a wise move. Similarly, if you have a small condominium or co-op and want to reproduce the feeling of larger homes, this may help differentiate your product.

Dividers and Platforms

There are some relatively low-cost approaches to building dividers that can create the impression of a separate dining area. By constructing a half-height wall along the length of the dining section, you will create a physical divider that will not significantly diminish the openness of the room. Capping it with oak or a darker wood to match your furniture will give it a coordinated look.

A more ambitious approach is to build a raised platform for the dining room furniture. This can be constructed with 2-by-4-inch framing and a half-inch plywood cover. The platform could then be carpeted or covered with hardwood or parquetry. An added touch would be to install a handrail with balustrades surrounding the area.

Expect the cost of this to run a minimum of $500, which can be justified only in a higher-priced house, condo, or co-op.

Lighting

By using different lighting fixtures, you can define a dining area.

A series of ceiling-mounted can lights above the dining room table can make this area look as if it was designed to accommodate a long table. Ceiling cans by Lightolier cost about $30 each, and installation will add another $25 a light. You are likely to need three or four.

A track light is another obvious way to highlight a specific area of the home. Both can lights and tracks are relatively inexpensive when compared with chandeliers, which are much more difficult to justify as a marketing tool.

CONCLUSION

For those who put a high value on entertaining, the dining room can be a real focal point of your home. By demonstrating how attractive and useful this room can be, you can help the buyer recognize its potential. And, in those instances where the dining room is stealing space from other areas of the home, don't be afraid to point out the room's versatility.

No matter how you position your dining room, make sure it looks as if it is used and enjoyed.

CHAPTER HIGHLIGHTS

1. Most buyers seek a feeling of elegance and formality in the dining room.

2. Certain colors — like peach and pastel yellow — are most appropriate for the dining room because they have been found to be appetite-enhancing.

3. Because most dining rooms are used less frequently than other rooms in the home, it is important to keep yours looking and smelling fresh.

4. The trade-up buyer looks at the dining room for its entertainment possibilities, so make sure it makes the right kind of life-style statements.

5. If your home does not have a separate dining room, take the necessary steps to define it by changing the wall color or building a half-height divider.

6. If the dining room seriously compromises the size of an adjacent living room, consider removing the wall and combining the two.

7. If the dining room is underutilized and robs needed space from other areas of the home, consider turning it into a dual-purpose room, like a combination study or library.

11

Heads-up
Bathrooms

Bathrooms have always been an important selling point in a home, but never have they received as much attention from buyers as they do today.

Most sellers know that the bathroom can be a very expensive room to replace and that a particularly weak one can seriously diminish the value of a home. But fewer people recognize the opportunities bathrooms offer to the seller who wants to make important life-style statements about a house and set it apart from the competition's.

"The bathroom is emerging as one of the most exciting and profitable home selling tools," states Dennis J. Hess, president of Merrill Lynch Realty, the nation's second largest residential real estate brokerage firm. Hess cites two reasons behind the bathroom renaissance.

First, because of the tremendous increase in the number of two-career families, there is a greater need for bathrooms designed to accommodate two people at once.

Second, there is a new awareness of the importance of fitness and relaxation today, and the bathroom can be ideal for this. Developers are taking advantage of this trend by installing luxury features in the bathroom that address this need.

By recognizing both of these demands, as well as understanding the basics of bathroom marketing, you can make your bathroom or bathrooms into an important selling point.

THE FIVE-STEP SYSTEM
Step 1. Consider the Competition

Take a good look at the competition's bathrooms. If you find your competition has ignored current consumer attitudes toward bathrooms, you'll have found an area in which to differentiate your product.

If there are newly constructed homes in your area, chances are they have some up-to-date features that your bathroom may lack, in which case creative packaging of your bathroom might come in handy.

In the event that no new homes are being built nearby, take a look at new homes in other areas to get an idea of what the latest bathrooms contain. If you see an inexpensive feature in another home that you especially like, consider applying it to your property.

Step 2. Consider the Buyer

Before you make any improvements to your bathrooms, you'll want to be sure that any alterations you decide upon will appeal to your prospects. Changes are improvements only if buyers like them. If the alterations you make don't appeal to prospective buyers, they can be considered unnecessary contributions to the asking price.

There are two levels of customer requirements to consider. Some are shared by all; others are specific to individual groups.

Of the universal consumer preferences, buyer surveys report that new fixtures and features are ranked at the top of the list, even if they are traditional in design. As always, newness is equated with low maintenance, value, convenience, and status. An old pull-chain water closet may look charming, but the plumbing problems it can suggest will more than offset this appeal.

Two other common requirements are ample storage and counter space and good lighting from new light fixtures.

First-Time Buyers

First-time buyers are usually the most cost-sensitive. Since the bathroom can be a costly room to upgrade, make sure yours does not suggest the need for major renovation. There are a number of inexpensive techniques we will describe with the first-time buyer in mind.

The environment in the bathroom, as in other rooms targeted toward the first-time buyer, should be bright and exciting. There are various decorating approaches you can adapt to achieve this effect.

Trade-up Buyers

The bathroom can have a special appeal for trade-up buyers if it makes the right kind of life-style statement and reinforces the fact that your home is indeed a trade-up.

There are a number of cosmetic and substantive measures you can take to make the bathroom especially appealing to this group.

Empty Nesters/Trade-down Buyers

Since many trade-down buyers are moving from larger homes to smaller ones, you'll want to maximize the efficiency of small bathrooms to make the adjustment easier—even the tiniest bathrooms may have wasted space.

Safety is another concern of older buyers. There are certain safety features you can incorporate into a bathroom that will make the buyer feel more comfortable and help differentiate your product.

Step 3. Evaluate Your Product

Use the feedback from your focus groups together with your appraisal of the competition to determine how much and what kind of work your bathrooms require.

If you conclude that major work is needed—the replacement of damaged or outdated fixtures or replacement of a badly worn floor or the repair of bulging or cracked tile—seriously consider completing this work before you sell the home rather than reducing the asking price. No matter what discount you offer, bathrooms that are badly in need of repair can hinder the sale of your home.

If your bathrooms are just tired or dated, you'll want to compensate with improvements that suggest newness and increased value. But before you do this, it is extremely important that you don't let small flaws obscure the overall picture.

Problems can be as small or as large as buyers see them. So it's best to correct any minor mechanical defects or surface problems on walls, floors, or ceilings before the buyer jumps to the wrong conclusions.

I once had a bathroom that had condensation stains on the ceiling, which the buyer immediately concluded were the result of a roof leak. A $10 half-gallon of paint and a half-hour of time would have preempted this reaction. Keep an eye on details like this so they don't detract from the packaging improvements you make.

Step 4. Eliminate Territorial Anxiety

The bathroom is one of the most personal rooms in the home and can cause territorial anxiety more easily than any other room. For this reason, the three most important rules to follow when preparing your bathrooms for a tour are cleanliness, cleanliness, and cleanliness. There is nothing quite as disconcerting as walking into a bathroom that either looks or smells as if someone had just used it.

Think about the way you feel when you use the master bathroom at someone else's home, even if you know that person well. When you walk in, you may feel uneasy about being in a place that is so closely associated with the private activities of another person. If the bathroom happens to be somewhat dirty or even a little pungent, this feeling is greatly magnified.

Keep all personal items in the bathroom out of sight. I once toured a home and, in the course of inspecting the master bathroom, I noticed a prescription for the treatment of a well-known social disease. Not only did I feel awkward at having seen this, but it also made me uneasy with the owner, who was showing me the property.

Alexandra Kira, author of a comprehensive book on the social and functional aspects of the bathroom, says, "There is no single space in Western culture where we place more value on privacy and seclusion than the bathroom." She notes that this is one of the only places where even spouses often require privacy from each other. So conditioned are people to privacy in the bathroom that, even when alone at home, most of us close the bathroom door.

Color can be another source of territorial anxiety which you should be sensitive to. We will show you how to deal with the problems color can cause and how to improve the purchase appeal of your bathrooms in the process.

Step 5. Maximize Packaging Power

There are a number of ways to take an ordinary bathroom and give it some marketing flair through packaging improvements. Suggesting that the bathroom is a luxurious retreat will appeal to many buyers.

But installing features like saunas or Jacuzzis is unlikely to pay off because of their expense. Consider impressing the buyer with cosmetic improvements instead. There are many ways to achieve the look of new installations at a fraction of the cost.

BATHROOM VARIATIONS

Some homes have three types of bathroom: the master bathroom, the second or third bathroom, and the half-bath.

The Master Bath

The master bathroom should be the target for most of your fix-up dollars because it is most important to the buyer. Many homebuyers fantasize about a luxury retreat off the master bedroom. While you may not be able to go this far, the more exciting the master bath, the better.

The Half-Bath

Under certain circumstances, the half-bath can be the second most important bathroom in the home. If it's located near the entry and is the first bathroom the buyer will see, it takes on special importance because of the first impression it will create.

The buyer will also realize that this is the bathroom his or her guests will be using and will want to make sure it makes the right statement.

Additional Bathrooms

In many homes, the second or third bath is used by children or occasional sleep-over guests. For this reason, it should look bright and well cared for, but does not need the sort of attention that the master bath does.

By following some of the general rules about making the bathroom look clean, and by incorporating some small packaging improvements, you should be able to make your second bath a perfectly marketable room.

This priority list will mean little, however, if any one of these bathrooms is in especially bad condition, because buyers cringe at the prospect of having to install a new one.

BATHROOM BASICS

There are major components common to full bathrooms: the tub, tile shower, toilet, and sink. Each of these fixtures makes statements about the quality, condition, and age of your bathroom, and we will show you ways to make these statements positive.

The Tub

For all practical purposes, the bathtub is a permanent part of your bathroom. Unlike the toilet, for example, it cannot be easily or economically removed because doing so will cause damage to the surrounding walls, floor, and plumbing. For this reason, it pays to make the most out of what you have, even if this means considerable work.

Giving It a Bath

The first step in properly presenting the tub is to make sure it is absolutely clean. No one wants to see hair or a buildup of film around the inside.

A tub that is stained or discolored by a buildup of bathtub film can be cleaned by pouring undiluted bleach onto a rag and scrubbing, or by filling the tub with warm water and letting a few cups of bleach soak away the stain. Make sure the room is adequately ventilated, since the fumes will be strong.

For more persistent stains, spread a mixture of peroxide and cream of tartar over the area, and then apply a small amount of ammonia. Let it sit for a few hours, and then scrub it off.

If your tub happens to be old porcelain and has become badly stained over the years, fill a small pail with hot water and combine ¼ cup of mineral spirits with a grated bar of naphtha soap. Let it all dissolve, and then wash the stains with the mixture as you would with a cleanser.

To make the chrome fixtures shine, you might try Dow Bathroom Disinfectant Spray. To help restore the shine to older fixtures, try any quality car wax.

If you have old or unattractive nonskid tub decals, soak them with mineral spirits to weaken the adhesive. Then scrub them off with an abrasive rag, and use Top Job or Fantastic to rub off any remaining adhesive.

Finish the job by using a lemon-scented cleaner to add a smell of freshness.

Dressing Up the Tired Tub

Sometimes, simply cleaning a tub isn't good enough. In older homes, for example, the tub may be visibly worn or chipped, making it and the rest of the bathroom appear in need of major work. You can restore the surface of an old porcelain tub by having it reenameled. This costs between $150 and $250 and eliminates all the unsightly surface cracks or worn areas that make a tub seem to be in need of replacement.

This may sound expensive, since you can probably find a new fiberglass tub on sale for about $250. However, fiberglass tubs are not of the same quality as older ceramic or porcelain tubs, and $250 will not begin to cover the hidden costs of tub replacement. When you pull out an old tub, be prepared to replace much of the wall and floor tile surrounding it, as well as some of the plumbing and subflooring. This is a very messy job and will probably cost somewhere between $1,000 and $2,000.

To find a refinisher, look under "Porcelain Refinishing" or "Appliance Refinishing" in the Yellow Pages. Or contact a national company called Perma Ceram by dialing 800-645-5039 (in New York State call 516-645-5039). And if all else fails, most Sears stores offer this service.

Updating with Color

If you refinish a tub, consider introducing a new color in the process. Like those of kitchen appliances, the manufacturers of bathroom fixtures update colors periodically. There are few more obvious tipoffs to the age of an appliance than an outdated color.

Consider the new pastels — like peach, rose, or even gray — since they are what major manufacturers like Eljer and Kohler are featuring in their new lines. If you want to be more neutral, try almond, sand, or the all-time favorite, white. Most tub refinishers should offer these colors and more.

The big catch here is that you will have to match the sink and toilet as well. Update with color only if all bathroom fixtures require the same amount of work or if your focus groups say that the existing color of your fixtures is absolutely intolerable.

Victorian Focal Point

If your tub is of the old Victorian variety with feet and white porcelain fixtures, you should think of it as an asset rather than a liability. In fact, some of the largest manufacturers of bathroom fixtures have introduced new versions of these tubs complete with brass "claw and ball" feet and very up-to-date prices.

There are many things you can do with an old and tired-looking Victorian-style tub to make it the star of your bathroom and help differentiate it from the competition's.

Begin by painting the outside of the tub with an authentic Victorian color like a deep red or green. You can use epoxy or porcelain refinishing paint, available through most large home-improvement stores.

Another way to treat the outside of the tub is to make a fabric skirt that wraps around it. Consider matching this color to your accessories — like the rug, shower curtain, or bath towels.

If you can find some attractive brass fixtures for the tub — for example, a clip-on soap dish, brass faucet, or brass ball-and-claw feet — you may well turn it into the luxury item that manufacturers are charging dearly for. There are many Victorian accessory stores where you can buy these products, many of which advertise in the annual *Old House Journal Catalog*. The Renovator's Supply offers an extensive range of brass and old-style fixtures. Write Renovator's Supply at Renovator's Old Mill, Millers Falls, Massachusetts 01349, for a copy of their mail-order catalogue.

Framing the Tub with Fabric

A clever idea that I saw in a condominium model unit was a fabric-covered valance over the tub. Hidden behind this was a shower rod with a pair of matching shower curtains tied back against either wall.

The valance was made from wood about 6 feet long by 18 inches wide and was mounted with L brackets from the ceiling. It was heavily urethaned on the back side and covered with a waterproofed duck cloth fabric on the front.

The result was a custom look that can be reproduced using less than $100 worth of materials. This approach is ideal if your bathroom has costly deficiencies that you do not choose to correct, and you want to create an attractive, but inexpensive, focal point. To create a designer's look, match the color of the fabric and the shower curtain with the color of the rug and towels. Remember to keep the colors neutral.

Special Safety Considerations

There are some relatively inexpensive features you can incorporate around the tub area that will appeal to the safety needs of the older buyer.

Consider installing a handrail along the wall leading to the tub. This can be both functional and aesthetically pleasing. An oak bar, coated with polyurethane and mounted with brass fittings, for example, can be purchased and installed for about $50.

A phone by the bathtub might also appeal to this group and to trade-up buyers as well. We will discuss this further at the end of the chapter.

Ceramic or Porcelain Tile

Bathroom tile can be a dominant feature of a bathroom and should always look its best.

General stains on ceramic tile can be removed by making a paste from baking soda and bleach. Scrubbing with a sponge or a thick cloth should do the trick.

To brighten old porcelain tile, use vinegar on a cloth and rub vigorously. This will return old, yellowed tile to its original white.

Cleaning the tile grout also helps make old tiles look newer. The bright white sets off the tile and is a particularly attractive frame to colored tiles. Try Grout Restorer by Super-Tek Products, Inc., Woodside, N.Y.

Tackling Troubled Tile

Problems with tile are common in the shower. They can also be among the most alarming to buyers because of the expense associated with their replacement. There are a number of different solutions.

Inexpensive Tile Solutions

If you want to spend as little as possible, run a second shower curtain along the wall to cover it up. But if you're masking a serious problem, inform the buyer.

Another inexpensive way to cover up badly stained, worn, or otherwise unattractive tile is to apply oil-based paint. To help the paint adhere, first rough up the tile a little with either sandpaper or coarse steel wool. When the paint is dry, apply a self-polishing wax so water spots will easily wipe off.

To prevent the paint job from calling attention to itself, take pains to match the color of the toilet, tub, and sink. If necessary, take the toilet seat to the paint store to make an accurate match.

If the tile is damaged and a cosmetic treatment like paint will not suffice, there are products available that you can apply right on top of the existing tile. Home-improvement centers carry simulated tile board as well as plastic shower wall kits that you cut to size and adhere to the wall. One of a number of companies that make these kits is called Plaskolite, Inc., which offers an interesting array of products to upgrade worn tile.

Refinishing Tile

Another alternative for substandard tile in the shower or throughout the bathroom is to refinish it. This can be expensive in large bathrooms, however, because refinishing costs about $4 to $5 per square foot. Yet it is much cheaper than buying new tile.

Remember that refinishing can be an opportunity to introduce one of today's colors to a dated bathroom, so think about taking advantage of this.

Tile over Tile

If new tile is needed, try applying the new tile right over the old. This will work fine as long as the original tile is firmly affixed.

I have done this on several occasions and have found it to be far less costly than ripping out the old tile and starting from scratch. To redo a shower stall, floor, and wainscoting in a 7-by-10-foot bathroom, I paid a contractor $900, as compared with a quotation of $2,600 for a totally new job. The perceived value of what appeared to be a brand-new bathroom made it a worthwhile investment. Especially if you are upgrading a master bathroom, this step can be particularly important.

If you have tile problems in other areas, make sure to address them. Replace broken or cracked tile, add grouting where necessary, and apply silicone or acrylic sealer in corners where gaps have developed. Dap Kwik Seal is ideal for this, as is an aerosol sealant called Tub'n Tile by Convenience Products Company.

Fiberglass or Plastic Enclosures

Because they are softer than ceramic or porcelain tile, fiberglass and plastic scratch easily. And even with normal use, the scratches often fill with dirt that highlights them.

Bleach will help remove these stains. Always use liquid cleaners on fiberglass, like Fantastic or Formula 409. A product called Gel-Gloss by TR Industries both cleans and waxes fiberglass.

The Shower

Showers come in varieties ranging from tiled stalls to one-piece fiberglass or plastic units to tub and shower combinations. The shower includes several elements that combine to create an overall look, and we will address each of these separately.

If your bathroom has a tub without a shower head or a separate shower enclosure, you can buy conversion kits to eliminate what could be a potential sales obstacle.

Alsons Corp. produces a 59-inch nonmetallic hose that attaches to a shower head and is referred to as model 410SPB. This mounts easily near the top of the tub wall and is connected directly to the tub spigot below. It does not block off the existing spigot. The cost is about $60.

Shower Curtains and Doors

Cleanliness in the shower is especially important since the bathroom can be a major source of territorial anxiety. Make sure that shower curtains are clean and free from mildew and that glass doors are spotless. Bleach, as previously discussed, should take care of any mildew problems and ammonia or vinegar on a sponge will eliminate dried water marks or film from a glass door.

If you have a particularly stubborn mildew problem, try Magic Mildew Stain Remover from Magic Chemical Company. To give the curtain a fresh smell and kill remaining bacteria, leave it out in the sun after washing it down. Since shower curtains are not very expensive, I recommend buying a new one if yours is in bad shape. It can be a dominant visual influence in the bathroom and have significant packaging appeal. For this reason, if you choose to do little else to the bathroom, buy the most attractive shower curtain you can find. A new curtain should also smell new, an aroma you will want to introduce at every opportunity.

Glass Enclosures

As attractive as shower curtains can look, their perceived value is not nearly as high as a permanent enclosure. Nearly half of all home purchasers expect glass tub or shower enclosures to be part of the bathroom.

There are many products you can choose from, some of which you can install yourself. The cost will be about $200, but if you want to increase the feeling of value or compensate for weakness in the shower or bath area itself, this can be a good investment.

Curing Common Shower Problems

Old and leaky shower heads and on-off valves raise some real concerns. Installing new ones can be an expensive proposition because it may involve pulling out old tile and then retiling.

If you can't cure the leak yourself by replacing a washer, call a plumber. Avoid the sight and sound of dripping. For a more substantial problem, you might take a look at Shower-Up by Delta. It is a one-piece, molded panel, complete with shower head, on-off valve, and tub faucet. By placing it over the holes created by the removal of the old fixtures, you can avoid expensive retiling. You can purchase this product for about $100 at any large home-improvement store.

Also, there is no excuse for clogged drains. If products like Drano or Liquid Plumber don't free the clog, have Roto Rooter snake the drain. The $40 or $50 charge may preempt needless buyer worries about major plumbing problems in your home.

Last, make sure the shower smells clean and fresh. If it has been thoroughly cleaned, there should be no odor, but if a lingering smell remains, the source could be organic matter in the drain. Apply a little drain cleaner to dissolve this problem.

Toilets

Of all the steps you can take to improve the toilet, few are more impor-tant than keeping it spotless and odorless. A dirty toilet can be a prime cause of territorial anxiety, so you will want to eliminate any offensive statements.

Clean it thoroughly and be sure that there are no rings in the bowl. To remove stains and leave a fresh smell, try Lysol Liquid Disinfectant Toilet Bowl Cleaner. If that fails, try scrubbing the bowl with a paste made of Borax and lemon.

In the event that ring stains have become imbedded in the porcelain and can't be removed, use a colored toilet bowl cleaner that can be dispensed every time you flush. The color of the water will help mask the flaw.

Toilet Improvements

There are steps you can take to upgrade the look of an old or worn toilet. The least expensive packaging improvement is to replace the seat. For about $15 or $20, you can buy a new seat and give the impression of a totally new toilet. For about $50, you can buy an oak seat, which sug-gests a higher level of detail to your bathroom.

If your toilet is badly stained or aged, you can have it refinished. This can cost almost as much as a new toilet, though, so consider it only if yours is special enough to save.

Toilet Troubleshooting

The toilet has the capacity to create a wide variety of disturbing sounds, all of which can make buyers nervous. These sounds range from running water, to high-pitched noises, to splashing.

Turning the tank's shut-off valve, located beneath the tank, eliminates high-pitched squeals. Running water can be cured by slightly bending the float arm attached to the float ball toward the bottom of the tank. If you are not a do-it-yourselfer, call a plumber and have the problem fixed by a professional.

The Sink and Vanity

The sink or vanity combination provides one of the best opportunities to upgrade the image of the entire room.

Keeping Them Clean

The sink itself should be free of hair or film build-up, and the faucet should sparkle. Bon-Ami Cleanser is good for cleaning the sink since it does not scratch like some of the more abrasive powdered cleansers. If the sink is old porcelain and has yellowed, vinegar will help restore its original color. Dow Bathroom Disinfectant will bring brightness back to a chrome faucet and drain cover.

The drain should flow freely. If the buyer decides to run the water to check the pressure, and the sink fills up, he or she will be concerned.

The countertop surrounding the sink should be clean and free of personal care products, prescription drugs, and various toilet articles. This will not only look neater and make the surface look larger, it will also reduce the risk of territorial anxiety.

Upgrading the Vanity

The vanity provides counter and storage space as well as aesthetic impact.

Vanities can range from free-standing units with a single sink to an entire counter stretching along a wall and equipped with double sinks. If your vanity is especially small, you should be aware that, with the tremendous shift in where people live and the increase in dual-career households, the design of the vanity is very important to the first-time buyers and trade-up couples. Double-sink vanities are among the hottest new products a bathroom can offer, especially among trade-up buyers, who frequently share the same schedules.

If you think this is your market, installing a second sink would be a logical consideration, except that it is expensive and you may not have room. Consider taking a halfway measure.

By extending the counter next to your existing vanity and putting a mirror above it, you will allow one person to put on makeup or adjust a tie while the other uses the sink. Also, the addition of the mirror will increase the perception of the room's size and make it seem brighter, too.

Making It Look New

If the vanity you have is old, there are measures you can take to avoid buying a new one. An old or worn sink requires the same refinishing

---

Do-It-Yourself Improvements under $100

1. Hang high-quality shower curtains ($35).

2. Add designer towels and throw rug ($50).

3. Put out imported soaps ($4).

4. Add a magazine rack with upscale magazines ($35).

5. Put in a wall-mounted, color-coordinated telephone ($50).

6. Use brass towel bars ($20).

7. Use brass accessories for a Victorian tub ($40).

8. Make a mirrored ceiling ($100).

9. Put in a new oak toilet seat ($50).

10. Install Hollywood makeup lights ($70).

11. Install a new medicine cabinet ($100).

12. Put a Levolor blind in the window ($75).

---

services you need for the bathtub. Another way to upgrade the sink is to put in a new faucet or simply add new handles.

If moisture has damaged the cabinet part of the vanity, either scrape and repaint it, or have the door replaced. The application of Val-Oil or polyurethane to a wooden cabinet will bring new life to the surface and introduce an effective "new" fragrance to the bathroom.

When to Buy New

If the overall appearance of your vanity is very weak, we highly recommend buying a new one. Because vanities are basically the only "furniture" in a bathroom, having a new one influences the buyer's perception of the entire room.

Vanities are not as expensive as you might think. A new Formica vanity with oak trim and a white sink, for example, should cost less than $200. If you have a large lumber supplier or home-products store in your area, look for an attractive, marked-down unit. As you probably won't have to match it to the other cabinets in the room, as you would in the kitchen, buying an orphan should not present a problem.

The Major Surface Areas

The floors, ceilings, and walls of a bathroom say a great deal about the room's age and condition. Since the bathroom is so often exposed to dampness, special problems can occur.

Colors, of course, have a major impact on the feeling of your bathroom. Darker colors can make the room look smaller, while brighter ones will make it appear larger. You might consider using one of the "in" shades to give your bathroom a contemporary look.

We will speak of each surface separately and discuss ways to make them enhance the perception of your bathroom.

Floors

There are a wide variety of floor coverings available for the bathroom, but ceramic tile is the most popular by a wide margin. Consumer surveys report that people prefer the look, durability, and ease of maintenance that tile offers.

If your floor is badly damaged and needs replacing, it will be well worth spending the extra money for tile rather than resorting to more economical alternatives like vinyl or carpet.

There are a variety of floor surfaces, but the general rule, no matter what you use, is choose light colors rather than dark ones. Bathrooms are generally too small to benefit from heavy colors, and the trend is toward light and bright bathrooms.

Ceramic Tile

This is the most durable, water-repellent, and practical floor surface available for the bathroom.

Clean your ceramic tile and the grout as well. Fresh-looking grout will make the entire floor look newer; bleach will help you do the trick.

If the tile is dull or has lost its sparkle, apply a thin coat of Val-Oil to bring out the shine. Remember, the smell of Val-Oil will give a feeling of newness to the room and certainly cover up any potentially offensive smells.

Rugs and Carpets

Wall-to-wall carpet in the bathroom is generally frowned upon because of its impracticality. If you are putting down a new floor, I strongly advise against choosing carpeting. But if you already have wall-to-wall, make sure it doesn't show the problems normally associated with carpet.

Throw rugs and wall-to-wall carpeting can soak up moisture and be a source of odor. Make sure these items not only look clean, but also smell fresh. Rugs should be shampooed to eliminate stains and bring back their original nap. Try do-it-yourself products first, like Woolite Carpet Shampoo. If the carpet needs more serious help, have it professionally cleaned.

If the carpet is in poor condition but the floor beneath it is in reasonable shape, consider pulling up the carpet and improving the floor.

Wood

Wood is gaining in popularity, especially in areas of the country with cold winters, because it is warmer on the feet. Wood floors can also create a softer and richer look.

With new pressure-treated materials and waterproof sealing agents, water damage is no longer a major concern. If you have to start from scratch, wood is an interesting alternative to a conventional floor, but it is most likely to appeal to the more progressive consumer like the young, professional trade-up buyer.

Marble Floors

Marble looks and is expensive. In some cases, however, its relatively high cost can be justified. If, for example, you have a small half-bath off your front entryway, a luxurious half-bath may be a real asset. If the cost of a tile floor is $15 per square yard and marble is $40 per square yard, and the total area is 3 square yards, then the difference in materials is $75. But that $75 will transform a conventional bathroom into one that clearly differentiates your product.

Walls

Whether you have tiled, wallpapered, or painted bathroom walls, they should look well kept and be neutral enough to prevent causing territorial anxiety.

Pepping Up the Paint

Peeling paint on walls and ceilings is very common in the bathroom due to the considerable moisture. Antifouling marine paint is designed to withstand moisture and retard fungus growth.

The color you select should either accent the color of the tub, toilet, and sink or match it perfectly. If you want a perfect match, remove your toilet seat and take it to the paint store.

Wallpaper

Again, the rule is to keep wallpaper neutral and the patterns simple so as to avoid causing territorial anxiety.

The reflective Mylar surfaces that were so popular in the 1970s are now out of style. If you have a dated color or style of wallpaper or simply feel it looks shabby, strip it and paint the wall.

There is a particularly effective product called DIP Wallpaper Stripper made by William Zinsser & Company. The product contains certain chemicals and enzymes that make the stripping process much easier. Your local wallpaper store may carry this.

Mirror Walls

A mirrored wall in a bathroom can dramatically increase the perception of size and light. Make sure the wall you select is visible from the doorway so it makes as dramatic a first impression as possible. Use either mirrored squares or sheet mirror sections and expect to spend around $3 per square foot, depending on the thickness and quality you choose.

A mirrored wall can not only change the entire complexion of a bathroom, it can also be a great way to cover up a wall in need of cosmetic work.

The Ceiling

Peeling paint is a common problem in bathrooms, especially in those that are not properly ventilated. There are several techniques to correct this problem and create a more marketable room.

Wooden Slats

The wood-slat ceiling that we discussed for kitchens can create warmth and visual interest in the bathroom, too. Place stained 2-inch wooden strips one inch apart along the length of the room, and you will either cover up a damaged ceiling or simply enhance the feeling of a bathroom.

Paint the ceiling black and nail the slats to black-painted 2 by 4's running the width of the room. Make sure either to urethane the wood or seal it so the moisture will not cause stains.

Mirrored Tiles

I once viewed a bathroom that featured square mirror tiles on the ceiling. I had always thought this would look tacky but in fact found it quite dramatic. As you can imagine, it increased the size of the room considerably. It is also a great way to cover up ceilings that have been stained by humidity or are otherwise unattractive.

If you decide to do this, make sure you have a strong waterproof bonding material so moisture will not loosen the mirror squares. Also make sure that the ceiling surface is secure.

ACCENT FEATURES

There are several smaller features in your bathroom that can make an important contribution to its selling appeal.

Medicine Cabinet

This is one of those bathroom staples that can be as simple or as elaborate as your tastes and wallet dictate. A new one can reflect positively on the entire room.

If you have an old medicine cabinet with either an antiquated or worn-looking door, you can save money by just replacing the door or having the mirror glass replaced.

But if your medicine cabinet is a prominent visual feature in your bathroom, it should look both substantial and in good condition. A rusty cabinet with a tarnished mirror is shabby.

There are a wide variety of cabinets available: oak, high-tech, mirrored. They start at about $40 and are a sure sign of a new or renovated bathroom. Because of this, if your medicine cabinet isn't in good condition, a new one will be worth the investment.

Shelves and Storage

All buyers want as much storage space as possible in the bathroom. There are a variety of places where you can create storage areas.

Corners are an ideal place to start. Building shelves for stacking towels, for example, can make the room more efficient. Adding shelves over the toilet can also provide extra space. The end of a boxed-in tub may be an ideal place for a floor-mounted cabinet or shelves.

Installing attractive brass or colorful ceramic hooks on a wall can suggest convenience at little cost.

Window Treatments

The most desirable window coverings or accents are those that are not affected by moisture and do not express strong personal taste. For this reason, I do not recommend fabrics.

Instead, consider wooden louvered shutters. They are very effective because they suggest permanence, and they go with just about any decor.

Levolor-style blinds are also a good choice because they give a custom look, especially if you're able to match or tie in their color with that of the major fixtures. These blinds create a new, high-tech look at relatively low cost. Expect to pay between $50 and $75 on the average, which is a bargain if it upgrades a tired or worn-looking window.

Designer Linens and Accessories

If you don't want to spend the kind of money it takes to make some of the improvements we're discussing—like painting, retiling, or wallpapering—consider buying a coordinated set of designer towels, shower curtains, and area rugs. They will give your bathroom a newer, more sophisticated look and can introduce splashes of color into an otherwise neutral environment.

If prominently displayed, they can make a strong impression on the buyer. In fact, linens and accessories can be the most effective low-budget packaging upgrade of them all, since they make a big impact at no real cost and you can take them with you when you leave.

Flowers

Another inexpensive yet highly effective way to introduce color into a bathroom is with flowers. They are considered a luxury touch and can create an upbeat feeling in the room.

Flowers like freesia or roses can introduce positive smells, which will add a feeling of freshness to the bathroom.

SHEDDING LIGHT ON THE SCENE

Lighting plays different roles in the bathroom. It must provide the illumination necessary to perform specific tasks like shaving and applying makeup. It can create a sense of atmosphere, and the fixtures themselves can make a statement about the age or quality of the bathroom as a whole.

Task Lights

The ideal placement of task lights is above and alongside the mirror over the sink. This will provide even and accurate illumination.

If you place lights over the mirror, make sure they extend across to each end of the mirror and create a balanced look. If you use a track or any type of directional light, make sure it doesn't shine into the mirror because it will be extremely hard on the eyes.

The "Hollywood" or cameo makeup fixture is both functional and attractive. It consists of a row of bulbs on a chrome or painted metal strip and was designed after the Hollywood makeup mirrors you see in movies.

These lights provide even, pleasing illumination. The fixtures range in cost from $50 for the basic three-bulb units to more than $100 for the larger name-brand products.

Fluorescent Lights

Remember that fluorescent lights seldom make people look as attractive as incandescents do. Fluorescents also can be harder on the eyes, especially first thing in the morning.

Always use soft white bulbs to minimize these problems. And always use either a diffusing cover or hide the bulb behind a valance. There are few clearer signs of an antiquated bathroom than an exposed fluorescent lighting fixture.

Track Lights

I've seen track lights used effectively as accent lighting in a bathroom. They highlight interesting objects in the room—like wall prints or hanging plants—and they are also attractive fixtures themselves, giving the room a high-tech feeling.

Track lights aren't normally associated with bathrooms, so they may provide more impact here than in other areas of the home. Install a dimmer to add the final touch.

Skylights

For the bathroom without a window, a skylight can add light without compromising privacy and can create an airy, spacious and contemporary look. Of equal importance, it can add to the buyer's perception of the room's value, create an interesting focal point, and set it apart from the competition.

But skylights, which score very high in consumer preference studies, are expensive. Although it will help the resale value of your home, a skylight can be justified only if you install it early enough to enjoy it yourself—or if you can purchase and install one for two or three hundred dollars. If the cost of a skylight, including installation, costs several hundreds of dollars, it is unlikely to pay off.

LIVING IT UP IN THE BATHROOM

Because buyers' expectations of the bathroom are still relatively low, as compared with the kitchen, for example, you have a real opportunity to grab their attention with surprising features that suggest the improved life-style your home offers.

Some of these ideas are aimed at the young, trade-up buyer who is very conscious of "the finer things in life." People from more traditional backgrounds—including older empty nesters—may consider these suggestions frivolous or inappropriate. Some ideas will appeal to all segments. As always, consider your market carefully before making any of these improvements.

Tantalizing Tubs

The tub can be far more than a place to scrub in. It should be a place to relax as well as provide an attractive focal point for the room. Here are a variety of ways to make your tub stand out from the competition.

Simulating a Sunken Tub

There are few more apparent signs of luxury and status than a sunken bath. These fixtures aren't for everyone, but they often appeal to the younger, trade-up buyer.

Although it is either extremely expensive or structurally impossible to install a sunken tub after the home is built, there is a way to simulate this effect. If your bathroom is large enough, consider building a deck or platform area around the tub to make the tub seem lower and provide a very attractive approach.

The platform, which requires 2 to 3 feet of space in front of the tub, can be constructed from ¾-inch plywood framed with 2 by 4's and then covered with a ceramic tile. Or it can be constructed with pressure-treated decking material. If you use wood, be sure it's carefully sanded so you won't spend your bath time pulling splinters from your feet.

Expect to spend between $200 and $600 on this sort of sunken tub, depending upon whether you do it yourself or hire a pro, as well as how elaborate you become. A well-illustrated paperback book that describes this project is *Design, Remodel and Build Your Bathroom,* published by Creative Homeowner Press.

The California Look

You can make a simple or cosmetically damaged tub quite exceptional by using a trick I once saw in an English home. The owner had taken a conventional white bathtub and applied urethaned redwood planks across the front. He had then attached a redwood rack to hold shampoo and various bathing tools.

The look he created was unmistakably Californian and transformed an everyday tub into a handsome fixture. The cost was also quite reasonable, totaling under $100.

You could also use birch, oak, cedar, or maple to get the same effect. You could use the wood you select as molding or trim in other parts of the bathroom — like a backsplash behind the sink or a chair-rail wrapping around the room — to establish a coordinated look.

Telephones

I once used a bathroom in a large New York investment firm and noticed a color-coordinated telephone next to the toilet. The thought of being so much in demand that a phone was necessary at all times did wonders for my self-esteem.

I later installed a phone in my own bathroom, and always got a favorable and slightly amused reaction from guests. Having a phone in the bathroom makes an effective life-style statement to those who consider themselves travelers in life's fast lane, and it's a real convenience besides. To the young professional, a bathroom phone insures that he or she doesn't miss calls while in the shower. The older buyer may find it a reassuring safety feature.

With the price of phones having come down so dramatically, you don't have to spend more than $50, plus installation. Buy a phone that is color-coordinated with the sink and tub so that it doesn't look out of place, and select a wall-mounted design to give it a built-in look.

Built-in Radio or Cassette Player

An attractive stereo radio or cassette player can easily be mounted on a wall or placed on a shelf. You could also mount the speakers on the wall to enhance the system's impact. Run the wires behind the wall so they aren't visible.

Do not permanently attach the stereo to the wall unless you want to include it with the sale.

Built-in Fixtures

Built-in features in any room suggest expense and custom design. It's quite easy and not very expensive to install built-in items like tissue holders, toothbrush dispensers, and soap dishes. These are small touches that suggest a higher level of detail and an abundance of amenities in your bathroom.

If you are at all handy with tools, building a small shelf and matching it with the room's predominant color will create a custom look. Be it a shower-accessories holder or a magazine rack, the cost of materials should not exceed $3 per item.

Bookcase

A bookcase can be an attractive and surprising feature. This is most appropriate in a half-bath designed for guest use, since it is more decorative than functional and the absence of a shower will prevent moisture damage.

Bar

This may evoke visions of decadence, but, if done tastefully, a bar or an approximation of one can add an interesting touch. Install a small shelf to hold a few bottles of your favorite drink or health juice and add a rack to hold glasses and mixing tools.

Plantery

Most plants thrive on the moisture present in bathrooms. If you have an abundance of natural light, set up an area with hanging plants or shelves for potted plants. If your bathroom doesn't have a window, you can install a grow-light, which may come in the form of an inexpensive light stick.

Whether you make your bathroom look like a tropical rain forest or simply add plants as accent features, you'll add color and freshness to the room while creating an exotic feeling.

Greenhouse Window

The same kind of "punch-out" greenhouse window we discussed in the kitchen chapter can be very attractive in the bathroom. Again, greenhouse windows are features you should consider only if you can enjoy them yourself or if you have to replace the window anyway and feel your bathroom could use an exciting focal point. The cost will be a minimum of $300, so review some of the other improvement suggestions before you decide on this one.

Sitting Area

Sitting areas are normally associated with bathrooms found in luxury hotels or large master suites, but they can be recreated in your home if you have a spacious bathroom or if you have adjoining master and guest bathrooms.

A wicker or wooden chair and a side table can add a nice touch. Tie in the color of the chair cushion with the rug or shower curtain so that the room is color-coordinated.

Built-in Heat- and Sunlamps

Today's health- and image-conscious young buyer likes built-in ceiling heat- or sunlamps. This is a bathroom feature that can help create the popular "health spa" feeling. These lamps are standard features in many new homes and may help suggest the newness of convenience features in yours.

A built-in Broan heatlamp will cost approximately $70, plus another $50 or so to install it.

Nostalgic Details

If you are trying to recreate or enhance a nostalgic or historic theme in your bathroom, brass can be a wonderful and relatively inexpensive addition. Products you might consider are brass towel racks, bathroom tissue dispensers, switchplates, receptacle covers, toothbrush holders, magazine racks, and storage shelves.

They look far more expensive than they are and can help make your bathroom distinctive. Plan to take these items with you after you sell your home or use them as negotiation tools at the time of sale.

You can purchase good, reasonable reproductions of the old brass fixtures that are made overseas. If you can't find these locally, pick up a copy of the annual *Old Home Journal Catalog* and purchase them through mail order.

Redwood Paneling

Fitting a bathroom with redwood paneling on the walls and ceilings can create the look of a sauna. This is an expensive proposition if you take it all the way, but there are products that enable you to reproduce this effect inexpensively. By purchasing veneer strips made just for this purpose and applying them to one or more walls with an adhesive bonding material, you can add warmth and suggest the type of bathroom it would take hundreds of dollars to create.

To cover two 10- by 12-foot walls will cost about $250. These strips are manufactured by Artistry Veneers and should be available at a specialty store or large lumberyard near you.

Before you consider creating a sauna in your home, you should realize that it's not likely to be a great investment unless your property is worth $400,000 or more and your market expects this luxury feature. Only 4 percent of all buyers express interest in owning a sauna and the remaining 96 percent are indifferent, so your $2,000 investment may simply dry up.

CONCLUSION

There are so many ways to upgrade a bathroom, it can be hard to choose among the various options. How much time and money you spend will depend largely on the present condition of your bathroom and how much you are asking for your home. Buyers of high-priced homes ($300,000 or more) expect more than buyers of homes under $100,000, for example.

As always, the more you concentrate on cosmetic packaging improvements, the higher the return will be from your investment. But remember that buyers know how expensive totally renovating a bathroom can be. If, by spending money on slightly more substantial improvements like tub refinishing, you can allay buyer fears of having to rip out part of the bathroom, it may well be worth it.

Also remember that the bathroom on which you should focus most of your attention is the one serving the master bedroom. The chapter that follows will cover ways to make sure the bedroom itself lives up to buyer expectations.

CHAPTER HIGHLIGHTS

1. The master bathroom should be as enjoyable as it is functional.

2. Take advantage of inexpensive extras like telephones to make the right life-style statement.

3. Remember that the bathroom is one of the most personal rooms in the home and can easily evoke territorial anxiety.

4. To minimize the risk of territorial anxiety, the bathroom should smell new and all personal objects should be out of sight.

5. If the tub and the tile surrounding it appear worn, consider refinishing rather than replacing them.

6. The quality of the vanity and light fixtures can influence the perception of the entire bathroom.

7. The proper use of mirrors can significantly increase the feeling of size in the bathroom.

8. Use the latest colors to suggest newness in the bathroom, but stay with the more neutral hues.

12

Dressing Up the Bedroom

The bedroom should be what homebuyers' dreams are made of. To fulfill those dreams, your bedrooms should project relaxation, comfort, and luxury. And because people spend about a third of their lives in bed, it's important that these rooms be among the strong points of your home.

From a marketing perspective, there is another important consideration about the bedroom — it's one of the most personal places in a house or condo. How do you present the room as warm and inviting without creating territorial anxiety by making it too personal?

The five-step system will help you recognize the most important aspects of the bedroom and suggest how you can avoid the critical mistakes homesellers most often make.

THE FIVE-STEP SYSTEM
Step 1. Consider the Competition

Of the many elements to consider when evaluating competitive properties, few are more important than the number of bedrooms. If two homes are equal in square footage but one contains two bedrooms and the other three, the latter will be easier to sell, usually for more money.

We will show you a number of ways to add bedrooms to your home or at least suggest how a room can double as one.

Step 2. Consider the Buyer

Buyers are very open about what they do and don't want in bedrooms.

According to the Housing Futures Consumer Survey conducted through the Harvard and M.I.T. Joint Center for Urban Studies, nearly a third of all homeowners feel their bedrooms are too small. Two thirds feel their home could use another room.

Privacy is another important aspect of the bedroom. Everyone wants a bedroom that's quiet, for example, so if yours is plagued by noise from neighbors or street traffic, we'll show you how to minimize this problem.

As always, some of the requirements of a bedroom cut across all market segments while others are specific to individual groups.

First-Time Buyers

A bright, cheery bedroom that is ready to be occupied is what the first-time buyer wants. As long as the fundamentals are sound, whatever inexpensive packaging touches you add will simply increase the room's appeal.

Trade-up Buyers

These buyers want luxury in the bedroom. They can be impressed with the small touches and creature comforts that create an air of elegance and relaxation. We'll show you how to make your bedroom stand out.

Empty Nesters/Trade-down Buyers

The major concern among trade-down buyers is the size of the bedroom in relation to what they formerly had. Specifically, adequate closet or storage space is important, as well as overall room size.

For the older empty nester, convenience and safety features also fill specific needs. We'll show you how to make the bedroom seem stronger in both of these categories while spending a minimal amount of money.

Step 3. Evaluate Your Product

There are few rooms in which you spend as much time as in the bedroom. For this reason, you are likely to become so familiar with your surroundings that you may no longer see small flaws or quirks in the room.

Peculiar smells from a musty rug, odd sounds from the heating or plumbing system, or small surface cracks around the door frame have probably become as much a part of the room as the view from the windows. But these elements can cause concern to prospective buyers.

Your focus groups can help point out aspects of your bedroom that you have become desensitized to as well as other weaknesses that may diminish the room's appeal.

Step 4. Eliminate Territorial Anxiety

As we have already mentioned, the bedroom is one of the most personal rooms in the home, and it can be difficult for an outsider to feel comfortable in this sort of environment. When certain clues are present in the bedroom that reinforce the fact that it is someone else's room, you can inadvertently make matters worse.

A lack of cleanliness or neatness contributes hugely to a buyer's discomfort. An unmade bed, for example, reaffirms that this is someone else's room. Prospects also have no desire to know that you wear boxer shorts, take Valium at night, or like to read spicy novels. This is your business, and you'll want to keep it that way. In fact, the less of your personal life the buyer can see in the bedroom, the better.

This doesn't mean that the atmosphere has to be cold and sterile, but there are more advantageous ways to suggest warmth and coziness.

Step 5. Maximize Packaging Power

The bedroom should have its own special atmosphere, and you can create this through certain packaging improvements. This room should emphasize comfort and warmth as well as luxury and convenience. We'll show you how to use color, mirrors, and lighting as well as certain small details to increase the value of all of your bedrooms.

BEDROOM BASICS

Before concentrating your efforts on luxury touches, make sure the basics are in order. This means focusing on the cleanliness and condition of the room so that the buyer can visualize the bedroom as his or her own.

Walls

As always, the walls and the objects on them should work to make the room more attractive and reinforce the overall feeling of quality.

Fill in hairline cracks, cover nail holes, and attend to other cosmetic flaws. Once the surface of the bedroom walls is in proper shape, consider the following ways to upgrade them.

Painting

A fresh coat of paint suggests care and newness.

The color of the paint should be neutral, but in the bedroom there is some basis for latitude. Blue, for instance, has a calming effect on people and can be especially appropriate in the bedroom. You might consider choosing pastel shades and using blue as an accent color. You could also try safe colors like antique white or beige and the soft, neutral pastels.

If you use pale yellows or a dusty rose, for example, consider highlighting the wood trim by painting it white. This will create visual interest but won't break up wall areas.

For children's rooms, brighter colors are appropriate. Yellow, red, green, or blue can create an atmosphere of fun. But because parents make the purchase decision and may impose their likes and dislikes on their children, play it safe by limiting bright colors to accent trim, and keep the walls neutral.

Mirrors

Size impresses buyers, and mirrors are the most cost-effective way of increasing the apparent size of your bedroom.

Closet doors provide an ideal place to install mirrors. Depending upon how many doors you have, this may cost several hundred dollars, but it is the single most effective way of making a room appear larger. Mirrored closet doors will also make the room seem more elegant and exciting.

If your closet will not accommodate this, you can try installing a full-length dressing mirror on a section of a wall. Mechanical Mirror Works of New York City offers a product designed for the do-it-yourselfer. The cost of covering a 60-inch-wide section of wall will be about $300. I would, however, stay away from a mirrored ceiling; it suggests a life-style that buyers might find objectionable.

Windows

Make sure windows are clean and that no panes are broken. Clear large objects from the sill to let as much light in as possible and to avoid obstructing the view. Also, when showing your home, be certain that the shades are up to let in as much light as possible.

If you do not live in the Sunbelt and you're selling during the winter, make sure all drafts are sealed with caulking or weather strip. And if you have a window-mounted air conditioner, remove it and store it in the garage or basement. Air conditioners are unsightly whether seen from inside a room or from the exterior of your home.

Next, you will want to determine the best way to enhance your windows. In a small bedroom, for example, you'll want to avoid bulky fabric window treatments that will break up limited expanses of wall space even more. Also, avoid painting window frames dark colors because they will make the walls look even smaller. As always, curtains that you select should be on the neutral side and should not express strong personal taste.

Louvered shutters are a safe bet because they have a very broad appeal, as do Levolor-style blinds, and you can probably take these with you after the home is sold.

Window Security

The security of windows is particularly important in the bedrooms since no one wants strangers climbing in in the middle of the night. Your local hardware store should have a variety of brass window-lock enclosures which you can install yourself.

If your home is an urban condominium or co-op, and is located on the first floor, you'll find that prospective buyers are more than usually concerned about security. If window grates or bars are an accepted approach in your area, consider placing them inside your windows and painting them the same color as your window frame so they call as little attention to themselves as possible.

Cast-iron grates can be expensive, but you can pick up Burglar Bars by Sterling for under $30 each. These are designed for the do-it-yourselfer and are quite easy to install. Women and older empty nesters are particularly concerned about security, so don't overlook precautions if your home seems vulnerable. Security problems can knock your house out of the running before the tour has ended, so they are well worth investment.

Ceilings

As long as the ceiling is in good condition, nothing more needs to be done.

Use the techniques we mentioned in previous chapters to fix cosmetic flaws. If you want to draw attention away from the ceilings and create a slightly more interesting atmosphere in the bedroom, try painting it blue. Because blue is the color of the sky as well as an appropriate bedroom color, this step may be considered proof of your creative sense of color instead of a cosmetic cover-up.

If your home does not have central air conditioning and your competition does, you might consider a ceiling fan. Keep the fan running when prospects tour your home.

Last, if you live in a condo or co-op and noise from those living above you is a constant problem, you may need to put sound-insulating tile on your ceiling. As discussed in Chapter 5, one product available for this is Gold Bond Decorator ceiling tile from Gold Bond Building Products of Charlotte, North Carolina.

Floors

Because a feeling of warmth and coziness is often expressed as the most desirable environment for a bedroom, carpeting is the favorite floor covering. Whether you have wall-to-wall carpet, hardwood floors, or a combination of the two, make sure the floor looks its best.

Carpet

Unless the carpet is brand new, shampoo it yourself or have it done professionally, whether it looks dirty or not. Carpets retain smells, and a thorough cleaning will eliminate them. Cleaning will also make the carpet look newer.

When you clean the carpet, don't forget the closet and the area under the bed, where dust or dirt often accumulates.

Hardwood Floors

Follow our advice in Chapter 10 about sprucing up tired hardwood floors. They can be a major visual influence in the bedroom and should look their best.

Appearance aside, the biggest problem created by hardwood floors in bedrooms is noise. Sounds will echo in the room and, if the house or condo happens to be noisy in general, hard surfaces only make this problem worse. We strongly advise an area rug and, if sound is a real problem, use an extra thick pad. You might be able to borrow one from friends, so you don't have to buy them.

Other floor sounds can also be very damaging to a sale. If you live in a condo or co-op, you may find that noise sometimes travels through heating and cooling ducts that lead to your floor or the base of the wall. Vibrations of sound that aren't damped travel easily through metal. You can muffle the noise by unscrewing the grate cover and gluing neoprene-covered insulation inside the duct, as far down as your arms can reach. Your local hardware store should carry this product.

Lighting

Natural light is always best, of course, but not all homes are blessed with sufficient sunlight. You can make artificial light in the bedroom dramatic and seductive but functional at the same time. Whether in their early twenties or late seventies, all buyers like a little atmosphere in the bedroom.

General Lighting

Obviously, general lighting is somewhat less important in the bedroom than in other areas of the home. The most important rule is to make sure that whatever fixture you have is clean, bright, and attractive.

Task Lighting

Reading or applying makeup requires specific lighting. There are a wide range of lighting options, including wall-mounted swing lamps that can be placed at the head of the bed or table lamps. If you buy lights for the purpose of marketing your bedroom, consider selecting only those fixtures that you can take with you when you sell your home.

If you want a more permanent look, consider a wall-mounted track light. When installed with a dimmer, these lights can be tremendously versatile.

Accent Lighting

Mood or accent lighting can highlight objects in your bedroom and set the right tone. Create a dramatic effect by placing portable can lights on the floor behind furniture — like bureaus or the headboard on your bed. Lights placed behind large floor plants will also create an interesting atmosphere.

This will, of course, only work if you are showing your home during the evening or there are dark corners in one or more of your bedrooms. Make sure all cords are carefully hidden.

Closets

How often have you wished you had more closet space in your bedroom? Chances are your buyer will ask the same question. Start by maximizing what you already have by weeding out any clothing and accessories you no longer need and donating them to your local Salvation Army or church. An uncluttered closet looks larger, and donated clothes provide welcome tax deductions.

Split-Level Storage

Once your closet has been cleaned out, try grouping all long items of clothing — dresses, coats, and suits — on one side and all shirts and skirts on the other side. Beneath the shorter clothes you may suddenly find enough space for a bureau or chest that was formerly sitting in the bedroom. This will give you added space in the bedroom. If you choose not to do this, use up the empty space by placing a second closet rod at a lower level. This will enable you to hang twice as many shirts, skirts, etc.

There is a product called Trapeze Bar from Closet King in New York City that serves the same purpose but does not require wall installation. It attaches to the closet bar that is already in your closet and hangs down like a trapeze about a yard lower. It costs about $20, for a 4-foot bar, can be taken with you when you move, and clearly demonstrates to the concerned buyer that there are creative ways to stretch limited closet space.

Purchasing stackable wire bins for storing smaller objects is an alternative to moving a dresser into the closet, and it will increase the utility of the space. You should invest in these only, however, if you can use them in your next home.

What happens if you feel that your closet is being used as efficiently as possible but you still do not have enough bedroom storage space? Fear not. There are storage areas in your bedroom just waiting to be discovered.

Corner Closets

For every corner of the bedroom, you have another potential closet. By building an enclosure with a door in a corner, thereby forming a triangular storage area, you can convert unused space into an ideal place for shelves that hold linens or other stackable items.

You can easily put up shelves along unused walls in your closet by installing the vinyl-coated wire systems available at many home-improvement stores. Sani-Shelf by Schulte is one such system and costs about $10 per 3-foot section. The beauty of the shelves is that you can take them with you when you sell the property.

Closet Doors

Take a good look at your closet doors and think of ways to upgrade them. This might simply mean replacing an old knob with one made of brass, porcelain, or cut glass, or installing a floor-to-ceiling mirror.

If you do need to replace a door, a new bi-fold louvered set will start at about $40. You should be able to install them yourself.

Eliminating Smells

Closets can become pungent because of the presence of laundry, footwear, or clothing that has been exposed to cigar or cigarette smoke. Buy one of the products designed to make closets smell fresher. Cedar Blocks from Eddie Bauer are perfect for creating a very desirable smell. They come in a set of twelve and cost $12.95.

Closets as Work Areas

If you have an especially large walk-in closet, you may be able to convert part of it into a small work area for sewing or putting on makeup. You might even have room for a small desk. Place a mirror above the area you have chosen and install some shelves alongside. By getting the most out of your closet, you can suggest how useful your bedroom truly is.

Furniture

The furniture in your bedroom should be dusted and wiped with either a lemon oil product or an aerosol spray like Endust. This will help make the room look better cared for and introduce a pleasant aroma.

The Bed

The bed is likely to be the dominant piece of furniture in the room. Make sure the comforter or bedspread is clean and attractive looking. Because what is covering your bed can be a major visual influence, don't take it for granted.

Take the bed covering to a dry cleaner if it is dirty or has absorbed odors from the room. If the cover is worn or the colors have faded, consider buying a new one that will help brighten up the whole room. Turning a matching sheet into curtains can complete the look.

If you only want to do one thing to enhance the appearance of your bedroom, investing in attractive bed linen is one of the easiest and least expensive ways to impress the buyer.

The Loft

A loft can significantly expand the usable area of a room and can provide an important selling tool. In studio condominiums or co-ops, a loft can make all the difference. And in children's rooms, it can turn a single bedroom into a double. You must have adequate ceiling height so that the loft is comfortable enough to sleep in and there is enough space beneath for practical use.

If a loft is to be constructed for an adult, allow about 6½ feet clearance beneath it, unless you are planning to have a desk area below, in which case 6 feet will be enough.

To construct a loft for a child, allow 5½ feet clearance beneath, but do so only if you must because of ceiling height limitations. Because you can never be certain who the buyer of your home will be, don't risk precluding a tall high-school student by building a loft that is too low.

Above the loft you will need a minimum of 4¼ feet, which will allow enough height for an average person to sit up. Constructing a loft is either a job for a pro or for an accomplished do-it-yourselfer. Remember, you can often do more harm by adding a feature that looks unprofessional than by not adding one at all. There is no middle ground.

If you feel up to the job, there is a helpful description of how to build a loft in *Your Bedrooms,* a book published by *Better Homes and Gardens.* Expect to spend about $1,500 if you hire a carpenter and less than half of that if you build the loft yourself. It is a very straightforward construction job that can add an entirely new dimension to a room.

In studio condominiums or co-ops, where the total space may not exceed 600 square feet, every inch counts, and a loft can be an excellent investment.

Concealing the Bed

In small condominium and co-op studios, the sight of a bed in the same room as the kitchen and living area can be unsettling. There are steps you can take to avoid this.

Start by considering a decorative wooden or fabric screen. The screen itself may become an attractive focal point; you might try placing a small furniture grouping in front of it.

A large shelf unit holding books, a television or stereo can be ideal for separating a bedroom from the rest of the space. And since you will be taking it with you when you leave, the wall unit won't be a selling expense.

If you want something more permanent, consider having a half-height wall constructed, just high and wide enough to conceal the bed from view from the entry. Mount shelves on the front of the wall and fill them with books or collectibles.

A wall made of translucent glass blocks is another consideration. It won't diminish light nor can it be seen through. Glass block is chic and should appeal to the sophisticated urban condo or co-op buyer. A wall 8 feet wide by 8 feet high will cost about $300.

Do-It-Yourself Improvements
under $100

1. Repaint the bedroom ($40).

2. Shampoo the carpet ($10).

3. Put out fresh-cut flowers ($5).

4. Suspend hanging plants ($20).

5. Put on a new bedspread ($50).

6. Use track lights ($100).

7. Install a mirror on the closet door ($75).

8. Install louvered window shutters ($75).

9. Use cedar-scented closet deodorizers ($5).

10. Install light dimmers ($8 each).

The Murphy Bed

This practical bed is making a big comeback in smaller living spaces. Murphy beds fold down from the wall when needed and fold back up into a vertical wall-mounted enclosure when sleep time is over.

Because a new one costs about $1,000, it's not an item that you will throw in lightly. But at a time when condo and co-op space in cities like Manhattan, San Francisco, Chicago, and Boston is selling at rates of $200 per square foot and more, an investment like this may open up a small unit to a broader segment of the buying market.

When you make an investment like this, make sure that you capitalize on it in your advertising, which we'll discuss in Chapter 17. Before purchasing a Murphy bed, ask yourself, "If the buyer doesn't want it included in the purchase price, can I use it in my next home?" If the answer is yes, you'll have all bases covered.

Special Groupings

A surefire way to make the bedroom stand out is to suggest several uses for it.

If you have covered a good-sized area of the wall with mirrors, you may have created an ideal backdrop for an exercise center. So if you already have an Exercycle, weights, a floor mat, jumprope, or other workout equipment, consider setting it up near the mirrored portion of the bedroom.

You can give your bedroom the feeling of a luxury suite by creating a separate conversation area. This can be done by placing two upholstered chairs in a corner of the room along with a small table. Some fresh flowers and glossy magazines on the table will complete the look.

A desk can also suggest that your bedroom doubles as a study. A set of bookshelves alongside will add the finishing touch.

Bureaus and Night Tables

As is often the case, the tops of these pieces become cluttered with small personal objects ranging from prescription medicines to creams and hairclips. Remove any items that could be considered too personal so as to avoid "marking" the room.

SPECIAL TOUCHES

Details can add to the utility and the luxury of your bedrooms at very little expense.

Conveniences

Empty-nesters appreciate special conveniences, and other buyers looking for extra luxury features will be especially attracted to wall-mounted telephones, dimmer switches, and shelf-mounted radios. If you can create the feeling that the bed is the command center of the room without going to great expense, do it.

Plants and Flowers

Large floor plants, hanging plants, or fresh flowers can make the room come alive. Plants add color and fresh scents to a room and can generally brighten up a dull bedroom, especially in winter.

CREATING AN EXTRA BEDROOM

As mentioned at the outset of the chapter, adding an extra bedroom or guestroom to a home can increase its value and speed up the sale of your home because your property will appeal to a larger segment of the market.

I do not recommend starting from scratch by building an addition onto your home, because the new construction costs are unlikely to yield much of a return. But if you're able to create a new bedroom by altering an underutilized area of your home, this may prove to be one of your best home-improvement investments.

How do you know how much an extra bedroom will yield on your resale, and how much you should spend to create an extra bedroom? As a general rule, the fewer bedrooms you have, the more you'll get out of adding an extra bedroom. A one-bedroom home or condo that gains a second bedroom will benefit much more than a five-bedroom home that gains a sixth. If it costs you the equivalent of 3 or 4 percent of your sale price to add an extra bedroom, which will enable you to attract a much broader market, my experience shows that the return is worth the cost. Most probably you can raise your asking price because your home will now be compared to more expensive properties.

Consider the economics of this for a minute. If new construction costs $75 per square foot and you are able to turn a 150- to 200-square foot area of your home into usable space at a cost of $3,000, you will have spent between $15 and $20 per square foot. This can clearly be a bargain.

To be sure, also get opinions from your real estate broker. Tell him or her what you are thinking of doing and ask how it would affect the marketability of your home. You may want to get several opinions on this, since you have so much at stake.

Where to Begin

First look for oversized or underutilized areas of your home. If you find one that can be converted into an additional bedroom, be careful that you are not doing this at the expense of another room.

I have seen, for example, large walk-in closets successfully expanded into small bedrooms that are ideal for an occasional guest. If erecting a single wall and installing a door will create a new room, then you will have discovered a hidden asset in your home. Even if you hire a contractor, you may be able to do this for under $1,000.

If creating an extra bedroom isn't simply a matter of adding a wall, consider what your other rooms have to offer. Although you may need to hire a professional, it may well be that a few pieces of bedroom furniture will do the trick.

The Den

Here's a room that can easily double as a guestroom with the addition of some bedroom furniture. If you don't have a sleeper couch in the den, consider setting a twin-size box spring mattress directly on the floor to create the look of a sofa bed. Position the sofa bed against a wall, use upholstered pillows for back support, and choose some colorful fitted sheets.

If you have a closet at least 2 feet deep and 4 feet wide, consider concealing a Murphy bed in it.

The Basement

This area of the home, as you'll read in Chapter 14, can provide an appropriate setting for an extra bedroom. The cost and practicality of doing this can vary, depending upon the condition and layout of your basement. If it's a finished basement, the job can be as simple as putting up a wall or sprucing up an existing room. If it's unfinished, however, you may need to add extra insulation, plumbing ductwork, and electrical service.

If you can add a bedroom by spending two or three thousand dollars, it's very likely to be a worthwhile investment. Keep in mind that unless your basement is substantially above grade and has a view outside, the value of a basement bedroom will be lower than the value of a bedroom on the first or second floor.

The Attic

Because the attic is above ground, converting it into a nicely finished room can carry significant weight at the time of resale.

If your attic is already finished, simply consider the cosmetic appearance of the room and the insulation. The ceiling should have 6 to 12 inches of fiberglass batting, especially if you live in the Snowbelt.

An operable skylight may also be necessary, because attics can get extremely hot and often are poorly ventilated. The cost and installation of a small skylight starts at about $300 and can go much higher.

If your attic is completely unfinished, you are looking at a more difficult issue. Have an engineer determine if the floor is strong enough to hold the additional weight of a furnished room and if there is enough ceiling clearance. You must then determine the expense of running heating, electrical, and plumbing systems up to the attic, as well as building an acceptable stairway.

If the cost exceeds 4 percent of your likely sale price, make sure your broker feels the market will reward you sufficiently for the major risk you are considering taking. The cosmetic conversion of an already upgraded attic is a better investment, because it will yield a much higher return.

The Porch

Converting a porch or sunroom into an extra bedroom can be a rewarding investment, especially if you already have a deck or patio. But, depending upon how substantial the existing structure is, it can also be a major job.

If your porch or sunroom is a simple framed area with screens, it will involve new construction. But if there are wiring and windows in place and there's reasonable access to heat, you may find the conversion feasible.

If the cost does not exceed 3 to 4 percent of your likely selling price, and you have thoroughly investigated this option, there is no reason not to proceed. But make absolutely sure that you are not robbing Peter to pay Paul by eliminating one desirable feature of your home just to replace it with another one.

CONCLUSION

The two most important points about bedrooms are how attractive they look and how many you have.

By taking steps to make up for limited closet space, compensate for a tired carpet, or increase the perception of size of a small bedroom, you will certainly make your bedrooms more salable.

The most significant improvement is to add an extra bedroom. By doing so, you can broaden the market to which your home will appeal and increase the price you will receive at the time of sale.

This can be particularly effective in condos and co-ops, where the additional cost of buying units with three bedrooms rather than two can be considerable.

CHAPTER HIGHLIGHTS

1. The number of bedrooms in a home can be a major determinant of its selling price and market appeal.

2. Creating an extra bedroom can be among the best home-improvement investments.

3. The bedroom can be the most personal room in the house, so special efforts must be made to eliminate sources of territorial anxiety.

4. The size of the bedroom is a major buyer concern.

5. Quantity of closet space is considered very important, especially among female buyers.

6. In studio condos and co-ops, creating a separate or defined sleeping area will add to the appeal of the unit.

7. Privacy and quiet are important in the bedroom and can be of particular concern in condos and co-ops.

8. Neutrality in color and design are essential in the bedroom.

13

Rooms to Relax in: Family Rooms and Dens

The family room and den can be the most enjoyable and utilized living areas of the home because it is here we kick off our shoes and relax. The more comfortable and relaxing these areas are, the more marketable they can be.

Because the look and design of family rooms and dens tend to vary widely from home to home, we will provide a more general marketing approach than would be appropriate for the kitchen, for example. But, as always, creating the right overall impression and targeting the rooms to the right market are essential.

THE FIVE-STEP SYSTEM
Step 1. Consider the Competition

Knowing what the competition is offering in family rooms and dens may help you determine what to focus on. But, because these rooms can vary so much from one home to another, direct comparisons may be difficult. In any case, keep your eyes open for especially attractive features or ideas that you may be able to apply to your home.

Step 2. Consider the Buyer

Different segments of the market have their own specific wants and needs with respect to family rooms and dens. By understanding these differences you can more efficiently allocate your improvement dollars.

First-Time Buyers

Many newly built starter homes don't have separate family rooms or dens. This space is often incorporated into a larger "great room" or may even be part of the living room. In the latter case, converting part of the room into a den or family room can make your home more appealing. You can do this with furniture groupings that suggest specific functions of the room. A desk, along with a reading lamp and file cabinets, will help the buyer visualize where, for example, a workplace might fit.

Trade-up Buyers

Let's start with the family room aspect, since trade-up buyers are likely to have children. This room should suggest comfort and suitability for family activities. Displaying leisure products, like a family board game or a stereo system, for example, can help convey this feeling. Showing the family room in use can help the buyer visualize the enjoyment of this area of your home.

The den may also have a special appeal to this group. Because so many trade-up buyers are career-oriented professionals, suggesting the use of the den as an office or study can provide an effective marketing tool. Home entertainment is another aspect of the den that can excite this segment of the market, and showing the possibilities your den holds as a home entertainment center will make it more appealing.

Empty Nesters/Trade-down Buyers

Since many empty nesters are retirees, a den that serves as a study, library, or quiet refuge for hobbies can help the buyer visualize what this room can be.

There is also another element that can make the den appealing to this market segment. According to Joan McClosky, building and remodeling editor for *Better Homes and Gardens*, "Among older buyers, who tend to spend more time in the home than other homeowners, the den can be seen as a man's refuge. The woman often lays claim to the kitchen but male buyers also respond to private space in the home."

The family room can also have special importance to the empty nester because of the casual life-style this group often adopts. Older buyers tend to do less formal entertaining than trade-up buyers, for example, and spend far more time relaxing at home. We'll show you how to make this room more appropriate for this purpose.

Step 3. Evaluate Your Product

Because dens and family rooms are so central to everyday life in the home, they can often look as if they have taken some abuse.

Adults are likely to be more casual about eating, drinking, and smoking here, and children tend to equate these rooms with indoor playgrounds. Ask your focus groups for their opinion on whether your den or family room looks worn, and then take the necessary steps to remedy any problem.

Step 4. Eliminate Territorial Anxiety

The sight of overstuffed pillows, warm colors, and a roaring fire in a fireplace can make a family room look like a three-dimensional greeting card. But a room that looks untidy, smells of cigarette smoke or yesterday's potato chips, or is filled with the sounds of a blaring television set can make it difficult for the buyer to visualize it as his or her own.

Your goal is to enable an outsider to picture him- or herself in the room alone or with the family. We'll show you how to keep personal statements from blocking the buyer's imagination.

Step 5. Maximize Packaging Appeal

Selling fun, comfort, and relaxation is your main objective in packaging the family room and den.

We'll suggest ways to give your den the aura of a high-tech center, for example, through various lighting, color, and decorating ideas, and how to determine if it makes sense to transform a family room into a "great room." We'll also show you how to eliminate common mistakes that can reduce the appeal of these rooms.

To maximize the packaging appeal, you'll want to assure that the quality of the room shines through.

THE FAMILY ROOM

This is a room that shouldn't take itself too seriously. It's a place for buyers to imagine themselves chatting with friends, playing with the kids, or watching a feature movie on TV. But it should also reflect the same kind of care and attention to detail that is present in the rest of your home.

Showing a family room that's too formal can detract from this message. In other words, there's nothing wrong with having Trivial Pursuit or another board game set up on the table, a bowl of Hershey Kisses sitting out for guests, or a pair of tennis rackets waiting for some action.

The Walls

As is the case in the other rooms of your home, the walls of your family room should be in good condition, and neutrality should be the underlying design theme. Personal color statements demonstrating the warmth of the room can be effective selling tools when limited to accent features.

Paint

It's best if this room sports beiges, antique whites, and light pastels. If the walls look at all faded or are in need of touch-up, repainting is advisable.

As previously discussed, a good test to determine the condition of your paint is to remove a picture that has been hanging on the wall for some time. If by stepping back, you notice that the area behind the picture is much brighter and cleaner than the walls around it, it's time to pull out the paint roller.

If painting isn't necessary or possible, make sure there are no fingermarks or assorted stains on the walls and around light switchplates. Fantastik spray from Texize is a good all-purpose cleaner.

Woodwork

It's very common for family rooms to have natural or stained wood paneling or accent trim. Wood can add to the warmth and coziness of a room and give it the kind of feeling many buyers are looking for. But there are some considerations you should be aware of if your room is paneled or has wood features.

If the wood has dried out and needs some life brought back to it, go over it with a lemon oil or a wood restorer. A product called Watco wood preservative can be particularly helpful if there are scratches, because it comes in different tints to match your wood. You can also use touch-up sticks, like Scratch Fix, by K. J. Miller Corporation.

If your paneling is curving away from the wall, secure it with color-coordinated nails, available from home-improvement centers and hardware stores.

Some wood paneling is considered out of fashion and can hurt the perceived value of a room. If your wood paneling happens to be the thin sheet variety with vertical grooves, for example, it may diminish the feeling of quality and substance in the room. This paneling may be fine for a basement, but in areas like family rooms and dens, it looks too inexpensive and is often too dark in color.

One alternative is to cover up the paneling with wallpaper. By filling the grooves and surface imperfections with spackle, you can create an even surface. First sand down all the areas to be spackled, and also give a light sanding to the wood itself so the wallpaper paste will adhere better.

I don't recommend painting over dark paneling because it gives the look of an inexpensive "quick fix." You're better off leaving it alone and making the most out of what you have.

Opening Up Walls

Taking down a wall or making other modifications can increase the impression of size of the house or condo in general.

For example, if your family room abuts the kitchen, consider creating a pass-through in a wall, similar to that discussed in Chapter 9. This pass-through will make the room seem larger and add convenience at the same time. And because snacks are so often eaten in the family room, consider a small eat-in counter beneath the opening.

If your family room is especially small and is adjacent to a small den or living room, you might consider taking down the wall dividing the rooms and creating one large "great room." Before undertaking this, however, ask a contractor or an architect to make sure you are not removing a load-bearing wall.

The Windows

You'll want the family room to be as bright as possible, so make sure the windows are spotless and there is nothing blocking the view. Curtains and drapes can add warmth to the room but are not essential, since they can also make rooms seem smaller by breaking up large wall expanses.

The Floor

Because this room often gets so much wear and tear, make sure carpets and hardwood floors look their best. Clean the carpets — if necessary call in a professional — or, if you have hardwood floors, consider a fresh coat of polyurethane. Chapter 8 discusses floor improvements in detail.

The Ceiling

If you have a conventional ceiling, be sure that it's free of cobwebs, dirt, water stains, and anything else that can cause concern.

If your family room has a special ceiling like a cathedral or beamed ceiling, take steps to highlight it.

Cathedral ceilings can have significant appeal because of the drama and feeling of spaciousness they add to a room. You can highlight this feature by using hanging plants to draw attention to the design. You might also consider installing track or spot lighting.

If your competition has central air conditioning and your home doesn't, a ceiling fan can be very effective against a cathedral-style ceiling.

Beamed ceilings need oil applied to them to look their best. If you have artificial beams — like molded plastic or Styrofoam — seriously consider either removing them or replacing them with the real thing. People today are looking for quality, so features that look temporary or lack substance can actually diminish the value of your property.

Lighting

Use artificial light to add warmth and coziness to a room. Even in daylight, warm artificial light that bathes your family room can make it look more inviting.

In addition to general lighting for the entire room, spot lighting can

Do-It-Yourself Improvements
under $100

1. Expose the brick behind a plaster wall or apply brick facing ($75).

2. Paper over old paneling ($70).

3. Place fresh logs in and alongside the fireplace ($5).

4. Hang colorful prints on family room walls ($30 each).

5. Place chair-rail molding in a den ($40).

help highlight particular areas. Track lights, for example, can draw attention to a fireplace, wall hanging, or other focal point in the room.

The Furniture

Your furniture should suggest comfort. If your current furnishings are stark, consider adding colorful overstuffed pillows. I've seen hammocks used effectively in family rooms, so if you have one in the backyard and feel it would have more impact indoors, bring it in.

Plants

Tall floor plants, hanging plants, or potted flowering plants can all add color and life to the family room. They also help freshen the air.

The Fireplace

A fireplace in the family room can have the same impact as a fireplace in the living room.

If you have a fireplace, make sure the fireplace screen and tools are clean — if you don't have any, perhaps you can borrow some — and you have logs in the grate. If it's appropriate to light the fire when buyers tour your home, all the better.

THE DEN

The den is often associated with richly paneled walls, impressive collections of books, and oversized rolltop desks. In today's high-tech world, though, it could also be conceived as a sophisticated entertainment center.

We'll cover the basic components of the den to establish the right look and impression of this room. Consider the buyer when making any of these improvements, because different groups have different ideas of what a den should be.

Walls

The walls can set the overall tone for a den. While neutrality is still the rule, you may need to be a little more expressive in the den to create the right atmosphere.

Paint

If you want to make the den into a study, consider darker shades of tan or beige. Dark green with natural-color wood trim or offset by wooden furniture will also look attractive. Be careful not to make a small den look claustrophobic by using dark colors that make the walls appear to close in. One thought might be to paint only one or two walls a dark color, and the other walls white. Using white trim on molding and around windows will also help.

If your goal is to give the den a high-tech look, choose high-tech color combinations. Gray walls with accents of maroon and white are considered chic, as are mauve, taupe, or dusty rose.

Exposed Brick

The look of exposed brick can be appealing to younger buyers and can create an attractive focal point in a room. If you live in an old brick townhouse or condominium unit, you can create this sought-after look by stripping the plaster off a wall.

But before you seriously consider doing this, there are several considerations. It's best, for example, to select a wall that abuts another building. Plaster acts as an insulator, and a wall that is exposed to extreme cold may make your room uncomfortable.

You'll want to work on only a small section to make sure the brick is attractive. You might find that low-grade brick has been used or that the wall has been patched. You will want to see what it looks like before going any further.

Because exposing brick is a messy job, you'll need to prepare for it carefully so the whole room does not get covered with a layer of plaster dust.

To remove plaster, put on protective goggles so the plaster will not get in your eyes, and consider a mask so you inhale as little dust as possible. Then simply take a hammer and chisel, and start chipping away.

Once you've exposed the brick, wipe it down with water and use a diluted muriatic acid solution to get it as clean as possible. Don't use polyurethane, because it will yellow and look unnatural.

If you feel the look of exposed brick would greatly enhance the look of your den, or if you have a wall that is in need of a cover-up, consider a high-quality brick facing.

There is a product called Real Brick by U.S. Brick that is about ½ inch thick and is real clay-fired brick. This type of product is preferable to simulated brick, which can often look unnatural. More important, you can install it yourself, and a wall 8 feet high by 12 feet long will cost about $200.

Windows

The style of window cover-ups or accents you select depends upon the theme of your den.

If you want to create a sleek, high-tech atmosphere, Levolor-style blinds can be ideal. They have a crisp, low-profile look and are available in a wide range of colors to match your decor. For a more sedate look, try installing wooden louvered shutters and staining them a medium shade of brown.

Floor

A clean-looking carpet or a well-maintained hardwood floor is as important in this room as in any other. If you want to suggest studiousness, an oriental rug can make the right kind of statement. If you don't have one or prefer to leave it in a more crucial room like the entry, consider borrowing one from a friend.

Ceiling

The same rules discussed for the family room apply here. Keep it as pristine as possible and make sure the molding or beams are in top condition and are not simulations.

Lighting

Lighting should serve two functions in the den. It should create a certain mood, and the fixtures should reinforce the theme of the room.

For a more studious look, use soft general lighting, with perhaps a desk lamp as an accent. To create a high-tech look, focus a track light on a stereo or video system. A track light aimed at an exposed brick wall will also add drama to the room. If you do install a track, make sure you put in a dimmer switch to complete the effect.

Furniture

The starting point for making the most of whatever you have is to make sure everything is dust-free and crisp looking. Endust or lemon oil will add a fresh smell and give a new luster to your furniture.

If you happen to have an ample array of home entertainment systems or a home computer, treat them as you would your best furniture because they can help make the kind of statement many home buyers seek. Place your stereo speakers in a prominent position, and make sure to open any built-in cabinets that may otherwise hide a video-cassette machine, audio-cassette desk, or laser disk player.

The Office Look

Because many people use the den as an office, creating a distinct working space here will increase the perception of utility. A wall-mounted task light will help define the space, as will mounted shelves above a desk. Using furniture — bookcases or file cabinets — to segregate the "office" from the rest of the den will also be effective.

If you have a computer that you do not actively use, place it on a desk and make it look like an integral part of your room. Have printouts, for example, sitting by the machine.

Shelves and Closets

Built-in shelves in a den are a feature which buyers respond to. If you already have these in your den, keep them uncluttered and well organized.

The same holds true for closets. Go through them mercilessly and throw out or give away whatever you are no longer using. If there is anything you want to keep, store it neatly in the basement.

Don't treat closets as depositories because the buyer will invariably stick his or her head in and discover the truth.

Dual Usage

The den can prove an ideal spot for an extra bedroom. As discussed in Chapter 12, pointing out to a prospect that, for example, you have a pull-out sofa will help him recognize the room's versatility.

Finishing Touches

The den provides opportunities to make subtle life-style statements that the buyer will want to see.

If you have a collection of leather-bound law books, classic novels, or an encyclopedia, make sure these volumes are in plain view. The same goes for upscale magazines like *Connoisseur, The Robb Report,* or *The Harvard Business Review.* Put a bookmark in them to make books or magazines look as though they are being read rather than just out for show.

A bottle of expensive brandy or a decanter and an attractive glass sitting on a desk will add an air of distinction.

If you have a collection of interesting pipes, antique collectibles like cameras, clocks, or art objects, make sure they can be seen.

Signs of participation in sports like horseback riding, sailing, or squash can be impressive, so dust off any photographs or trophies you may have.

CONCLUSION

The family room and den should not be taken too seriously, but should reflect fun and relaxation. Improvements that reinforce this impression will make dens and family rooms more appealing to the buyer.

The family room and den are not the only places in the home that are primarily recreational, however. The deck and patio also exist for this purpose and, in the next chapter, we will show you how to make the most of them when marketing your home.

CHAPTER HIGHLIGHTS

1. The family room and den should suggest comfort and relaxation.

2. Make sure the wear and tear often seen in family rooms do not show.

3. A home entertainment center in either the den or family room should serve as a focal point.

4. The fireplace, if you have one, should be the focal point of the room.

5. The den can have special appeal to the man in the house because it can represent his personal space.

6. The den as an office, library, or study can be of particular interest to professional trade-up buyers and retirees.

14

Delightful Decks and Patios

The concept of treating outdoor space as an extension of the interior of a home is becoming increasingly popular, and many developers are incorporating decks and patios into new homes. Decks and patios located off sliding glass windows or rear-entrance doors can make a home seem more expansive and provide more living area.

Although this appreciation for outdoor living space is strongest in younger buyers, it cuts across all groups in all parts of the country. Outdoor decks, which were once regarded as a trademark of California living, are now popular just about everywhere. A survey by *Builder* magazine confirms that 64 percent of those seeking luxury features in a home want a deck.

Patios, while not quite as trendy as decks, are also experiencing renewed popularity and are now being thought of as landscape architecture that can transform a dull yard into something special.

We'll show you ways to enhance the appeal of a deck or patio, if you already have one, or the circumstances under which you might consider building one for your house or condo.

THE FIVE-STEP SYSTEM
Step 1. Consider the Competition

Once again, it will pay you to examine what the competition is offering. If the major difference between your home and the competition's is a deck, for example, and brokers agree that this will make the other home far more marketable, the installation of a deck might be a worthwhile investment.

Although a deck can set two properties apart, the expense of adding one could be less than you think. And if the cost of a deck is too high, a less expensive patio might be a consideration.

Step 2. Consider the Buyer

While decks and patios have the greatest appeal among young, affluent trade-up buyers, they do score points among all categories of buyers.

First-Time Buyers

All buyers appreciate more living space, but to the first-time buyer, who may have limited finances, decks or patios not only provide extra space but add something special to a starter home.

Trade-up Buyers

While basement recreation rooms were popular with the previous generation of trade-up buyers, outdoor space is what today's generation is looking for.

One primary reason for this change is that today's young people have a renewed interest in the outdoors that they like to reflect in their homes. Why spend time underground when you can bask in the sun?

Because the size of a home can mean status to the trade-up buyer, the deck or patio can make it seem more impressive. And the larger it seems, the more likely you'll be to receive the premium price you will have assigned to your property.

Last, the trade-up buyer considers entertainment to be an important use for a home, and the deck or patio opens up new entertainment possibilities. We'll show you how to point these out to the buyer when you are ready to show your home.

Empty Nesters/Trade-down Buyers

The deck or patio can fit the special needs of this group in several ways. Relaxation, to the empty nester, is of prime importance, and the ability to enjoy it outdoors is a big plus.

Research has also shown that one of the reasons empty nesters move is to avoid the maintenance that the large backyards of their former homes involved. Decks or patios can be the perfect compromise because like first-time buyers, trade-down purchasers appreciate as much space as possible, as long as it's not expensive to buy or keep up.

Step 3. Evaluate Your Product

If you don't have a deck or patio, your focus groups should help you determine how much more attractive your home might be if one or the other were included. This is a very important issue that you'll want to put to as many brokers as possible.

If you do have a deck or patio, your focus groups can indicate what's right and wrong with it, as well as what you might do to improve it.

Step 4. Eliminate Territorial Anxiety

Outdoor space is less likely to contain personal statements than interior areas of your home. The basics of cleanliness and order always apply but, by and large, territorial anxiety in this part of the home isn't a concern.

Step 5. Maximize Packaging Appeal

One of the beauties of decks and patios from a packaging standpoint is that they're relatively inexpensive to construct, yet they can significantly increase the perceived value of your home, set it apart from the competition, and create an attractive focal point, all at once.

We'll cover ways to make the deck or patio an integral part of your home and add value to it. These include making the existing deck look newer and using furniture to suggest the usefulness and enjoyment of the space. We'll also offer ideas to achieve the Common-Area Upgrade Multiplier Effect for condominiums and cooperatives.

HOW TO APPROACH DECKS AND PATIOS

Because decks and patios add more living space to a home, they need to be designed to work as an extension of the home itself. Ideally, they should be placed directly off interior living areas of the home.

By showing the deck or patio with chairs, chaises longues, or even serving tables with food on them, you'll emphasize the potential of these areas and make a compelling life-style statement about your home. A deck or patio doesn't have to be elaborate to create this feeling.

You simply want to suggest how this feature can add a new dimension to your home. If the buyer can visualize that, he or she can also visualize expanding the deck or patio at some later point.

Decks in Condos and Co-Ops

The installation of a deck along some exterior point of a condo and co-op can be a particularly rewarding investment. Because these types of home are often sold on a cost-per-square-foot basis, the deck may be assigned a much higher value than it would in a detached, single-family home.

I once converted a deck from a fire-escape platform, made obsolete by the installation of a new fire egress in another area of the building. Since the interior living space of the unit had a market value of over $175 per square foot, the addition of an extra 75 feet at a total cost of $400 was a tremendous bargain.

Of course, I didn't expect to receive the same value on the deck as on the interior space, but my experience has shown that decks yield far more than their construction cost.

Some developers include the deck in the measurement of the unit, but this is unfair. The deck will, however, increase the overall value of the unit, and the smaller the condo or co-op is, the more relative impact the addition of a deck will have.

We'll discuss decks and patios separately and provide some basic ideas on how to get the most out of them.

THE DECK

Decks can range from small areas built atop a roof of an urban co-op to a sprawling, multitiered platform off the den of a suburban ranch house. Whether you already have a deck or decide to install one, there are many ways to package it. We'll start with the basics and build up from there.

The Deck Surface

Decks can be constructed from a variety of woods. Redwood and cedar are probably the most desirable because of their combination of good looks, decay resistance, and strength. But they are also the most expensive, running about 50 cents a board foot. Less expensive choices include spruce, hemlock, and Douglas fir, which cost about 30 cents a board foot.

No matter what kind of surface you already have or select, the deck should look well maintained. Remove bird dropping stains with light sandpaper and replace any split boards that are plainly visible.

If it's been more than three years since you last stained your deck, consider staining it again. This will give it a fresh, new look and minimize any surface imperfections which occur over time. Try to use the same color and brand as before so you don't get any surprises as a result of combining two different mixtures.

If you're staining for the first time, keep the wood looking as natural as possible. Heavy staining that masks the grain can defeat the purpose of having an outdoor look. Semitransparent stains, by companies like Olympic Stain or Cabot Stain, will tint the wood enough to give it character yet keep it natural looking at the same time.

If you have installed a new deck that doesn't have pressure-treated wood, prime it with pentachlorophenol preservative first. Wait several weeks before staining so the wood fully dries out.

I do not recommend painting a deck because this robs the wood of character and also suggests the need for frequent maintenance. If your deck is already painted, then apply a fresh coat if needed, but otherwise you're best off keeping it the way nature intended.

Design Basics

The great variety of deck and patio styles available to you are beyond the scope of this book. We'll confine our discussion to basic ideas on how decks and patios are best used as a resale tool. This means spending as little as possible to generate the highest return on investment. There is definitely a point of diminishing returns on improvements like this so when in doubt, keep it simple.

Once you understand this, there is an excellent, inexpensive book by Ortho Books, *How to Design & Build Decks and Patios,* that offers a broad range of ideas on building decks yourself.

Deck Locations

The deck should be as much a part of the home as possible, so actually attaching it to the house's structure is obviously the best way to go. If for some reason you cannot locate it right next to the home, consider building a small bridge or walkway to the main body of the deck.

Also make sure your deck is situated so that it gets the sun. If the home itself blocks the sun or the area is covered with heavy shade trees, the deck's usefulness may be limited. There's a significant difference in temperature and mood in sun-soaked areas and those cast in shadow.

If you're lucky enough to have sliding glass doors off a living room or a den, they can add even more value because they will increase the viewer's perception of size of one of the most important rooms of the home.

If possible, position the deck so that it takes advantage of attractive views and doesn't look onto those sights you would prefer to avoid. (We'll show you later how to screen unpleasant views.)

Deck Patterns

When constructing a deck, you have alternatives to simple parallel plank patterns. To create more interest and a more expensive look, consider a herringbone or parquet pattern.

If you're building the deck yourself, these patterns will take more time but cost little or no additional money. Hiring a professional will boost the price.

Railing

Railings serve several functions. First and foremost is safety, especially if there is a drop from the deck to the ground. If the home is likely to contain children or empty nesters, some sort of rail is essential.

If your deck can be easily seen by others, a railing can help to create a feeling of privacy. It can also be used to obscure unattractive views.

Do-It-Yourself Improvements
under $100

1. Restain an existing deck ($30).

2. Buy potted plants ($30).

3. Install a hammock ($75).

4. Plant flowers around the patio ($25).

5. Install an outdoor spotlight ($50).

Latticework can provide an ideal screen without giving the deck a closed-in feeling. If you need more privacy, canvas duck cloth might do the trick. You can also make the railing double as a bench. This alternative requires more construction and added expense but will also increase the deck's perceived value and usefulness.

Plantings

Plants can be an excellent addition to the deck because they add color and make the area more comfortable and inviting, yet are relatively inexpensive.

We recommend using potted plants like geraniums or hanging baskets of fuchsia, as you can take them with you when you sell your property. It's hard to go wrong with attractive plants, so feel free to use them abundantly. They also provide another ideal way of blocking an unpleasant view.

Furniture

Furniture will let buyers know whether your deck is there for show or is really a useful area of your home, so if you have attractive lawn furniture and the weather permits, set it up to suggest that you use the deck as much as possible. A table with a bowl of fresh fruit or a pitcher of iced tea will help make this point.

When you bring serious, qualified prospects outside, invite them to sit down and share refreshment with you. Giving them a chance to pause on the deck should create a lasting and positive effect in their minds.

If you have any furniture that suggests relaxation—a set of large overstuffed pillows, a beanbag chair, or, especially, a hammock—make sure they are in place. All furniture should be clean and in good condition. If it isn't, consider borrowing some from your friends. Shabby-looking lawn furniture will detract from the appeal of your deck.

Special Features

There are some added touches to the deck that are not essential, but will certainly set it apart from the crowd and appeal particularly to the trade-up buyer.

Telephone

If you have a cordless remote phone or can discreetly place a regular phone on the deck, you'll reinforce the practicality of this area. A few upscale magazines like *Town and Country* or *Architectural Digest* alongside the phone will suggest the sort of life-style that some people may be striving for.

Grill

A grill, preferably gas, will call to mind enjoyable gatherings. We don't recommend cooking a steak at the time of the tour because the smell can filter into the home and become a distraction, but leaving the grill cover up or having utensils out can suggest that the grill is used often.

Bar

If you have a portable cart on wheels, you can create the feeling of a bar by having the cart stocked with your favorite libations. This should be out only on weekends or late in the day so the buyer doesn't get the wrong idea about your living habits.

Music

Indoors is not the only place for music. If it's a warm, sunny afternoon and you have a quality FM radio or cassette machine, a little background music targeted toward your particular buyer may add the final touch to your deck. Chapter 5, which discusses sound, will help you determine which music is most appropriate for your market.

THE C.U.M.E. EFFECT

The deck can provide an ideal opportunity for the Common-Area Upgrade Multiplier Effect you can achieve in condominiums and co-operatives. Patios don't have the same level of appeal in this setting as decks do, so we'll confine our discussion to decks.

In urban condominiums or co-ops, where outdoor space can range from rare to unheard-of, deck space can add significant value to each unit in the building. Some buyers simply will not purchase a co-op if it has no roof deck, yet the cost to each unit owner can be negligible.

Of course, the nature of your building will determine the cost, feasibility, and appeal of a deck. Many buildings have flat roofs that are empty. If there is a central staircase leading to the rooftop or an elevator leading to a top-floor lobby, chances are that everyone can have access to the space.

If your roof can withstand the load of a deck and the people on it, the deck can be an excellent investment. And the larger your building is, the lower the cost per unit.

A 20- by 20-foot rooftop deck might run to $5,000, but if divided among 20 units in the building, it will cost $250 per unit. This small charge can add a feature to each unit that could ultimately influence the outcome of a sale.

If the roof is not an option, look for other areas around the property where a common-area deck can have a multiplier effect on all the units in your building or complex.

PATIOS

Like decks, patios can come in just about any size, material, and layout imaginable. They can range from small gravel-covered areas to expansive combinations of stone and wood.

What often comes to mind when you think of a patio is the conventional concrete slab that sits outside the back entrance to a house. I do not recommend installing this kind if you're starting from scratch. There are simply too many more interesting approaches available that will increase the perceived value of your home and help make it more marketable.

Some of these alternatives can be expensive and even exceed the cost of a deck. Therefore, we'll limit our discussion to ideas that require the least investment and yield the highest return.

As with decks, your patio should be an extension of the living area of the home. Locate it off the main entrance to the rear or side of your home.

The Basics

If you already have a patio, make sure it looks well kept and has no weeds growing through it. Cracked concrete or brick areas should be repaired or replaced. Stains from fruit trees or bird droppings should be removed with muriatic acid.

Signs of work in the back area of your home should not be visible. Remove clotheslines, trash cans, lawnmowers, and garden tools. Garden hoses should be neatly coiled up. The yard should suggest relaxation. Anything to the contrary won't make the right life-style statement.

Materials

The almost limitless range of materials you can use to create a patio can range from flagstone to tile pavers to simple gravel.

Brick

Each material has its own advantages and disadvantages, but I find brick comes out on top. It combines moderate cost with high perceived value and complements homes that range in style from period to postmodern. You can also put down brick on your own, and it comes in a wide range of colors, shapes, and sizes.

Laying brick in sand is the easiest and least expensive installation method. Simply select the area you plan to cover, remove all grass and weeds, and level it out while removing enough soil to make the brick flush with the area surrounding it.

Cover the soil with perforated black polyethylene to inhibit weeds from growing through. Then cover the polyethylene with 2 to 3 inches of sand and dampen with the mist spray from your garden hose. Starting from one corner, lay the bricks in rows, and force them into the sand. Occasionally place a large board on top of the bricks to assure a uniform height. When you're finished, sprinkle dry sand on them and sweep the surface with a broom, so that the sand acts as grout.

For a more detailed explanation, you could refer to *How to Design and Build Decks & Patios*. To find a brick supplier, look under "Brick" in your Yellow Pages.

Gravel

Gravel doesn't have the substantial feeling and the value of brick but because gravel is less expensive, you can afford to cover a wider area.

If time is an issue, you can put down a simple gravel patio very quickly. Prepare the surface as you would for brick but use a grass-retardant chemical instead of polyethylene, because the plastic is likely to show through the gravel and might feel odd underfoot.

Gravel doesn't look as substantial as brick, so be sure to use a high-grade variety. White crushed stone, for example, will cost about $4 per square yard of coverage and looks more attractive than conventional gravel.

Edging

A crisp and defined edge to a patio will make it more attractive and look as though it has been put down by a professional.

One alternative is to use pressure-treated wood beams. Once you've determined the layout of your patio, dig a long narrow border so the top of the beams will lie flush with the top of the brick or other surface material. Beams are preferable to railroad ties because they have more of a finished look and the color is not as harsh as dark creosote.

Another alternative is angled brick set vertically. The bricks will probably have to be anchored in mortar so they don't fall over, but this may take more work than you are prepared to do. Simply laying brick down as an edging can also work as long as it is laid out in a pattern that's different from the rest of the patio. For example, if the patio bricks are lined up in a north-to-south direction, the border should define the end of the patio by running perpendicular to the edge.

There are a variety of edging products that make it simple to establish a defined edge. One such product is called Landscape Lawn Border, from Patrician Products, Inc., of Westbury, New York. It's made of a thick but flexible plastic material available in 20-foot rolls in a variety of colors. This is ideal for preventing gravel from spreading beyond the confines of an area but can be used with a variety of patio surface materials as well.

Furniture

The same rules discussed with the deck apply to the patio. Make the area look as if it is used and enjoyed, though the furnishings will probably be somewhat less luxurious.

You wouldn't, for example, put overstuffed pillows or a beanbag chair on the ground, especially on gravel. Outdoor tables and chairs are still appropriate, as are hammocks and chaises longues. A free-standing umbrella might also add a colorful touch; if you don't have one perhaps you can borrow one.

Plantings

Small plants along the border of a brick or crushed-stone patio can make a great difference. They will help define the area and add necessary visual relief to the expanse of unbroken color. Cineraria, marigolds, impatiens, variegated coleus, and standard fuchsia are all suitable for this.

CONCLUSION

If you have the choice between spending the same amount of money on a deck or on a patio, we would advise choosing the former. It has a higher perceived value and more status appeal. In most cases, of course, a deck will be more expensive.

In either case, keep the deck or patio simple. Avoid spending more than $2,000 on a deck, and spend that amount only if the home needs it because of an unusually small interior living area or if the competition is so strong that your home pales in comparison.

If you install a brick patio on your own, your cost should run between $250 and $450. A handy rule to follow on this or any other significant expenditure is "When in doubt, do without."

CHAPTER HIGHLIGHTS

1. Outdoor living space has become one of the most popular features of new homes.

2. Sixty-four percent of those buyers seeking luxury features in a home want a deck.

3. The perceived value of a deck can far exceed its cost, especially in condos, where units are often sold on a cost-per-square-foot basis.

4. If you have a deck, take the steps to make it seem as utilized and enjoyable as possible.

5. The Common-Area Multiplier Effect (C.U.M.E.) can come into play with the installation or upgrade of common area decks in condo or co-op buildings.

6. The patio is another way to take advantage of outdoor living space but does not have the same timely appeal as a deck.

7. You can create a patio yourself at minimal expense, yet add a feature that will enhance your yard.

15

Sprucing Up the Service Areas: The Basement and Garage

The basement and garage are seldom thought of as being among the more important selling points of a home, but they can have far more influence than you realize. Seldom do people end a tour saying to themselves, "What a handsome heating system!" or "That garage floor was outstanding!" But these areas can play a significant role in your home sale.

The basement can suggest a great deal about the condition of your home and, if you choose to add special features, can increase the perception of its value. And the garage can fill the specific needs of certain groups and help differentiate your product.

The basement, including the heating and electrical systems, and the garage can also make some distinctly negative statements about your property, and you will want to take the necessary steps to prevent these from undermining your sale. We will demonstrate how to convert these areas into surprise selling points and how to correct potentially costly mistakes.

THE FIVE-STEP SYSTEM
Step 1. Consider the Competition

The most important difference you are likely to find between your home and the competition's is the level to which the basements are finished. If two homes are equal apart from the condition of the basement, the one with the finished basement is likely to win out.

A finished basement can be converted into an additional bedroom, playroom, or exercise area, thereby increasing your home's versatility. It's not an all-or-nothing situation, however, so if you lack a finished basement and your competition offers it, there are steps you can take to narrow this gap.

The competition can also gain a slight upper hand if, for example, their garage holds two cars and yours holds only one. Although there's little you can do to increase the size of your garage, there are several ways to improve the buyer's perception of what you already have.

Step 2. Consider the Buyer

Despite the fact that women have become increasingly concerned with the mechanical aspects of a home, men still show more interest in these areas. According to Joan McClosky, building and remodeling editor of *Better Homes and Gardens,* "When couples shop for a home, it is still the man that insists on looking at the heating system, plumbing and electrical service, even if he doesn't know the first thing about them."

For this reason, be especially sensitive to needs of the male purchaser when showing your home. Provide him with the reassurance he's looking for.

But don't ignore the female buyer either, because when a woman is buying a home on her own, the mechanical systems may become an issue. And you might come across an instance in which the woman is the informed partner and the man is not.

First-Time Buyers

The condition of the basement and garage is of major concern to the first-time buyer. Fears of surprise expenses can make this usually nervous buyer even more anxious.

By showing that your service areas are well maintained, you can help give this group the confidence they are looking for.

Trade-up Buyers

You can add features to both the basement and garage which will appeal to trade-up buyers, whether you live in a house, condo, or co-op. By suggesting that the basement can be converted into an exercise facility, for example, you can increase the appeal of this often underutilized area.

And because trade-up buyers frequently own expensive cars, you can offer security features in the garage that will be of special interest to this market.

Empty Nesters/Trade-down Buyers

Specific safety and labor-saving features will make your basement and garage more appealing to older empty nesters. And because trade-down buyers often bring too much furniture from larger homes, properties that offer extra storage space are more appealing to this group.

We'll describe these features and how to incorporate them into your house or condo.

Step 3. Evaluate Your Product

The condition of your basement and garage can be of real concern to the buyer.

For example, you may know that the oil stain by your oil tank resulted from a spill that occurred years ago, but the buyer is likely to decide it is evidence of a current problem. Or the buyer might see condensation marks on the walls of your garage and come to the conclusion that you have a roof leak. And there may be sounds and smells in the basement that you no longer notice but that a buyer might pick right up.

Have your focus group evaluate your basement and garage and point out potential problems before the prospective buyer does.

Step 4. Eliminate Territorial Anxiety

Neither the basement nor the garage is an especially personal place in the home and both are therefore unlikely sources of territorial anxiety. As always, however, pay close attention to color, cleanliness, and smell.

Step 5. Maximize Packaging Appeal

Cosmetic packaging improvements can transform a dull, depressing basement or garage into an area with strong sales appeal. An upgraded basement, for example, adds to the usable area of the home and should also suggest the overall excellent condition of your property. Bolster the buyer's confidence by making sure the basement looks as impressive and versatile as it can.

The garage should also be a positive selling point, and we will show you how to make certain yours is.

Last, there are certain considerations regarding basements that relate specifically to condominiums and cooperatives. We'll discuss how the Common-Area Upgrade Multiplier Effect (C.U.M.E.) can be applied to this area of your home.

THE BASEMENT

If you have a finished basement, you're way ahead of the game, and some of our suggestions won't apply to you, but if your cellar looks like a dungeon, we'll offer some simple yet effective remedies. The following ideas do not cover major structural or renovation work but are limited to the low-cost, high-perceived-value improvements that are likely to yield the greatest return at the time of sale.

The Clean Sweep

Your first step, no matter what kind of basement you have, is to make it clean and orderly. Given the way many of us keep our basements, the thought of a major clean-up is enough to make us want to mow the lawn. To get top dollar for your home, though, you'll need to clean up this area.

Begin by going through all the objects you've accumulated over the years and discard them or donate those you no longer need to your local Salvation Army branch or Goodwill store. It may be hard to separate yourself from that old collection of clothing or your grandmother's black-and-white television, but now's the time.

Organizing the Basement

After you have cleared out this area, create a feeling of order and efficiency. Enlarge the look of your basement by utilizing hidden storage areas. Every inch of unused wall and ceiling space should be thought of in terms of its potential use.

If you have bicycles or large toys sitting on the floor, consider mounting them against the wall with heavy-duty wall hooks. These are large rubber-covered, screw-in hooks available at most hardware stores or bicycle shops.

If you have paneling in the basement, find a stud on the wall and screw the hooks in. If you have cement or masonry walls, ask your hardware store for the appropriate bit for drilling the hole. You will also need a threaded anchor to insert into the hole and provide the necessary grip for the screw.

Use heavy-duty shelf brackets to hold large objects that are too wide for hooks. Cover the brackets with adhesive tape so the metal will not scratch the objects you are hanging, and wrap extra tape at the ends so people cannot be injured if they inadvertently bump up against them.

If you have long ladders that are lying on the floor, attach them to exposed ceiling joists with bicycle hooks. You will need more than two hooks to ensure that large objects are secure. All other large objects — unused foldable tables, chairs, and large trunks — should be neatly stored.

Many homes have an open area beneath the basement stairway. This can provide excellent storage space that would otherwise be wasted. Rather than simply cramming objects into this space, give it a finished look by sealing it off from view with a door and a piece of plywood.

Clearing Up Problems

The next step in upgrading the basement is to eliminate common problems that may be of concern to buyers. These are often easy to correct and are well worth the effort.

Pests

The basement is a perfect breeding ground for insects, silverfish, and assorted creatures. If you suspect you have any infestation problems here, be sure to take care of them before you put your home on the market. For potentially serious problems, call in a professional exterminator.

The cost of fumigation depends on the size of the area, but expect to spend $100 or so for a comprehensive job. Don't show the home until several days after fumigating to allow the smell of pesticide to disappear completely and to give you time to sweep up all pests that may have been killed. The sight of even one dead termite or carpenter ant can be enough to kill a home sale, even if the problem has been eradicated. Buyers almost always fear the worst in these cases, so don't take any chances.

Mildew

Mildew is a far more common and less threatening problem than pests, but can cause concern in the buyer's mind. As previously discussed, eliminate mildew by using bleach or Magic Mildew Stain Remover by Majic American Chemical Corp. If the problem is caused by leaking in the basement, correct the source.

Leaks

Common leaking sources include window wells that fill up during heavy rains, or improper grading of soil around your foundation. Window-leaking problems can be corrected by installing plastic bubbles that divert water away from the house. Window bubbles can be purchased in hardware stores or through the mail-order section of home magazines and range in cost from $15 to $40. The grading can be improved by adding soil or gravel to areas around the foundation that are pitched the wrong way.

If you've made these improvements but still find water is seeping through your walls, consider using one of a variety of products available from hardware stores. A company called Thoro System Products offers two waterproofings, one called Waterplug and the other Thoroseal. The former is designed to stop water running from wall cracks and joints, while the latter totally seals porous surfaces.

An all-purpose product by Weldwood called Waterproofing Sealer is also designed to seal a wide variety of porous surfaces. A gallon covers about 150 square feet, though the surface should be painted twice. Or you might consider a waterproof paint called Enterprise Latex Waterproofing Basement Paint, which contains a water-repellent shield.

If you have a more serious problem, like water seepage through the floor, call in a mason to find the source of the water.

Once this problem is corrected, wash off any white rings on the floor with a detergent, and discard any rugs that have become water damaged. A sure sign of a leaky basement is objects that are propped up on blocks so they will be protected against any flooding. If this scene sounds familiar, eliminate the cause and then the evidence of the leak.

Electrical Problems

Bad wiring in a home can zap your sale. If it's old and inadequate, all the packaging in the world isn't going to help. In fact, if it's very old or inadequate for the needs of the home, the buyer should be made aware of this for safety reasons.

A 60-ampere service in a 4-bedroom home, for instance, may cause lights to dim when the refrigerator goes on or fuses to blow frequently. You might consider upgrading the service to 120 amps, which will cost about $300. You don't have to do this, but if you don't you will be risking a damning inspection report if the home is ever examined by a professional.

In any case, make sure your fuse box is in good order and is covered by a panel. Wipe down the box to make it look clean and well maintained.

Soot

Oil furnaces often create a residue of soot in the basement. In fact, oil is not the cleanest of fuels, and a buyer may know this. So wash down floors, table tops, and other surface areas to make sure your basement doesn't look or smell like a refinery.

Mechanical Sounds

Every home has its own sounds and, after a while, you recognize which ones are "normal" and which are not. But to the unitiated, any odd mechanical noise can be disconcerting. A banging water pipe caused by an air-lock or a high-pitched squeal caused by loose washers in shutoff valves can create unwarranted concern among buyers who are not familiar with these easily correctable problems. Call a plumber, who will either explain how to correct this or will do it for you.

Gas Smells

The smell of gas can be a major problem, for it can be a sign of serious trouble, especially in a confined area.

To avoid causing the buyer concern, and to ease your own mind, call the gas company and have any leaks fixed. Oftentimes a faulty pilot light on a water heater or a furnace will cause this problem. It's not advisable to try to solve this yourself; rather, it should be brought immediately to the attention of a repairman.

Creating a Star Cellar

With a little money, some time, and lots of imagination, you can make your basement a cut above the competition's. There are a number of practical ways to accomplish this.

Paint

Without question, the most inexpensive way to increase the perceived value of your basement is to apply a new coat of paint. If your basement walls have grown dingy over the years, one or two coats of white paint will make the basement look newer, larger and cleaner.

But don't stop at the walls. The basement floor can also benefit from painting. It must be absolutely clean before you do this or else the surface will show all the dust and dirt you failed to wipe up.

I recommend using a glossy oil-based gray to give the basement a crisp, clean look. If you want to create a softer feeling, go with either a glossy dark brown or dark green. Oil paint is easier to clean and reflects more light, but if you're in a hurry, latex will dry more quickly. And to make the job easier, apply the paint with a roller attached to a long handle.

Don't forget to paint the stairs and walls leading down to the basement, as this is where the all-important first impression will be created.

And if any of your steps are broken or badly worn, fix them. A carpet

---

Do-It-Yourself Improvements under $100

1. Paint the walls and floor of the basement ($70).

2. Paint exposed ceiling pipes bright colors ($20).

3. Carpet the stairway leading down to the basement ($75).

4. Repaint an old heating system ($15).

5. Buy insulating blanket for water heater ($15).

6. Put up additional fluorescent lights ($40 each).

7. Hang sporting goods and ladders on wall hooks ($5 each).

8. Paint garage walls and floors ($70).

---

runner may be a cost-effective alternative to more substantial work on the steps themselves.

Lastly, if you have exposed pipes running along the ceiling, turn them into an asset rather than an eyesore. Paint hot water pipes red, for example, and cold water pipes blue. Use oil-based glossy paint, and have some fun with the colors you select.

Carpet

One sure way to give an unfinished basement a more finished look is by laying down carpeting. Combined with freshly painted walls, a wall-to-wall carpet will suggest a great deal about the condition and utility of the basement.

It's much easier for a buyer to visualize spending time in a basement that is comfortable than one that feels cold and forbidding. Carpet also suggests a dry basement, and the smell of newness can be an added plus.

The cost of basement carpet is generally lower than that of living room carpet, for example, and starts at about $5 per square yard. If your competition has a finished basement or you simply feel that a more attractive basement will help your sales effort, carpet might be the answer.

Lighting

To highlight the work you've done, make sure you have sufficient illumination in the cellar. It is very common for basements to have a few simple, single-socket fixtures that hold an exposed bulb. Basements are dark enough and certainly need more light than two or three incandescent bulbs can provide.

Fluorescents are more appropriate. They are brighter and longer-lasting and require fewer fixtures than incandescents. If you want to transform a dark and depressing basement into a bright and usable space, consider installing several fluorescents. The open double-bulb variety will cost about $20 each, and installation will probably more than double the cost. Higher-quality fixtures with a plastic diffusing panel over the bulbs start at about $40.

The Heating System

There aren't a lot of interesting things you can do with a heating system. It will not be the focal point of your home or fill any life-style needs, but it can certainly enhance the buyer's perception of your property's quality. At the very least, a well-maintained heating system, especially an older one, may reassure the buyer that the system is not in need of immediate replacement.

There are ways to improve the buyer's perception of an old heating system without having to make expensive repairs or modifications. All it takes is a little repackaging.

I once put on the market a home that had a heating system that was in good working order, but looked old and dull. To make matters worse, the furnace room itself was covered in soot, and oil stains spotted the floor.

When I learned that the person interested in the house was an engineer, I knew he would be inspecting the furnace room carefully. I proceeded to clean the room from top to bottom and used a product called Degrease-All to clean up the oil on the floor.

The next step was to make this antique furnace look modern. I washed it down with a detergent and cleaned the burner, which was the system's only relatively new component. I then applied Armor-All, a polymer surface rejuvenator, to all the metal and cast-iron pieces, and polished all the gauges. Then I spray-painted the old oil tank with a product called Stove Black by Illinois Bronze Paint Co.

By the time I was done, the room was immaculate and even the furnace looked respectable. After the buyer examined the system, he said, "They sure don't make them like this anymore."

I don't advocate going to this extreme in most cases unless you feel it's important to compensate for the age of the system. Just painting the room itself will probably do the trick.

The Basement Door

Bulkhead-style basement doors, the type that rest at a 45-degree angle to your home, can take a gradual beating from the weather. Wooden ones can peel, crack, and even rot, while metal bulkheads can rust.

If your basement door needs help, either repaint it or replace it. The door can make a statement about the security of your home and will affect the exterior appearance of your property. You'll pay about $150 for basement doors, and you can install them yourself.

Beyond the Basics

If you have a finished basement or have taken the steps to make it look habitable, there are features you can add that will increase its utility and perceived value.

An Extra Bedroom

As discussed, one of the main factors determining home prices is the number of bedrooms. If your basement is already finished or looks attractive because of the cosmetic upgrades you've made, adding an extra bedroom can be well worth the investment.

If you already have a bathroom in the basement, this may involve simply putting up walls, laying down carpet, and adding some wiring. The total cost could range anywhere from $2,000 on up, depending on how elaborate you plan to be. But if it means selling your home as a three-bedroom rather than a two-bedroom, converting the basement will give you a decided edge over the competition.

Playroom

If your market is likely to include families with children, a defined playroom in the basement can be seen as a big plus because it can take pressure off limited space upstairs. Carpeting on the floor, colorful graphics on the wall and a well-lit Ping-Pong table can all suggest this area's versatility.

To create your own wall graphics, paint a colorful double horizontal stripe around the room. Place one strip of masking tape along the wall about 30 inches off the floor and a second strip one foot above the first. Paint the area in between the tapes red and remove the tapes when the paint is dry. Repeat the process of taping the wall so a second stripe will border along the top of the first one and paint it yellow.

Exercise Room

Because basements often have open expanses, they are ideal places for exercise rooms, which can be particularly appealing to the young professional or trade-up buyer. If you have weights, a jumprope, an Exercycle, a padded floor mat, and other fitness equipment, you can easily create the feeling of a little gymnasium in the basement. Hang a pull-up bar from the ceiling, and place a scale on the floor. Installing a mirror along part of a wall will make it ideal for aerobics. It will also increase the apparent size of the basement and create the atmosphere of a fitness center.

Consider painting the walls and floor different colors in this area to separate it from the rest of the basement. Bright colors like red and yellow will make the basement livelier, and a track light will make it seem more substantial.

The Workshop

Creating a defined workshop area may appeal to certain buyers. If you have tools spread all over the place, organize them by mounting a pegboard to the wall and neatly hanging them up. Again, by moving all related objects to this area and defining it with special task lighting, you will suggest how useful your basement can be.

The Laundry Room

First, make sure that the washer and drier are clean and free from lint, hair, or caked detergent. If the machines show signs of rust or have dated colors, consider either touching them up or having them refinished. These are high perceived-value items in your home and should be packaged as such.

Add to the convenience of the laundry room or area by building shelves and counterspace around the washer and drier. A place to store detergent and fold clothing can be a welcome feature, especially for a buyer with a large family. If you have painted the floor with glossy oil paint, put down adhesive nonskid strips to avoid accidents. And don't hesitate to accent the area with bright cheery colors to make the laundry room seem less mundane.

The Wine Cellar

If you have a closet by the base of the stairs, you can turn it into an inexpensive wine cellar by installing store-bought modular wine racks. There are products on the market that can be expanded like Tinker Toys and let you fit the rack to your closet.

Before you install the rack, paint or stain the inside of the closet and put down dark-color carpet on the floor to give it a more finished look.

Warming Up the Sale with Insulation

Energy conservation has moved from the headlines into a part of our daily lives. People have added energy-efficiency to their purchase criteria for products ranging from refrigerators to air conditioners, to automobiles, to homes.

A study published in *Builder* magazine reports that among trade-up buyers and empty nesters, improved energy efficiency has become one of the single most important motivating factors when buying a new home. With evidence like this, it is crucial that you prove that your house or condominium is in step with the times.

There are two general rules I use when determining which energy-saving features to install. The first is to use features that the buyer can see. It's always harder to sell intangibles, so if you have a choice between blown-in insulation between the walls, which is invisible, and fiberglass insulation that is installed between the open ceiling joists in the basement, and can be plainly seen, go with the latter.

The second rule about insulation is to install features that are low in cost. A solar roof panel is highly visible but you won't even come close to recovering what you paid for it. On the other hand, a hot-water tank blanket may cost $10 and it, too, can clearly be seen.

What to Insulate

The basement is an ideal place to show off how much you have done to make your home a model of energy conservation. Start by covering your hot water tank with an insulation "blanket." These cost about $10 and can also make an old hot water heater look new. The Water Heater Insulation Weather Seal from Stanley Hardware of New Britain, Connecticut, is a good choice.

Then install fiberglass insulation between the exposed joists in the ceiling of your basement. The vapor barrier, which is the foil or thick paper attached to the fiberglass, should always be facing the heated area. The cost of this insulation varies with the insulation and width, but you can expect to spend 50 cents per running foot. If you have a finished or drop ceiling, I do not recommend installing insulation because what the buyer cannot see will not add to the value of your home.

Your electric company probably publishes free guides on installing insulation; you could also write to Owens Corning Fiberglass Corporation, Fiberglass Tower, Toledo, Ohio, 43659. If your home is very old and has a dirt floor in the basement or a dirt crawl space, put down sheets of 6-millimeter polyethylene, and hold it down with bricks. You can purchase this at any home-improvement center.

Whether or not you have insulation, your home should be warm when it is shown on cold days and vice versa. Saving fuel bills when your house or condo is being toured is a big mistake that can create an immediate concern in the mind of the buyer that your home is inefficiently heated or cooled.

The C.U.M.E. Effect

The Common-Area Upgrade Multiplier Effect also applies to basements in condos and co-ops. The basement can provide the space for valuable amenities, thereby increasing the value of all units in the complex.

If your building is large enough, you can create a fully equipped exercise room at little cost to the individual owners. Because this feature is so popular among young professionals, who happen to be a major market for condos and co-ops, it would clearly be viewed as an attractive feature.

If you have 50 units in the building, for example, and each one is assessed $200, you will be able to buy much of the same equipment that a club offers, and there won't be any membership fees.

Separate storage space is another desirable feature. Because the value of living space in condos and co-ops is at such a premium, anything that can free it up is greatly valued. For empty nesters moving from larger to smaller homes, secure storage space in the basement takes on even greater importance. Deeded storage space is a definite advantage and should be mentioned when you advertise.

TUNING UP THE GARAGE

The garage is another section in the home that the buyer approaches with minimal expectations. Surprise him or her by making your garage unusually well kept and offering special convenience features.

Incidentally, if you don't have a garage, don't consider adding a makeshift carport. These seldom look attractive and the investment required to build a substantial one isn't likely to pay off.

Keeping It Clean

Start by eliminating old or unwanted objects that are taking up space, and sweep the garage thoroughly.

Make certain that it is spotless and free from oil or gasoline. Then you can consider applying a fresh coat of paint to the walls and floor to give it a feeling of newness and care. White walls and a glossy oil-based gray floor will make your garage seem more suited to a Ferrari than a Ford.

Then organize the area by hanging garden tools, brooms, sporting goods, and automobile accessories on the walls.

One of the most visible objects in your garage is your car. Have it cleaned and waxed, so that the buyer can take note of the pride you take in your possessions.

Electric Door Opener

The garage does not generally lend itself to luxury features that enhance the marketing value of your home. Indoor-outdoor carpeting is not really practical, heaters are considered wasteful in these energy-conscious times, and special lighting is generally unnecessary.

But one feature that consumer surveys show is very appealing to empty nesters is a remote-control electric garage opener. In fact, because older people may have difficulty managing heavy garage doors, this amenity may help address an important buyer need.

The cost of these doors ranges between $80 and $300 depending on what type you buy and how much horsepower you need to open the garage door. You can install them yourself, but they are not quite as easy as the television commercials suggest. Having one professionally installed will run about $100.

If you're quite certain that this is the market you are targeting and your home is in the middle to upper price range, an electric garage door opener might be an effective marketing device.

The C.U.M.E. Effect

There are aspects of the garage and parking in general that relate to the Common-Area Upgrade Multiplier Effect for condominiums and cooperatives. If your condo or co-op has a common garage, certain improvements will add to the value of all units in the building.

If the basement lacks storage space, adding storage bins to the garage will take up the slack. These can either be deeded to each unit, granted as an exclusive easement, or assigned to each unit on a more casual basis. A lawyer can help unit owners determine how to handle this.

If the garage happens to be underground and the property is located in an urban area, a closed-circuit television camera that hooks up to an existing central TV antenna or cable system can provide assurance to those with expensive automobiles. The cost of a black-and-white camera plus installation will run about $1,000. This would be most appropriate in especially exclusive condos or co-ops, where auto theft may be a larger concern.

Security is also a primary concern in establishments with outdoor parking. To provide comfort for people walking to and from cars at night and to deter thieves, extensive lighting is essential.

Lighting systems vary tremendously in price depending on whether the lights can be mounted alongside the building or whether lampposts need to be erected. This is well worth investigating, because if the building develops a reputation for security problems, all units will suffer.

Again, a closed-circuit camera can appeal to the security needs of all buyers.

CONCLUSION

The basement and garage are too often overlooked when marketing a home. While there is little glamour to these areas, they can say a great deal about the condition of your home and how well you have cared for it.

These areas also provide a way to differentiate your product by offering features that other homes may lack. For these reasons, view the basement and garage as opportunities to build the buyer's confidence about your home and to increase its perceived value.

CHAPTER HIGHLIGHTS

1. The condition of the basement and garage can reveal a great deal about the care and quality of the home in general.

2. In the basement, any evidence of pests or rodents can kill a sale. Additionally, the condition of the heating system and overall dryness of the basement can be important to the buyer.

3. Offering attractive living space in the basement can significantly add to the value of the home.

4. Showing how the basement can be used as a workshop, an exercise center, or an office will suggest versatility.

5. At the very least, the basement should be as neat and well organized as possible.

6. The Common-Area Upgrade Multiplier Effect (C.U.M.E.) can be applied to basements in condos and co-ops.

7. Like the basement, the garage should reflect the overall care and maintenance of the home.

8. C.U.M.E. can be applied to garages through features like common storage, security systems, or outdoor lighting if the parking facilities are outdoors.

16

The Selling Process: The Bucks Start Here!

Y ou have arrived at the moment of truth. This is where all your research, focus-group testing, target marketing, packaging, and product differentiation will make your home sell more quickly and for more money.

But this last step can also be the most critical. If your home is presented properly, it can make it far more marketable. But showing your home incorrectly can seriously diminish its appeal.

We'll show you how to apply the advice of sales experts to ensure a successful showing and how to avoid common mistakes that can snatch defeat from the jaws of victory.

First, you must determine if you're going to sell your home through a broker or on your own. This chapter addresses the advantages and disadvantages of using a broker and of selling the home yourself. You'll also learn how to make your choice more profitable, as well as ways to sell your home under difficult circumstances.

SHOULD YOU HIRE A BROKER?

This is one of the most important questions you must face. Your answer will affect how much time you devote to selling your home and perhaps how much money you get for it.

According to the National Association of Realtors, 77 percent of all sellers seek the help of brokers, and an additional 8 percent start out selling on their own and ultimately decide to use a broker. This association also reports that 12 percent of homeowners sell on their own, while another 3 percent start with a broker and end up selling by themselves.

The statistics suggest that selling through a broker seems the way to go, but arguments can be made on both sides.

The Case for Brokers

If you're one of the 12 percent who have tried selling on their own and come up empty-handed, the case for brokers can be strong.

Save Time

If you are a single professional or are part of a dual-career household, showing your home during the week can be difficult. You can schedule all your tours on weekends and evenings, but you risk losing a prospective buyer who may not be able to bend to meet your schedule or could find another home in the meantime.

When you do sell your home, there's a tremendous amount of follow-up work — arranging financing, meeting with appraisers, interacting with the bank, obtaining tax bills and legal documents — which the broker will handle for you.

Save Money

Time is money, and because the broker can be more effective than you at finalizing a sale, he or she can actually save you money. If you are carrying two homes at once or if you have an especially high mortgage you want to be rid of, the quicker you sell your home, the more money you will save.

If you personally urge a buyer to put in an offer, it will sound as if you are either anxious or pushy. And if you say something to prompt an offer, like "There are other people interested in the property," it will sound like the oldest line in the book, even though it may be true. This sort of statement will have more credibility coming from a broker because he or she is more impartial than you are.

And don't forget that the broker has more time to determine if the buyer is qualified. The broker can do this by finding out the buyer's income, the value of his or her present home, and any other information you may feel awkward about asking. There are few selling experiences more frustrating and costly than taking your property off the market for a month only to find that your buyer has failed to qualify for a mortgage.

Get a Higher Price

Market coverage is another edge the brokers have over the owner-seller. The broker's livelihood depends on his or her ability to pull in new prospects all the time. A good broker or brokerage office should also have a stable of ready buyers waiting for the right property to come along. For these reasons, the broker may be able to sell your property for more money because he or she has more people to choose from.

The Broker as Informant

The most important aspect of the third-party relationship is that the buyer is much more likely to express his or her feelings honestly to a broker than to you. In fact, this is where the broker's conflict of interest can work for you.

A prospect may leave your home absolutely poker-faced, then turn to the broker and say how fantastic the property is and admit that he or she doesn't want to lose it. This information, which you should learn through the broker, could be worth thousands of dollars because you may not have to be as flexible as you thought about the asking price. Without the broker, a smart buyer will be able to keep his or her feelings a mystery.

The Broker as Buffer

The buyer may feel more comfortable using a broker because it's often easier to negotiate through a third party than directly with a seller. The buyer might also feel easier about asking negative questions about the property of a broker than of an owner. If the buyer keeps concerns to him- or herself when a straightforward answer might allay them, the sale could be jeopardized.

If you want to play tough, you might feel more comfortable using a broker as a buffer, and some brokers are very effective at presenting your case and helping the buyer see your point of view.

Emotional Detachment

The fact that you know your property better than the broker can work against you. The broker will be more objective and will not have the same intensity of interest in little details — like the shelves you so proudly put up in the den or the new floor you installed in the kitchen. Nor will a broker be as sensitive to criticism.

The broker can also help to alleviate territorial anxiety. If a buyer tours a home with the broker and the owner is not there, the buyer will feel much more at ease. This will make the visualization process easier and the tour more relaxed — and it is likely to make it last longer, too.

Lastly, if you're selling because of financial difficulty or because of death or divorce, the broker might be able to keep this information under wraps. If you show the home yourself and reveal that there are problems behind the sale, some buyers may use this knowledge to get a better price on the home.

The Case Against Brokers

There are several arguments against using a broker, the most compelling of which is to save money.

Too Expensive

Why should you have to pay a broker's commission, which is often 6 percent of your sales price? After all, you've done all the work by making your home look terrific and have taken all the risk by investing your hard-earned money.

In some cases, the commission may exceed the cost of a new car, which certainly doesn't seem commensurate with the amount of work involved or the fact that the broker has nothing at risk.

You Can Do the Same Job

The second part of this argument is that there is no reason you can't do exactly what the broker does. You know the house better and therefore can present it more effectively. What's more, you can probably write a classified newspaper ad just as impressively as a broker. And you don't need a license to sell your own home.

Conflict of Interest

Last, there is a conflict of interest. The broker is being paid by you, of course, but often it's unclear whose interests are being represented. If the broker takes a hard line and represents only the seller's interest, it may take longer to sell the home and longer to get his or her commission. So a broker might not take as hard a line as you would like.

A broker might also let the buyer know how much the seller will concede because that information could expedite the transaction. It's not always easy to know if the broker is on your side or just looking out for him- or herself. So which way should you go?

If you do decide not to use a broker, the seasoned buyer may well discount the price of the property by factoring out the brokerage commission. People know that you are making more by selling it on your own and will feel they have more room to bargain.

Clearly, there are more reasons to use a broker than not. This doesn't mean that it is necessarily a better idea, but a broker can be well worth his or her commission.

We will review both approaches to selling your home and provide ideas on how to maximize your success.

SELLING WITH A BROKER

Using a broker can make selling your home much easier, but you can't simply hire a broker and wait for the offers to roll in. You must first choose the right broker and then motivate him or her as much as possible to sell the property. A little preparation up front can make a big difference to the final outcome of your sale.

Selecting a Broker

Taking time down the road to pick the right broker will save you time and money. One of the easiest and best ways to find a good one is through personal referral by friends. You might also consult your attorney or accountant. If this doesn't produce results, check the real estate pages in your newspaper and look for the most professional ads.

Some brokers specialize in certain locations within a city or town and in particular types of homes — like condos or co-ops — so focus on brokers who seem most experienced with your type of property.

I was once told of an excellent method of finding the best brokerage company in a particular area. Select five brokers from the Yellow Pages, call them and ask, "I've heard that you're the best broker in town — could you tell me who you think is second best?" You should be able to discover who brokers consider their most respected competition. If one name keeps coming up as the "second best," chances are it's *the* best.

If you decide against this method, try taking a look at the real estate classified ads in your local paper to see which firm does the most effective promotion. Because classified ads can be such an important part of the sales process, a broker's advertising approach should be considered.

Once you've narrowed down the choice of firms, find out who the top producing broker is by asking the manager of the offices you select. After meeting top brokers in different offices, pick the one who looks the most professional. Strange as this may sound, the way a broker dresses and presents him- or herself can affect the perceived value of your property.

Studies conducted by John T. Molloy, author of *Dress for Success*, reveal that the broker is seen as a reflection of the property he or she is showing and the more upscale the broker looks the better the property will seem. For this reason, the major national brokerage companies are investing a substantial amount of money in determining how to improve the appearance of their brokers.

The Listing Alternative

There are basically three ways to sell a property through a broker, each of which has its benefits and drawbacks.

The Open Listing

Virtually any broker can list or advertise the property if you have an open listing.

At the outset, this may generate a flurry of broker activity, but because so many people have the listing, their interest is likely to fade quickly. Although the selling broker will get a full commission from an open listing, the property can also get overexposed and become "shopworn" if it is shown indiscriminately.

Another disadvantage is that "everybody's business is nobody's business." This suggests that if no company or individual is made specifically accountable for selling your property, you can't expect the same sort of commitment that you might from an exclusive agent. If the property doesn't sell right away and the brokers begin to lose their enthusiasm, you're not in a position to crack the whip.

Shared or Multiple Listing

The second alternative is to give the listing to several brokers in town, and let each of them advertise and promote it as they see fit.

By choosing only a few, you will have somewhat more control over them and you may get more exposure than if you pick only one. But because you have spread the wealth, the brokers will still not feel the same sort of commitment that an exclusive agent would.

Don't confuse "multiple listing" with the Multiple Listing Service, which some brokers offer. The Multiple Listing Service is designed to expose your home to more prospects and therefore help sell it faster. MLS publishes on a regular basis a directory that is distributed to member brokers. A broker who is a member of a local MLS network will add an extra dimension to his or her selling capability. Depending upon the strength of the MLS in your area, it might well be worth considering a broker who is a member of this network.

The Exclusive Agreement

The third alternative is to sign an exclusive listing agreement with one brokerage office. This will bind you to them for a certain length of time, during which the broker's right to a commission will be protected, even if the property is sold by another broker. (This is known as a "co-broke," and the commission is split.)

In return for an exclusive listing, the broker often puts in a certain amount of money for advertising and perhaps holds an open house. If the broker doesn't perform to your satisfaction and show enough interest in selling the property, you are in a strong position to voice your displeasure.

The primary disadvantage with an exclusive listing is that you are locked in with one broker for a certain amount of time and, if you're unhappy with the level of performance, you're stuck until the agreement expires.

The decision on which approach to take with one or more brokers depends on several variables. If you feel very good about one company and think that an exclusive listing will enhance their performance, go with them. But I advise you not to make them the exclusive broker for longer than 8 weeks. If there is no clear choice, I would give an exclusive to one broker on a very short basis, say 3 weeks. The time pressure will motivate that person or firm.

A second alternative is to select two of the best firms and let them battle it out. Selecting more than two will reduce the enthusiasm of all firms to a point where you might as well have an open listing.

Motivating the Broker

Just because you've hired a broker doesn't mean you should rest easy. You want the broker to be excited about the property so he or she will convey that enthusiasm to the buyer.

Invite the broker or the entire office to your house or condo for coffee and pastry. Take them through the property and point out all the features and benefits just as if they were prospects.

Never tell a broker a price you'll settle for because, invariably, that is the price you'll get. If you say to the broker, "I'm going to list the condo at $110,000 but I'd probably accept $95,000," then $95,000 or thereabouts is almost surely what you'll be offered. The broker will use this cushion to help close the deal. Always tell the broker you are quite firm but want to see every offer made. Keep your magic number a secret.

Motivation Tips

The broker has an obvious incentive to sell your property, but he or she has a similar incentive to sell every other listed home. So differentiate the way in which you reward the broker just as you tried to differentiate your product.

Imagine that you were a broker and had listings on two identical houses in similar areas. One owner was offering a standard 6 percent commission and another was offering the same commission plus an airline ticket to a major city in the U.S.A. to the broker who sold the home. As objective and professional a broker as you might be, it would be difficult not to be influenced by this latter offer.

There is no law that limits what a broker can be paid and, by adding a little extra incentive, you'll put yourself at an advantage over the competition.

Although the commission may already seem high, spending a few hundred dollars more on a broker may yield several thousand additional dollars on the sale of your home. And, if the broker doesn't perform, you'll have spent nothing.

Conversely, one of the quickest ways to kill a broker's enthusiasm is to negotiate a reduced commission as a provision to giving a listing. This move may be very common with sellers, but it is very much unappreciated by brokers. It can work against you, especially if you're competing with a similar property whose owner is offering a full commission.

If the broker does his or her job by presenting a high enough offer to you, then that broker deserves the full commission. But if there are a few thousand dollars separating the deals, then you may look to the broker to reduce the commission. Your leverage with the broker is greatest at this point because if the broker holds out for everything, he or she may end up with nothing. Wait until the concluding stage of a deal to suggest reducing the commission. Never reduce it beforehand.

SELLING ON YOUR OWN

Selling on your own can be a profitable experience and well worth the time and effort. But it can also turn out to be frustrating and disappointing, and you may wish you had contacted a broker in the first place. By following certain selling rules and avoiding common mistakes, however, you can increase your chances for success.

Before you start the process, think about specific instances where you have been impressed by a salesperson and then again where one has actually dampened your buying interest.

For example, have you ever walked into a new-car dealership to get a firsthand look at that beautiful machine you've been dreaming about, only to be turned off by an overzealous salesperson?

Conversely, have you ever encountered one of those salespeople with a sixth sense about the appropriate time to provide you with information or give you space to browse?

And have you ever been to a country antique store and become frustrated by a stubborn owner who refused to bargain at all over an item you really wanted? Compare the frustration you felt with the pleasure you probably would have had from successfully negotiating even a few dollars off the piece.

Or, to take a slightly different approach, have you ever gone shopping for an expensive item like a stereo or color television and known more about the product than the salesperson selling it? On the other hand, have you encountered a salesperson who has been so totally versed in the features and benefits of a product you were interested in that you felt more confident about buying it?

You can benefit from the many experiences you've had with salespeople by emulating their best techniques as you prepare to meet prospective buyers for your home.

Success Factors

When people make major purchases, they want to feel good about actually buying them. If buyers think they have won price concessions, they will feel victorious. And if salespeople treat buyers in an especially helpful manner and show a strong knowledge of the product, buyers are more inclined to purchase.

But if the focus of your transaction shifts from the home itself to a battle of egos, a question of trust, or a difference in style, it is likely to harm the sale. And if the buyer actually becomes annoyed during either the tour or the negotiations, it may kill the deal altogether.

There are several key rules to follow when selling your home and specific mistakes to avoid.

Know Thy Product

Know as much as you can about your product. This gives you credibility, and it gives the buyer confidence.

You'd be surprised how many people don't know the number of amperes their electrical service has, how many gallons their hot water tank holds, or whether or not their windows are thermal-paned. Some buyers may not care, but the one who does will feel better about other things you say if you show a comprehensive understanding of your property.

If you don't know this information, have a knowledgeable friend come over to take a look at the systems you want to learn more about.

You should also know the brand names of the major systems in your home, including the furnace and central air-conditioning unit, and have warranties available. You should know if your plumbing is copper, PVC, or another composition. Have at your fingertips information on utility costs and property taxes. And if you live in a condominium, learn a little about the construction of your building — whether or not there is sound insulation between the walls, the age of the roof, and the type of heating system you have.

Know Thy Competition

You should know what other properties are on the market in your area in case another home comes up in conversation. This will enable you to field questions on why your home is a better value than others.

If the buyer says, "The home on Walnut Street is larger yet is nearly the same price," you can be prepared to reply, "I agree, but it doesn't have a finished basement like ours, and from what I hear, the kitchen needs a lot of work." The right piece of information about a competitive property may be worth thousands of dollars to you. So take the time to familiarize yourself with at least some of the other homes on the market in your area.

On the other hand, be careful not to "negatively sell" your home by putting down others. It will only force the buyer to take a position against your property. Be diplomatic when bringing up the weaknesses of other homes.

Sell No Home before Its Time!

Never put a home on the market until you have completed all necessary work. If you are in the middle of painting a room, redoing a floor, or cleaning the yard, wait until it's finished before marketing your home.

Your first shot should be your best shot. Make sure the buyer falls in love with your home, and then he or she will be more tolerant of small quirks that may surface later.

Additionally, the buyer shouldn't get the feeling that you've worked too hard to make your home look terrific. Your house or condo should give the impression of being a natural beauty, but, by your revealing work in progress, the buyer will know it's being done simply to sell the property.

Sell in Season

You may not be able to choose when to sell your home, but spring is the best time to put it on the market. Psychologically, people are in good spirits, trees and lawns look their best, and the weather is often ideal. It is also an easier time for people to move than the winter and is less likely to interfere with school schedules.

Showing your home on a sunny day can also make a significant difference to how people perceive your property. As discussed in Chapter 4, sun has a physiological effect on us and can significantly improve our mood. Although you can't be absolutely sure of the weather on any given day, if you know the forecast calls for sun early in the week and rain later on, try to schedule showings accordingly.

Look Successful

As you know, when people are shopping for a home, they are also shopping for a life-style. So when they meet you, they will be looking for the same kind of positive statements that they will seek from the home itself. For this reason, you must package yourself as well as your property.

Wardrobe expert John T. Malloy suggests, "Clothing that suggests an upper-middle class lifestyle is what the homeseller should aim for." He indicates, "Quiet elegance and tasteful, casual attire are most appropriate."

Specifically, in spring or summer khaki or poplin pants and a short-sleeved polo shirt are good for the man in the house. A cheery but classic-style sundress would be fine for a woman. To suggest an active life-style, wearing tennis attire would send the right message.

In the fall or winter months, corduroy or gray flannel pants for the man, along with a sweater and a blue blazer or tweed jacket, would project the right image. For the woman, anything from a conservative silk or oxford blouse with a gray flannel A-line skirt to a wool challis or understated silk cocktail dress will work fine.

As with color selection of walls and exteriors, the colors of your clothing should be on the neutral side. It is fine for a woman to put on a little jewelry, but she should do so in an understated way.

Listen Carefully

Some of the most effective salespeople are those who talk the least and listen the most. Prospects will provide purchase decision clues throughout the tour if you listen to what they say.

If a couple asks a question about the quality of the schools in the area, chances are that they would also respond to other features that would benefit their children. At appropriate times in the tour, point out what nice children there are in the neighborhood, how your basement could easily be turned into a playroom, or how your driveway would make an ideal basketball court.

The more questions that are asked, the clearer idea you will have about the buyer's interests and the likelihood that he or she will make a good offer.

Be Positive

Every home has weaknesses, but chances are that you are more sensitive to them than the buyer. By pointing out an item you're concerned about, you may bring attention to something that otherwise would have gone unnoticed. You will have also provided the buyer with ammunition to reduce the price.

I recently toured a property where the owner said, "I was not pleased with the way this skylight was installed." I agreed with him, even though I would never have thought twice about it, and I used it as a bargaining point when negotiating for the property.

Be Candid

Establishing trust and credibility is very important when selling any product, and particularly one as expensive as a home. Don't try to fool the buyer by exaggerating a feature's value or minimizing the expense of correcting a problem. Be honest and candid, and you will go a long way toward making the buyer feel good about you and your property.

The prospect will be on guard anyway because of the nature of the buyer-seller relationship. If you come up with one statement that the buyer knows to be false, it will cast doubt on whatever else you say.

Schedule Appointments

You'll accomplish two objectives by scheduling appointments. The first is to avoid surprises — like your home's being a mess when someone pops in for an unannounced tour. And second, scheduling tends to weed out the "tire kicker" who is just looking for a way to kill a Sunday afternoon.

When you get the chance to speak to prospects over the phone, you can provide enough information about the property to let them decide if they want to set up a tour. If they don't, you'll both have saved some time.

On the other hand, if you have a sign up in front of your house, you have to expect people to ring the doorbell at just about any time, and your home should always look its best.

Show the Most Attractive Rooms First

Map out your tour before it starts, with the goal of enhancing the first impression.

Once the prospect has entered your home and you've met, proceed to the closest strongest room. If it's the living room, stop there to give a brief introduction to the home or exchange pleasantries. The more time you spend there, the stronger and better the first impression will be.

Without making the tour seem awkward, proceed to the next most attractive room and continue this strategy until the last room you visit is the least impressive and the place in which you spend the least amount of time.

Make the Buyer Feel like a Winner

Winning the battle and losing the war is a good way to describe a failed negotiating strategy. If you negotiate so hard that the prospect walks away feeling like the loser, you have a much higher chance of the deal's falling apart at a later date. The buyer's sense of commitment to the deal will have been damaged.

I once negotiated for a home with a particularly determined seller. I couldn't get her to budge on anything and began to look for concessions just for the sake of winning something. I was about to give up when she decided to give me a credit for some extra legal expenses incurred during the transaction. In the grand scheme of things, the money meant very little except that I had finally gotten something out of a tough negotiator, and my ego was satisfied.

One relatively inexpensive way to make concessions is by including a specific piece of personal property with the house — like certain ceiling fixtures, a microwave oven, or a fireplace screen. I've found that material objects take on a higher value than their actual worth, simply because you're giving away something tangible.

Common Selling Mistakes

Most of the mistakes salespeople make seem to come naturally. For example, you are likely to be anxious to sell your home but, by acting anxious, you'll hurt the sale. You will also want to tell the buyer how great your house is, but in so doing you can appear overbearing. And when you finally do get an attractive offer, your natural instinct will be to accept it right away, but even this can be a mistake.

The following are common mistakes that you'll want to avoid.

Don't Appear Anxious

It's hard to act relaxed when there's so much at stake in selling a home quickly. But by revealing that you are anxious to sell, you risk losing your negotiating power and possibly thousands of dollars in the process.

It's easy to read an anxious seller, so be careful. Avoid asking questions like "Well, what do you think?" or making remarks like "We'd be willing to make some concessions if we could close before the end of the month."

Also, if you indicate the circumstances surrounding your sale — the fact, for example, that you have already purchased a new home and can't afford two mortgages — the buyer will be the stronger.

Last, don't offer to call the buyer to find out what his or her decision is. If a buyer wants the property, he or she will call you. Have confidence in your product and in yourself.

Don't Overstate the Facts

While it's fine to say, "We love this condominium and are going to miss it," it is not all right to say, "This is without a doubt the best unit in town." If it is, the buyer will probably already know that, and if he or she doesn't, your word isn't going to be convincing.

By bragging about your property, you risk forcing the buyer to disagree with you.

More important, if you make specific references to the condition of certain features of your home — the roof, heating system, or plumbing — be prepared to back them up. These can be construed as representations, and if they are shown to be inaccurate, the buyer can try to hold you accountable.

This does not mean that you can't "sell" the benefits of your home, but be realistic and subtle. For example, don't be afraid to tell the buyer that you used premium paint on that exterior so it won't need repainting for many years. Or that the skylight you put in helps plants grow like weeds. And it's fine to say that you're an energy-saving fanatic who has made a point of spending money on insulation and not on fuel.

Don't Prejudge the Buyer

It's natural to judge buyers on their looks alone. But, as I have learned from experience, assumptions can be costly.

A qualified buyer can be hard to read, so it's dangerous to assume that a prospect with a modest car and old clothes is a waste of time. Of course, you don't expect prospective buyers to look as if they've just walked out of a soup line, but some people choose not to display their wealth at all.

One of the more common prejudgments sellers make is that the man is the dominant decision maker. When selling to couples, you may find that the man is more interested in the exterior and the mechanical systems, while the woman is more sensitive to the features of the rooms themselves. This difference in orientation has been supported by a study conducted by the renowned psychiatrist Erik Erikson, who demonstrated that, even at early ages, boys and girls show this role difference.

But it takes two to make a purchase decision, and assuming otherwise can be a costly error. Direct the conversation equally to both buyers, whether you are talking about the kitchen or the furnace. If you sell one prospect on the home and alienate the other, you're less likely to generate a sale.

You should always be careful when showing your home to the general public because you want to beware of a burglar posing as a buyer. Use your judgment, and don't let a prospect wander around unattended.

Don't Crowd the Buyer

When touring your home with prospects, respect their personal space. Show them around the house and be available to answer questions, but give them enough space to feel comfortable and speak privately.

If you happen to overhear something confidential, don't respond to it because they'll know you've been eavesdropping. Wait until after the tour to volunteer any related information.

Don't Fight Criticism

It can be hard to accept criticism from perfect strangers about something as near and dear to you as your home. But becoming defensive will only add credibility to what they are saying. More important, view criticism as a good sign, especially when it becomes petty.

When I'm selling a property and a buyer starts saying things like "The plumbing under the sink looks like it could use replacing" or "Would you be fixing the broken hardware on the bedroom door?" I know I have a solid prospect. If people have no interest in your home, they will not bother criticizing it in front of you.

Look for motives in questions and comments. Either the buyer is genuinely bothered by some aspect of your house or condo, or he or she is trying to figure out how to buy it for less.

Defuse negative comments by either agreeing with what the prospect is saying or by countering with a positive response. If a person rightfully states, "The ceiling appears quite low in the bedroom," don't reply, "It seems as high as any bedroom ceiling I have ever seen." It's more effective to respond, "It definitely is, which is one of the reasons our heating bills are so low." If the prospect says, "The heating system looks old," agree by saying, "I had the same reaction when I first saw it, but it's been as reliable as could be."

Don't Become Discouraged

Rejection is a necessary part of the sales process. If you show your home to ten people and one buys it, you are doing well, even though it is still a rejection rate of 90 percent.

There are no firm numbers on how many times you should show your house before you can expect to receive an acceptable offer, nor is there any definitive research on how long it should take. On the other hand, while you shouldn't view a little rejection as a statement about your property, if it goes on too long, step back and assess the situation.

If after 10 or 15 or 20 tours, the same criticisms recur, reevaluate either your packaging or pricing strategy. And if your property has been on the market for an unusually long time, say four months, consider taking it off for a while. If prospects read the same ad or "For Sale" sign week after week, they'll begin to wonder, "Is something wrong with this property?"

Don't Negotiate Too Early

Never offer concessions during a tour. If a buyer walks into your den and asks if the ceiling fan is included, say, "We were planning on taking it with us, but it might depend on the offer."

By showing your cards too early, you will lose bargaining power down the road and suggest weakness as well.

Don't Assume It's a Deal

No matter how well a tour goes and what a buyer says, never assume you have made a sale. To paraphrase Yogi Berra, "It's not a deal until it's a deal."

If a buyer gives you verbal assurance that he or she loves the home and will be back later in the week to give you an offer, keep showing the house to prospective buyers until an offer has been signed and a check has been deposited in an escrow account.

After you sign an offer or a purchase-and-sale agreement, you cannot rightfully show the property to another prospect. But you can tell people who express interest in the home that it's under agreement, and you'd be happy to take their names in case the deal falls through. If the buyer can't get financing or doesn't approve the inspection report, for example, and the deal dies, it's far better to have a list of backup prospects than to start again from scratch.

Never Immediately Accept an Offer

If a buyer submits an offer and you immediately accept it without any negotiation, you create problems down the road. Buyers like to feel as if they have bought property at the best possible price. And by accepting the buyer's first offer, you make him or her immediately feel that the home could have been bought for less.

There's often a period that follows a major purchase decision, called "postpurchase dissonance," "buyer's remorse," or, more simply, cold feet. If the buyer feels he or she could have negotiated a better price, this feeling is very likely to occur.

Even if the bid you received is an attractive one, my advice is to offer some token resistance at least. Say, for example, that you'll accept the offer only if the deal is closed by a certain date. This is really meaningless because it will not cost the buyer any more, and you can extend the offer if the deadline comes and goes.

Another approach is to come back to the buyer for an additional three or four thousand dollars and then settle for half of it. If the buyer remains firm, accept the deal but shorten the time in which he or she has to sign the purchase-and-sale agreement.

SELLING UNDER DIFFICULT CIRCUMSTANCES

The sale of a home does not always occur under happy circumstances. Someone may be forced to sell by a death in the family, illness, divorce, financial problems, or sudden job relocation. And sometimes the market itself can create obstacles to selling your home for the largest amount of money in the shortest amount of time.

One or more of these situations can often result in a substantially reduced sales price because the buyer may realize that he or she has the upper hand. If there is any evidence that yours is a "distress sale," you're likely to be in for a rough time.

The following are some general rules and specific considerations to bear in mind that may help you to avoid paying a price for selling under difficult circumstances. This discussion applies whether you're selling your home on your own or through a broker.

Keep Your Reason for Selling to Yourself

Don't let the buyer know why you're selling if your reason might suggest you are under pressure to sell.

One of the best ways to prevent an unfortunate situation from reducing the value of your home is to dissociate yourself from the selling process by using a broker. Because it's often hard to hide strong emotions or cover up the reason behind your move, the broker can be an effective screen.

If you do use a broker, exercise caution in telling him or her about the situation. With the knowledge that you are under pressure to sell, the broker may inadvertently handle the selling process differently by encouraging people simply to make offers rather than suggesting that offers should be close to the asking price. You might also be asking the broker to put on an Oscar-winning act that would test the most skilled salesperson.

Only if you know the broker very well or find yourself in an extreme position should you suggest to the broker that you are willing to do whatever it takes to make a deal.

Keep the Atmosphere Upbeat

Make sure you don't let the unhappiness of the situation cast a pall over the atmosphere of your home. Remember, people are buying an improved life-style and are looking for happiness.

I once knew of a home whose owners were killed in a highly publicized airline crash. The home went on the market and sat for nearly a year until an out-of-towner finally bought it. People just did not want to consider a home associated with this sort of tragedy.

Avoid Selling an Empty Home

When it comes to furnishing a home, there are two extremes that can hurt its marketability.

The first is any type of decor that is overdone. Remember, strong personal statements can make the visualization process difficult because people cannot project beyond what's already there.

The second is the home that has no furnishings at all. Buyers can have difficulty imagining the home furnished. This is another reason why model units usually sell before empty units in the same housing developments.

If you are transferring to another city or have bought another home, delay removing your furniture as long as possible.

In some selling situations, the home may be put on the market after all the furniture and other personal property has been moved out. This can make a home sell for less money in more time than is necessary.

I had a recent experience that clearly reinforced this point. I placed a property on the market that was occupied by a tenant who had furnished it attractively and kept it absolutely immaculate. The house sold within days, but later the deal fell through. By the time I put it back on the market, which happened to be even stronger than it had been before, the furniture had been moved and it took nearly six weeks to sell.

The brokers who conducted the tours were in total agreement that because it was empty, buyers simply couldn't imagine how attractive it could look, especially in comparison to the furnished properties I was competing with.

One solution is to furnish key rooms in your home with rental furniture. The cost of furnishing a front hallway and a living room, for example, may be about $150 per month and requires at least a two-month minimum, but compared to the carrying costs of any empty home, it may be worthwhile. If there is a furniture leasing company in your area, it should be listed in the Yellow Pages.

If you already have a new house and must carry two mortgages at once, the idea of an additional expense may be out of the question. A compromise might be to leave at least some furniture in the house and take essentials to your new address.

Specific Problem Situations

Each one of the circumstances behind a distress or pressured sale has its own special considerations.

Divorce

Many divorces are less than amicable. If the buyer thinks that this is why you're selling, he or she may assume that you have to move the property in a hurry.

When buyers tour the home, be careful about saying things like "This was my husband's workshop" or "The kitchen is so well equipped because my wife was a gourmet cook." If the buyer asks why you're selling, indicate you want to pull the equity out of the house to reinvest elsewhere.

Put away pictures of the spouse. If the buyer asks if you are married, say that you're single rather than in the throes of a divorce.

Death

A sale prompted by the death of a homeowner can have two unfortunate effects. First, because estate sales are notorious for providing buyers with bargain opportunities, a prospect might immediately assume he or she is negotiating from a position of strength. Second, a recent death can create a feeling of uneasiness about a home.

Combating the feeling of emptiness in the home is important in creating the kind of life-style message you want to convey. Plants and cut flowers should be in the home so that fresh smells fill the air. Place copies of recent magazines on the coffee table, and put on some upbeat background music. The lawn should be trim, and the mailbox should not be stuffed with uncollected mail.

One of the biggest mistakes is to cover up furniture with sheets. This is sometimes done to prevent furniture from getting dusty when homes are left vacant for a while, but it creates an eerie look that should be avoided.

Illness

If the home is being sold because a previous occupant has been hospitalized or institutionalized recently, the buyer is better off not knowing this.

Prospects may feel uncomfortable, for example, with the knowledge that a very sick person has been living in what may be their bedroom. This can create territorial anxiety and make the visualization process more difficult.

There is no reason to explain why the home is being sold, and if for some reason it surfaces, do not go into detail. The look and smell of fresh paint and polyurethane along with the aroma of fresh flowers and lemon oil will brighten the atmosphere.

Financial Difficulties or Sudden Job Relocation

Both sets of circumstances should be kept "close to the vest" because a seasoned buyer will interpret your situation as a bargain opportunity. Use your discretion in confiding in your broker, because if the rest of his or her office finds out, chances are someone will let the information slip.

Difficult Market Conditions

The curse of high interest rates, a weak economy, or a surplus of housing in your area can make selling a real challenge. At no time is it more important to differentiate your product and creatively package your home than when the market is not cooperating.

But even in bad economic times, there are ways you can fight fire with fire through creative financing techniques.

Making Your Home Affordable

Helping a person afford a home is one of the most effective sales incentives. There are an almost infinite number of financing ideas that can combat high interest rates or help a buyer qualify to purchase your home. There are also many financial incentives you can offer which will ease the mind of the nervous buyer.

Many of these ideas should be considered last resorts because they can be costly. But under difficult market conditions, it may make the difference between making or losing a sale.

Buy-downs

This refers to a cash subsidy paid to the buyer to cover the difference in monthly payments between high interest rates and more affordable levels. For example, if your buyer can only find a 16 percent mortgage when 12 percent is an affordable level, you can offer to pay the 4 percent difference for a period of one year, after which rates may have dropped and the buyer can refinance.

If the mortgage is $90,000, for example, and has a 30-year amortization, this will cost you about $3,400. That's a lot, but it may be the difference between selling your home and not.

Prepay Condo or Cooperative Association Fees

If you're selling a condo or co-op, consider offering to prepay the association or maintenance fees for 6 months or a year, depending on how high they are and how much room you have to play with on your selling price. This may run you a few thousand dollars but will make the property more affordable up front.

Buyers generally assume that they will be making more money in the future and will figure out a way to afford the higher payments when they arrive. If they like the property, up-front savings can be very effective.

Take Back a Second Mortgage

The need to come up with the down payments prevents many buyers from being able to purchase a home. By offering to take back a second mortgage, you enable the buyer to put down less cash to buy your property. This is done by having a lawyer draw up a note using the home as collateral.

My advice is not to write the mortgage for any longer than 3 years, and keep the interest rate near market value just in case you have to sell the note to generate some cash.

Offer a Buyback Guarantee

This is a bold move, but for the nervous first-time buyer it can spell great relief. You offer to purchase the home back from the buyer at the price he or she paid if the buyer isn't happy with it after 2 years. The buyer won't have made any money if he or she takes you up on it, but he or she will know there's no way to get badly hurt either.

From your perspective, in the rare event that a buyer decides to sell the house back to you, it should have appreciated and you stand to profit. Of course, you should never make such an offer if you're not in a position to take the buyer up on it. It's essential to use a lawyer to draw up this type of an agreement.

Offer a Lease-Purchase Agreement

If you're in a real bind — like owning two homes at once — and can no longer bear the cost of an empty home, consider offering a lease-purchase agreement. This enables a buyer to lease your property and gives him or her the option to buy it at a specific price at some future date.

The rent should be higher than the market rate, but you should offer to credit a percentage of it toward the purchase price if the tenant decides to buy. The longer the tenant stays and the more purchase credit he or she accumulates, the more incentive the tenant has to exercise the purchase option.

You should not do this for much more than a year because chances are the conditions that made it difficult to sell your home will have improved, and you'll be able to move it without any special incentives. This, too, can be very complicated, so using a lawyer to draw up an agreement is essential.

CONCLUSION

Preparing your home for sale and actually selling it are two different steps. The effort you put into the first will pay off only if you take time to select the right broker or fully prepare yourself to sell your home on your own.

No matter how good a product is, the salesperson can make or break a sale. Make sure the way you sell impresses the buyer as much as your home does.

If you do sell your home on your own, you will want to come up with as many qualified prospects as possible. This requires the proper advertising approach, which is the subject of the following chapter.

CHAPTER HIGHLIGHTS

1. The decision whether or not to hire a broker is the first and most important step when putting your property on the market.

2. The broker can save you time in finding a prospect, touring the property, and closing the sale.

3. The broker may also be able to generate a higher price by exposing the property to more buyers and being an effective buffer in the negotiations.

4. The primary disadvantage to hiring a broker is the expense, usually around 6 percent of your selling price.

5. If you do use a broker, try to get referrals from friends who have had firsthand experience.

6. If you can't get referrals, go to the two or three leading real estate brokerage offices in your area and ask to speak with their top broker.

7. Of this group, select the one broker that presents him- or herself the best because he or she will reflect on the quality of your property.

8. Never negotiate the brokerage fee until late in the transaction because it will reduce the motivation of the broker.

9. Avoid signing one long exclusive listing contract; and instead sign short, renewable contracts.

10. If you decide to sell without a broker, be careful not to oversell your product.

11. Be knowledgeable about your home and its competition and be ready with informed answers. But be a good listener and avoid pressuring the buyer.

12. Dress like a winner when you sell your home, since you are a part of the life-style statement the buyer is looking for.

13. Schedule tours to weed out casual buyers and always be honest and candid.

14. Never accept a first offer even if it is what you want. Always offer some candid resistance so the buyer does not feel he or she paid too much.

15. If you are selling under difficult circumstances like divorce or financial problems, keep the reasons from the buyer and, if possible, from the broker. Knowledge of a distressed sale may cost you thousands of dollars.

16. Avoid selling an unfurnished home if possible.

17. Under difficult market conditions, take advantage of the many "creative financing" options available to you.

17

Advertising: The Madison Avenue Home Sell

The same advertising principles used to sell anything from soap to soda can be applied to selling your home. There are proven principles and techniques that you can easily apply and make the difference between the success and failure of your advertising effort. You can have the best product on the market, but if no one knows about it or it is not well presented, it won't sell. That's why advertising has evolved into a multi-billion-dollar business and why top copywriters can earn more than the man sitting behind the big desk in the White House.

THE PROBLEM WITH ADVERTISING

Between waking up to the morning radio and reading the paper at breakfast, seeing billboards on the way to work and watching television in the evening, the average American is bombarded with an estimated 1,800 advertising messages per day! If your brain absorbed all this information, you probably wouldn't have enough room left to remember your name. This type of advertising overload is known in the ad business as "clutter."

Fortunately for all of us, most of this clutter goes in one ear and out the other, while only a very small percentage of the messages actually stick. Thus, the test of truly effective advertising is to break through the clutter and leave a lasting image in the mind of the consumer.

One of the best examples of clutter is the classified section of your local newspaper, the place where three quarters of all home-buying prospects look for information on what's available. There can be more words per square inch in a typical classified page than anywhere else in a paper, making it very difficult for any one ad to stand out. This is complicated by the fact that so many of the ads describe similar products. But because so many people rely so heavily on classifieds, you must cut through this clutter with proven advertising techniques like the use of white space, for example, or short, bold headlines.

The classifieds are not the only place where you can find prospects. There are many creative ways to target prospects that most home sellers rarely consider. In the same way that you target your home to a specific audience, you should also target your advertising message to those who are most likely to buy your home. An essential element of effective advertising is therefore to identify your audience and select the right media for reaching it.

Once you've determined who you want to reach, how you want to reach them, and what to say, be prepared to handle the responses. If you can't convert the inquiry into a tour, all your efforts will be lost.

The home advertising process, therefore, involves four basic steps which apply no matter what kind of property you're selling. The following discussion will cover each of these steps and provide specific ideas on how to make your message stand out from the crowd.

THE THREE-STEP SYSTEM
Step 1. Identify Your Target

This step is easy because you have already performed it in your initial market research. The combination of input from brokers, a look at recent sales in your area, and your own observations will give you a good idea who is likely to buy your home. The price of your home will also help you determine the target audience.

The purpose of identifying your target market is to help select the most appropriate place to advertise and to determine what to say in your ad. The following is a partial list of types of properties and likely prospects for them.

URBAN CONDOMINIUM

A. SMALL ONE BEDROOM OR STUDIO

1. Young single professional
2. Divorced or single homeowner
3. Downtown executive looking for an in-town residence
4. First-time buyer

B. TWO-BEDROOM OR LARGE CONDOMINIUM

1. Downtown corporation looking for an alternative to hotel use
2. Empty nesters
3. Young married professional couple

SUBURBAN HOUSE

A. SMALL RANCH HOUSE

1. First-time buyers
2. Young couple without children
3. Young family
4. Divorced or single homeowner

B. LARGE COLONIAL

1. Trade-up professional
2. Relocated executive
3. Growing family

VACATION HOUSE

1. Executive family
2. Retiree looking for a primary residence
3. Successful young professional couple

Step 2. Where to Advertise

There are one overwhelming choice and several secondary options for advertising your home. A combination of the two is probably the best approach.

Classified Ads

The dominant real estate advertising vehicle is the newspaper classified section. According to research conducted by the Newspaper Advertising Bureau, on an average Sunday 57.5 million people read classified ads. Of this total, 7 million are actively looking for a house, condominium, or co-op. Nearly three quarters of all prospects who want to buy a home read the classified real estate section, and two thirds of those who have sold their home have advertised in them.

The demographics reveal that two thirds of these people are college-educated and have incomes well above the national average. For these reasons, classified advertising is almost a must in promoting the sale of your home.

The cost of classified advertising depends on the circulation of your newspaper. The *New York Times* costs about $10 per line, while the *Des Moines Register* charges $4.75 per line. If an ad is 14 lines, then the cost will range between $60 and $140.

There are many different types of newspaper, ranging from major metropolitan dailies to small suburban weeklies. If you live in an area that is well covered by both, consider taking out classified ads in each. It's not worth skimping on the extra advertising cost to save money — the cost of your property sitting on the market will far exceed the cost of the ad.

And don't save pennies on the size of your ad. Compared to how much extra you will make without a broker, the added cost will be insignificant.

There are both advantages and disadvantages to using classifieds. The advantages are that for a relatively small amount of money, you can reach an enormous number of people. And based on readership studies conducted by the Newspaper Advertising Bureau, chances are the kind of person reading the classifieds is the kind of prospect you are looking for. Also, you can generally call in an ad just days before you decide to run it. Last, you know that you have a receptive audience because people seek out this information rather than having it forced on them.

The primary disadvantage, as discussed, is making your ad stand out from the crowd. Also, because people generally throw away their newspaper shortly after reading it, you have very little time to get their attention. This short retention time means that if you don't get a response right away, you probably won't get one, so you'll probably have to run your ad several times. And if your home is very expensive or appeals to a specialized market, the classifieds are not likely to reach that market.

Local Magazines

In general, the only magazines that make sense are those that have very specific geographic markets, so you don't pay for readership beyond your area. A person reading a magazine in Memphis is not likely to be interested in a house for sale in Atlanta.

There is a growing breed of monthly magazines that are targeted toward very specific markets in different parts of the country. These include *Texas Monthly, Boston Magazine, Chicago, San Diego Today,* and *Washingtonian,* and all appeal to a young professional, established or upwardly mobile group.

Advertising a home in these publications assures that you reach an affluent, well-educated market and is particularly appropriate if your home is expensive. Another benefit is that there is generally not a great deal of real estate advertising in these magazines, so your ad will stand out. Because these are monthlies, the retention value is higher and the chances of your ad getting read more than once is greater.

One disadvantage is that the cost is quite high compared to the newspaper classified. A fourteen-line ad may range anywhere from $150 to $500. The circulation of the magazine is also likely to be much less than a newspaper, which means you will probably get a smaller response. The primary disadvantage is that it may take several weeks before your ad appears in print because of infrequency of the publications.

My advice is to use these publications along with classifieds if your home is in the upper end of the market and if you're under pressure to sell. This is a good way to cover your bases and reach qualified buyers.

Professional Trade Publications

Almost every major city has local professional trade publications that are "must reads" by people in specific fields. These publications may be directed toward lawyers, accountants, advertising professionals, bankers, stockbrokers, and financial managers.

While few people advertise homes in these newspapers or magazines, they can prove very effective. First, there is virtually no clutter. And second, because the incomes of the readers are high, they are ideal for advertising either an expensive first home, a downtown home as a second residence, or a vacation property.

The disadvantages include the fact that many people are too busy during the day to call about a home and may forget to do it in the evening or on a weekend. The publications may be expensive to advertise in and their circulation is limited. This will mean fewer but probably better-qualified responses.

Bulletin Boards

This may sound like a demeaning place to advertise your pride and joy, but don't jump to conclusions. An attractive photograph of your home and a brief description placed on the bulletin board of a country club pro shop, a yacht club lobby, a doctors' cafeteria in a hospital, or an expensive antique shop can reach as impressive a demographic group as any elite magazine. If your target market is not quite as rarefied as this, try a local bookstore, a library or community center.

The cost of this type of advertising is minimal, especially when compared with the potential benefits. Make sure the photo does justice to your home and use color.

Signs

In relation to its cost, a sign can reach more prospects per dollar than any other form of advertising. A "For Sale" sign on your lawn can be seen by hundreds of people per day depending on how busy your street is.

The biggest advantage of a sign is that it's inexpensive and tends to reach those who are already familiar with your area or neighborhood. It also lets your neighbors know you are selling and can help the word-of-mouth process. For these reasons, many homes are sold by signs.

The disadvantages are that you lose control over who sees your home and when. Even if you have a sign with a phone number and clearly state "By Appointment Only," people will still come up and ring your doorbell. Not only may your home not be in showing condition at the time, but you may also attract some undesirables you don't want inside your home.

Another problem with signs is that they do not effectively qualify the buyer. A person who answers an ad and takes the trouble to set up an appointment to see your home is much more likely to be interested than someone passing by on a nice afternoon. Last, signs can suggest weakness in your selling position. Because they are so visible, the longer they are up, the more apparent it is that you haven't sold your home right away.

The compromise is to put up a sign after you have advertised and see how it works. Don't leave it up for more than 2 weeks. If it draws the kind of prospects you are looking for, then you will be pleasantly surprised.

Step 3. Creating Your Message

What you say and the way you say it can make all the difference between an ad that works and one that doesn't. Exhaustive research has been conducted over the years by just about every major consumer products manufacturer, consumer publication, and advertising agency on what it takes to make a successful ad.

Although advertising is not a science, there are some principles upon which almost all experts agree. The following information is based on the results of a special study conducted by the National Advertising Bureau and advice from advertising professionals.

The Bigger the Better

It probably comes as little surprise that the bigger the ad, the more noticeable it will be. Especially in the classified section where so many ads are the same size, the bigger ones definitely stand out.

Consider using larger headline type, more detailed body copy to describe the property, or more white space surrounding the ad. These alternatives will help fill larger space and give the ad more impact.

The Headline is the Key

The headline is designed to catch a buyer's attention, so you can then sell him or her with the body copy. But if the prospect misses the headline, chances are the body copy will go unread.

Research has shown that the most effective headlines are those that emphasize low cost or unusually good value. Seventy-five percent of those who read real-estate advertising do so to find price information, so let the buyer know what he is already looking for. But while appealing to the pocketbook has proven to be the most persuasive approach to generating buyer attention, it is not always appropriate. In high-priced, executive estates, for example, focusing too much attention on price can actually work against the image you want to get across. Use your judgment but remember that, whenever appropriate, mentioning money grabs attention.

Terms like "good value" have been so overused they've become meaningless. You must go one step farther and clearly suggest unusual value in order to catch the buyer's interest. A headline like "Superb

Features, Unbeatable Price!" would draw far more interest than would "A Real Suburban Value."

Second in effectiveness to the economic appeal is a consumer benefit. Comfort, convenience, privacy, cleanliness, brightness, and proximity to schools all help to bring inquiries. Always select the benefit that has the most impact on your target market. If in doubt, use one in the headline and others in the body copy.

Make sure that the headline stands out clearly. Bold or large type or short headlines surrounded by white space will increase the visual impact of the headline. You can request this when you call in your ad, or draw it up and send it to the newspaper or magazine.

If you can find an existing ad with a headline that caught your eye, cut it out and ask the ad salesperson to duplicate its look.

Always keep the headline brief. The shorter the headline, the more quickly it can be read, and the better it will stand out. If you try to communicate too many points in a headline, you probably won't succeed in any. Select only one or two points to make, and let the body copy sell the prospect on the rest of the details.

By saying "Ranch House Surrounded by Trees and Near Town Center," you're asking too much from the reader. Replacing this with "Ultimate Ranch Privacy with Convenience" will require half the time.

If you can come up with a catchy 2- or 3-word headline and have it set in bold type, it will pop out from the page. Let's say you're lucky enough to have a vacation home on the water. "Oceanfront Retreat" will register much more quickly than "A Beautiful Vacation Home on the Water."

Also, make the headline specific. Why say, "You'll Love This Charmer" if you can say, "Authentic Colonial with Carriage House."

Always avoid snobbishness. If a home is truly exceptional, saying so in a boastful manner can actually cheapen it. The buyer of a very expensive home is generally sophisticated enough to read between the lines, and spelling it out can suggest the opposite of what the prospect is looking for. Understatement can be the most powerful approach for the luxury market.

An English Tudor home with a library, wine cellar, solarium, and circular driveway that sits on a sprawling, architecturally landscaped site should not be described as "The Ultimate Statement in Luxury Living." A more effective approach would be "A Tudor Home in the Grand Tradition."

Also avoid exaggeration. By doing this, you will not set prospects up for disappointment when they see your home. If you live in a comfortable but conventional suburban two-family, don't describe it as having "Exquisite Old World Charm." By the time the prospect pulls up to your house, he or she will not only be annoyed but also will not believe a word you say.

The same applies to location. If the town in which your home is located borders a more prestigious area, don't lead the prospect to believe your home is in that section. I have answered ads like this and immediately felt that the seller was trying to pull a fast one. It also makes the buyer feel the price should be discounted to compensate for the less desirable address, even if the asking price has already accounted for this.

The Body Copy Should Support the Headline

The first line of the copy works to "pay out" the headline. It immediately begins to detail the facts that give credibility to the headline statement and starts to paint a picture of what makes your home special.

If your headline reads "Move-in Condition," the copy should begin by saying something like "Newly renovated with new carpet, paint and systems." The buyer who is attracted by this headline will be most interested in the specifics of its move-in condition

The copy should also be easy to read. Good copy flows easily and encourages further reading. To save money, people often use abbreviations, to the point where an ad can look like a secret military code. How many times have you seen a classified ad similar to this: "2 bdrm. condo w/frpl., w.w.cpt, kit.w d+d., pkg., bsmt. and more." You need to call in a cryptographer to figure out what they're talking about.

Not only do abbreviations make ads more difficult to read, they also make them look like every other ad on the page and do little to create the type of visual imagery that can excite a buyer. Spending the extra money to make the ad readable will be worthwhile.

Keep the copy informative. It's fine to tease the reader a little to motivate further inquiry, but if you withhold too much, the reader may move on to another ad. According to the Newspaper Advertising Bureau, the type of information readers look for, in order of importance, is as follows:

> Price
> Number of bedrooms

Lot size
Location/neighborhood
Number of baths
Style of house
Details about extras
Type of construction
Closeness to schools
Type of heat/air conditioning
Number of rooms
Cash required

The ad should close with the price and your phone number clearly displayed. It's important to indicate the times you can be reached so the prospect does not lose interest by calling when you're not available.

The more information you provide, the larger the ad will be and the more attention it will attract. The home may also seem to be a better value if you include a detailed list of features, especially when compared to a comparably priced property that gives sketchy details.

The word "new" has proven very powerful in advertising and should be used when appropriate. Newness suggests value, good working order and convenience. It's especially effective when describing a kitchen, bathroom, heating system, or roof.

If you are running the ad for several weeks, consider two versions. When people start seeing the same ad over and over, it may suggest that the house is just sitting and puts you in a position of weakness.

If the ad is generating a great response, there's no need to play with it — but the fact that it's running for several weeks suggests that it could use a fresh approach.

Headline and Copy Suggestions

The following is a list of ideas for creating headlines and body copy. You can interchange these and adjust them to more accurately describe your home.

HEADLINES

A. STARTER PRICE HOMES

1. Affordable Comfort
2. Expansive, Not Expensive
3. An Irresistible Buy!
4. Enormous Potential

5. Low Monthly Payments
6. Little Cash Needed
7. Rich in Value, Not Price
8. A Do-It-Yourselfer's Dream
9. A Perfect Starter

B. MIDDLE-PRICED HOMES

1. Elegant But Economical
2. Affordable Luxury
3. A Life-Style Leap
4. A Growth Investment
5. Privacy and Comfort
6. A Blend of Old and New
7. Newly Renovated
8. Below Market Value
9. Convenient Luxury
10. Wooded Seclusion

C. UPPER-MIDDLE PRICED HOMES

1. Dignified Elegance
2. Wooded Seclusion
3. Country Living
4. Park-like Setting
5. Exceptional Detail and Ambience
6. Quality and Substance
7. An Extraordinary Value
8. Spaciousness and Value
9. Pristine and Private
10. Uncompromising Investment

D. HIGH-PRICED HOMES

1. A Home of Distinction
2. When Luxury is a Necessity
3. Historic Beauty
4. Understated Elegance
5. High on a Hilltop
6. Quintessential
7. In Search of Excellence?
8. A World unto Itself
9. Elegance Redefined
10. A Classic Contemporary

COPY POINTS

A. Cleanliness/ Convenience/Condition

1. Maintained by a perfectionist
2. An investment in convenience
3. A 21st century worksaver
4. Designed for tomorrow
5. Impeccable condition
6. Walking distance from downtown
7. A homemaker's fantasy
8. Move-in condition
9. A house that works for you
10. A lazy man's dream

B. Living Room

1. For gracious entertaining
2. Expansive views
3. Warmth and elegance
4. A grand fireplace
5. Bright and elegant
6. Newly carpeted
7. Breathtaking ceilings
8. Built-in bookcases
9. Exquisitely detailed woodwork
10. Hardwood floors add to overall ambience

C. Dining Room

1. Formal elegance
2. Adaptable for formal and casual occasions
3. Designed for gracious entertaining
4. Ideal for family gatherings
5. Bathed in sunlight

D. Bedroom

1. Master suite with private bath
2. Enormous closet space
3. Luxuriously proportioned
4. Warmth and elegance
5. Cozy and comfortable

E. KITCHEN

1. State of the art convenience
2. Efficiency at its best
3. High-tech kitchen
4. Charming country flair
5. A model of efficiency
6. New counters and cabinets
7. New no-wax floors
8. Bright and spacious
9. Designer styling
10. Latest appliances

F. EXTRA ROOMS

1. Room to grow
2. An office for the busy executive
3. Ideal for in-law apartment
4. Perfect for extra bedroom
5. Ideal for a library or study

G. SPECIAL FEATURES

1. Spectacular cathedral ceilings
2. Rich in Old World detail
3. Charming period fixtures
4. Gleaming brass hardware
5. Custom wainscoting throughout
6. Elegant french doors
7. Handsome marble fireplace
8. Newly refinished parquet floors
9. Richly carpeted
10. Authentic wide pine flooring
11. Dramatic stairway
12. Inspiring view
13. Charming multipaned windows
14. Built-in wet bar
15. Exciting recessed lighting

H. SYSTEMS

1. State-of-the-art efficiency
2. Air-tight thermo-paned windows
3. Top-of-the-line heating system

4. Fully insulated
5. New plumbing throughout

I. DESCRIPTIVE FEATURES

1. A relaxed environment
2. Artfully landscaped
3. Atop a rolling hill
4. Built with craftmanship
5. Lush gardens
6. Striking appearance
7. Stately design
8. On a winding lane
9. Surrounded by natural beauty
10. Historic charm

HANDLING THE RESPONSES

When your phone rings with an inquiry about your home, get serious. Don't handle calls casually, because dropping the ball at this point is like marching all the way down the football field only to fumble the ball on the opponent's one-yard line. The following thoughts address ways to help convert your caller into a live prospect.

The first rule is obvious: you can't answer a call if you're not at home. If you're running an ad in the newspaper, be home during the days when it appears. As discussed, newspapers are an immediate response vehicle, and the calls you get are likely to come right away. If you're not going to be home to receive them, save your money and don't advertise at that time. Or, specify in the ad to call during evenings, if that is when you will be home. Use a work number also but ask your employer for permission first.

Telephone answering machines are a partial solution, but people often don't like to leave their name and phone number with someone they don't know. If a person can't reach you right away, you run the risk of losing them altogether.

Once you begin to field calls, don't act too anxious. Calmly answer questions and be as open and as pleasant as possible. People don't want to be smothered on the phone any more than they do in person. Use the same sales techniques in your conversation as recommended in your tour.

Make sure there are no unpleasant background noises like barking dogs, screaming kids, or loud appliances. Some music in the distance may convey the kind of peace and tranquility that your home should project.

Motivate the Tour

You will encounter three types of phone experiences: the one in which the prospect learns a key fact that makes him or her lose interest, the one that makes the prospect more interested and request an appointment, and the one in which the prospect is undecided. The latter is the only one in which you need to apply a little consumer psychology.

You're either dealing with a nervous buyer, a casual buyer, or simply one who just may not know what he or she wants. Your job is to make the idea of a tour as nonthreatening as possible. Suggest to the prospect that he or she come by and, if all else fails, he or she will gain a better perspective on the market. The less pressure you apply, the more comfortable he or she will feel.

CONCLUSION

If you are selling on your own, effective advertising is essential. Especially in the case of classified advertising, there is no more efficient way of getting the word out about your property.

Resist the temptation to save money by making ads too small or not running them often enough. Remember, you may be saving a 6 percent brokerage fee, so don't let a few dollars influence the outcome of your largest personal investment.

CHAPTER HIGHLIGHTS

1. Many of the same advertising principles used to sell consumer packaged goods can be applied to selling your home.

2. Newspaper classified advertising is the single most effective vehicle for selling real estate.

3. Consider supplementing classified advertising with advertising in special publications that are specifically targeted to your market

4. "For Sale" signs can reach more prospects per dollar than any other form of advertising.

5. The primary disadvantage of signs is that they do not tend to generate as selective or qualified a buyer as targeted advertising.

6. In print advertising, the bigger the ad is, the more effective it will be.

7. Headlines that emphasize good value are most successful in generating buyer response.

8. Bold headlines and ads surrounded by white space are most noticeable.

9. Always avoid language that sounds snobbish.

10. Don't be penny-wise by saving money on short, abbreviated ads in favor of longer descriptive copy.

Conclusion

You can have tremendous control over how much money you will make on your home sale and how much time it will take. By carefully packaging your product rather than just putting it on the market, you can reap thousands of additional dollars on your sale.

Making the right packaging improvements does not necessarily mean spending a great deal of money. It can mean correcting a small problem detected by your focus groups, like an unpleasant smell or the addition of an inexpensive improvement, like upgrading the front doorway. There are instances where more costly improvements can produce a positive return, like exterior repainting or creating an additional bedroom, but spending thousands on the wrong improvements can often yield nothing.

Your overall goal is not to change the entire character of your home but to give the buyer confidence in your product and help him or her visualize it as their own. But you should never use packaging techniques as a way of hiding serious problems or defects in your home. Rather, packaging should be used as a positive means to maximize the perceived value of what you already have.

By thinking like a marketing professional and applying the points covered in this book, you will find yourself at a distinct advantage over most home sellers. Whether you use a broker or sell on your own, effective packaging is the key to getting the most out of your largest personal investment.

Acknowledgments

The information in this book is derived not only from the field of real estate but other areas, including psychology, consumer behavior, sociology, advertising, sales, interior design, and landscaping. Without the cooperation of people from a wide range of disciplines, this book would not have been possible. We would like to acknowledge some of those who provided us with the necessary support to complete this project.

Mr. Allan Sabbag, president of Better Homes and Gardens Real Estate Service; Mr. Joe F. Hanauer, chairman of Coldwell Banker Residential Real Estate; Mr. Robert A. Dyson, chairman of the board, Red Carpet Realty Corporation of America; Mr. Edward G. Gresham, president of Electronic Realty Associates; Ms. Toni Reuter, director of training of Century 21 Real Estate; Mr. Saul Cohen, president of Hunneman Residential Real Estate; Mr. Keith Romney, president of Keith Romney Associates; the National Association of Realtors.

Mr. Brooke Warrick, director of the Values and Lifestyles Program of SRI International; Professor Pierre L. van den Berghe, Department of Sociology and Anthropology, the University of Washington at Seattle; Mr. William C. Apgar, Jr., director of the Housing Futures Consumer Survey at the Joint Center for Urban Studies of M.I.T. and Harvard University; Mr. David Snyder, Systems Librarian, Mugar Library at

Boston University; Professor Irwin Altman, Sociology Department at the University of Utah; Ms. Barbara B. Brown, Assistant Professor of Psychology at Texas Christian University; Ms. Debra Marino, Assistant Professor of Management Science at M.I.T.; Ms. Judith Wurtman, research scientist, Department of Applied Biological Sciences at M.I.T.; Rose E. Steidl, Professor Emeritus, Department of Design and Environmental Analysis, Cornell University.

Ms. Nancy Christiansen, General Electric Lighting Institute; Ms. Jean Niederberger, bathroom design and color director of Eljer Plumbing Corporation; Mr. Ken Charbonneau, color merchandising director of Benjamin Moore and Company; Ms. Beverly Trupp and Ms. Ava Busby of Color Design Art; Mr. Everette Call, director of the Color Marketing Group; Ms. Bonnie Bender, color consultant; Ms. Marina Muntenau, director of research at International Flavors and Fragrances; Mr. Robert Furlong, Muzak International; Mr. Edward Barz, senior vice president, Simmons Market Research Bureau, Duro-Test Corporation; Joanne Fitzgerald, office manager of the Newspaper Advertising Bureau.

Mr. Steve Cosmopolis, president of Cosmopolis, Crowley and Daley; Mr. Nick DeSherbinin, senior art director, Rizzo, Simmons and Cohn; Mr. Bob Thompson, president of Thompson's Nursery; Mr. Wayne Stoddard, research director, Greater Boston Real Estate Board; Mr. Roland Hopkins, publisher of the *New England Real Estate Journal*.

Special thanks to our editors, Mary Tondorf-Dick and Stephanie Holmes; our literary agent, Felicia Eth; and our research assistants, Brenda Thomas and Jennifer Berry. We would also like to thank the people close to us who gave us support over the many months of writing, including Merrill and Sheela Percelay, Alicia Lee Trowbridge, Marjorie and Jessica Arnold, and Derek Goldman.

Bruce A. Percelay
Peter Arnold

Index

Brass fixtures, 91, 106, 118, 186–187
Brasso, 136
Brass Wax, 91
Brick(s)
  exposed, 214
  as facing material, 88–89
  as patio material, 228
  for walkway, 75
Broker, 6
  case against hiring, 252–253
  case for hiring, 250–252, 267
  commission, 252, 253, 256–257
  conflict of interest of, 251, 252–253
  motivating, 256–257
  selecting, 253–254
  selling with, 253–257, 267
Broun Heatlamp, 186
Brown, Barbara, 72
Builder magazine, 219, 243
Built-ins
  bathroom, 185
  kitchen, 148
Bulletin boards, advertising home on, 280
Burglar Bars, 93, 194
Buyback guarantee, 271
Buy-downs, 270
Buyer(s)
  burglar posing as, 264
  empty-nest/trade-down, 9–10, 20, 65, 68–69, 98, 113–114, 132–133, 153, 165, 191, 208–209, 220–221, 234
  first-time, 8–9, 19, 64, 68, 98, 113, 132, 153, 164–165, 191, 208, 220, 233
  identifying, 8–10, 276–277
  male/female, 132, 208, 233, 263–264
  needs of, 10–11
  negotiating with, 262, 265, 266
  prejudging, 263–264
  trade-up, 9, 20, 65, 68, 98, 113, 132, 153, 165, 191, 208, 220, 230
Buyer, considering the
  bathroom and, 164–165
  bedroom and, 191
  color and, 19–20
  deck/patio and, 220–221

  dining room and, 153
  entryway and, 98
  exterior and, 69–70
  family room/den and, 208–209
  kitchen and, 132–133
  lighting and, 35
  living room and, 113–114
  service areas and, 233–234
  smell and, 48
  sound and, 58

Call, Everett, 27
Care, Dr. Morley, 49
Carpeting
  basement, 240, 242
  bathroom, 179
  bedroom, 195
  cleaning, 56, 121–122, 178, 195
  dining room, 156
  living room, 121–122
Cedar Blocks, 198
Ceiling fans, 120, 146, 195, 212
Ceiling medallions, 120
Ceiling moldings, 103
Ceilings
  bathroom, 180
  beamed, 212
  bedroom, 195
  cathedral, 212
  color of, 24–25, 103, 120
  den, 215
  dining room, 155–156
  dropped, 148–149
  entryway, 102–103
  family room, 212
  high, 42
  living room, 119–120
  low, 42
  metal, 103
  mirrored, 158, 180, 193
  repairing, 103
  uneven, 42–43
Ceiling tile, 196
Cellar. *See* Basement
Chandelier, 157
Charbonneau, Ken, 22
Children, house tours and, 60
Children's rooms, 193, 199
Classified ads, 254, 276, 277–278
  abbreviations in, 283
  responses to, 288–289
  writing, 281–288

Hardware, kitchen cabinet, 137
Heating system, 240–241
Hedges, 74, 79
Hess, Dennis J., 163
Home entertainment center, 208, 215
Home marketing
  five-step system, 6–16, 19–21, 34–36, 47–49, 58–59, 98–99, 112–114, 131–134, 152–154, 164–166, 190–192, 207–209, 220–221, 233–235
  mistakes in, 2–4
Housing Futures Consumer Survey, 191
Hughes, Dr. P. D., 37

Illness, as reason for sale, 269
Insulation, 243–244
Interest rates, 270

Job relocation, as reason for sale, 269
Joint Center for Urban Studies (Harvard/M.I.T.), 8, 10, 191

Kira, Alexandra, 166
Kitchen, 131–151
  color accents in, 28
  do-it-yourself improvements, 141
  five-step system and, 131–134
  luxury, 148–149
Kitchen cabinets, 136–139
Kitchen counters, 139–142

LaGuisa, Frank F., 37
Lampposts, 74
  municipal, 84
Landscaping, 76–84
Laundry room, 243
Lavender Scented Moth Sachet, 106
Lawn, 76–78
Lawyer, creative financing and, 271
Leaks
  gas, 238
  water, 237
Lease-purchase agreement, 271
Lemon oil, 56, 126, 156, 198, 210, 215
Levolor-style blinds, 119, 155, 181, 194, 215
Library, gourmet, 149
Life-style statements, 11, 126, 216–217, 221, 226, 227, 259–260, 269

Lighting, 36–45. *See also* Lights
  accent, 39–41, 124, 144, 196–197
  basement, 240
  bathroom, 182–183
  bedroom, 196–197
  categories of, 38–42
  den, 215
  dining room, 157, 160
  entryway, 104, 109
  family room, 212–213
  five-step system and, 34–36
  general, 39, 123, 143, 196
  ground rules of, 37–38
  kitchen, 143–145
  living room, 123–124
  natural, 145
  outdoor, 80, 91, 246–247
  solving problems with, 42–44
  task, 41, 42, 144, 182, 196
Lights
  can, 40, 124, 160, 196
  ceiling-mounted, 39, 104, 109
  floor lamps, 41
  floor spots, 40–41, 124
  fluorescent, 143, 182, 240
  hanging, 39, 144
  heat/sun, 186
  light sticks, 41, 144, 186
  picture, 40
  spot, 123, 212
  table, 124
  track, 40, 123, 144, 160, 183, 196, 213
  valance, 41, 44
Linens
  bathroom, 181
  bedroom, 199
Listing(s)
  exclusive, 255
  multiple, 255
  open, 254
Living room, 112–130
  color accents in, 32
  do-it-yourself improvements, 121
  five-step system and, 112–114
Locks, 105–106, 109–110
Lofts, 193, 199
Lub-A-Lite, 62
Lusher, Dr. Max, 21

McClosky, Joan, 208, 233
Magazines, advertising home in, 279

Rooms
    dual-use, 15-16, 158-159, 201,
        216
    narrow, 43
    small, 43
Rustoleum, 127

Sabbag, Allen, 67
Safety, 10-11, 165. *See also* Security
    bathroom, 170-171
Sandblasting, 88
Sani-Shelf, 198
Scratch Fix, 137, 210
Sealants, 55
Second mortgage, taking back, 271
Security, 10-11, 69
    basement and, 241
    in condos and co-ops, 109-110
    door, 105-106
    garage/parking area, 246-247
    window, 93, 194
Security, economic, 11
Selling your home, 249-274
    avoiding discouragement in, 265
    with a broker, 253-257
    common mistakes, 262-266
    negotiation in, 262, 265, 266
    timing in, 259
    under   difficult   circumstances,
        266-271
    on your own, 257-266
Septic tank, 53
Service areas, 82, 227, 232-248
Settling, 26
Shelves
    in bathroom, 181
    built-in, 216
Shower, 172-174
Showing. *See* Tours
Shrubs, 79-80
Shutters, louvered wooden (interior),
    119, 155, 181, 194, 215
Shutters, wooden exterior, 92-93
Sidewalk, improving, 71-72
Siding
    aluminum, 89
    brick, 88-89
    vinyl, 89
    wood, 86-89
Sink
    bathroom, 175-177
    dry, in bar, 128

kitchen, 149
Sitting area, in bathroom, 186
Skylights, 43, 145, 183, 204
SLA Cedar Scented Spray, 106
Smell(s), 47-57
    to avoid, 49-54
    in closets, 106, 198
    cooking, 50, 134
    gas, 52, 238
    kitchen, 50, 134
    lemon, 52, 56
    medicinal, 51-52
    "model" or "new," 14, 47, 54-57
    musty, 52
    pet, 51
    smoking, 51
Smoke detectors, 147
Soot marks, 26, 238
Sound(s), 46, 47, 57-65. *See also*
    Noises
    to avoid, 60-63
    effect of, 59-60
    floor, 195-196
    to sell by, 64-65
SRI International, 69, 85, 97
Stains, semitransparent, 223
Steidl, Rose, 132
Stereo, 128, 185, 215
Storage. *See also* Closets; Shelves
    basement, 235-236, 245
    bathroom, 181
    bedroom, 197
    split-level, 197
Stove Black, 241
Street, improving, 71
Strypeeze, 90
Study, 213
Sunlight, 36-37, 56-57

Tamp 'N Set Driveway Patch, 81
Target market, identifying, 276-277
Telephone, 171, 184-185, 225-226
Television, 61
Territorial anxiety
    bathroom and, 166
    bedroom and, 192
    broker and, 252
    color and, 20-21
    deck/patio and, 221
    dining room and, 154
    entryway and, 99
    exterior and, 70

ABOUT THE AUTHORS

Bruce A. Percelay has combined his experience in consumer marketing and real estate investment to become a specialist in real estate marketing. A former advertising professional and marketing director at a major New England real estate firm, Mr. Percelay has spent the past seven years developing an effective system to merchandise residential property. Using this system, Mr. Percelay has personally profited from his marketing approach, as well as helping others to maximize the resale value of homes, condominiums, and cooperative apartments. Mr. Percelay is the president of the Mt. Vernon Company, a Boston-based real estate investment and marketing consulting firm.

Peter Arnold is the author of many nonfiction books on a wide variety of subjects. He also writes business articles for a number of trade publications. Mr. Arnold lives in Boston with his family.